PART I

CONCEALED CARRY BASICS

CONCEALED CARRY CONSIDERATIONS

There's more to concealed carry than strapping on a gun.

BY RICHARD NANCE // PHOTOS BY ALFREDO RICO

There's a lot of thought that goes into carrying a concealed firearm on a daily basis—or at least there should be. Sure, you could slip a compact revolver or drop a .380 into your pocket and go about your day. But there's more to concealed carry than just having a gun with you.

From choosing the right gun, carry location, holster, supplemental equipment and clothing to knowing when to draw your gun, the simple notion of carrying a concealed firearm can become quite complex. At a minimum, these are the questions you should be asking yourself with regard to concealed carry.

Photo by Alfredo Rico

Have you considered whether you could draw your concealed carry gun with your off hand? An injury could require a test of an unusual set of skills.

WHICH GUN WILL YOU CARRY?

Once you decide to carry a concealed firearm, your first step should be to select a gun that's right for you. In a perfect world, your carry gun would fit your hand like a glove. It would be compact and lightweight for comfort and concealment, yet powerful enough to stop even the most determined attacker. This perfect gun would be so accurate that it almost shoots itself. And, of course, this gun would be offered at a price you could manage without consideration.

There are some handguns on the market that come pretty close to filling this bill, but in the real world, there's no perfect gun. Some cringe at the thought of carrying anything less than a cocked-and-locked full-size Model 1911 in .45 ACP, while others opt for a much smaller-caliber pocket pistol. If you live in a relatively cold climate and typically wear a jacket, concealing your 1911 may be no big deal, but that 1911 might stick out like a sore thumb if you live in a beach community where a T-shirt, shorts and flip-flops are the norm.

Everyone always thinks about caliber first. A .45 caliber is better than a .40 caliber or a 9mm, right? Well, the .45 will make a slightly bigger hole, but it may be in a frame that's too big for your hand, too bulky for you to conceal or too difficult for you to shoot accurately. When it comes to concealed carry guns, bigger isn't always better.

When selecting a handgun, be sure to look for one that fits your hand. Ideally, when you achieve a proper grip on the gun, it should align with the middle of your forearm and still leave you plenty of room to reach the trigger. If your index finger can't comfortably reach the trigger when the handgun is properly aligned in your hand, you would have to grip the gun improperly to shoot it. This would be detrimental to your accuracy and make it much more difficult for you to manage the gun's recoil.

On the other end of the spectrum, if you have catcher's mitts for hands, shooting a subcompact handgun as your little fingers dangle below the mag might not be too comfortable either. The most important consideration when choosing a handgun is finding one that fits your hand and your needs. Don't focus solely on caliber. A well-placed hit with a .22 caliber beats a miss with a .45 caliber any day of the week.

Here the defender is reaching for his pistol, holstered in a DeSantis Tuck This II.

Photo by Alfredo Rico

WHERE TO WEAR YOUR GUN?

Deciding where to carry your concealed carry gun will influence the type of holster you'll need and the style of clothing required to conceal it. While there are numerous options when it comes to concealed carry, the most secure method (which also facilitates the fastest draw) is to carry your gun in a belt-mounted holster. But at what position along your waistband should you wear your holster?

When you wear your gun on your hip, it's comfortable and easy to get to, but it tends to stick out from your body, which can make concealment a real problem.

Wearing a gun in front of your hip, in what's sometimes referred to as

> **"FROM CHOOSING THE RIGHT GUN, CARRY LOCATION, HOLSTER, SUPPLEMENTAL EQUIPMENT AND CLOTHING TO KNOWING WHEN TO DRAW YOUR GUN, THE SIMPLE NOTION OF CARRYING A CONCEALED FIREARM CAN BECOME QUITE COMPLEX."**

appendix carry (at about the 2 o'clock position for a right-handed shooter), is a much better way to conceal a firearm than hip carry, but the draw from this position is arguably more difficult. However, with practice, appendix carry can lead to a very fast draw because the gun travels less distance to the target than from any other location along your waist.

Another popular carry location is behind the hip at about the 4 o'clock position for a right-handed shooter. This produces a similar draw as hip carry, but keeps your gun closer to your body for added concealment.

Small-of-the-back (SOB) carry is yet another option for a concealed firearm. Your gun could be positioned either vertically or horizontally, depending on the holster. SOB carry makes it pretty easy to conceal a gun, and if a lesser-armed bad guy were to order you to give him your wallet, you could draw your gun while he assumes you're reaching for your wallet.

One of the main drawbacks to SOB carry is that sitting with a gun pressing against the small of your back can become rather uncomfortable. Another concern is that, unlike with the other carry methods, SOB carry (especially when your gun is oriented horizontally) can make drawing with your off-hand next to impossible.

WHAT TYPE OF HOLSTER?

Wearing a gun on your hip in an outside-the-waistband (OWB) holster is probably the most comfortable and accessible way to carry your gun, but it's definitely not the most efficient way to conceal it. Unless you're wearing an overgarment such as a jacket that conceals your waist really well, this mode of carry won't work well because the outline of your gun and holster will tend to print, revealing to anyone taking note that you're armed.

Inside-the-waistband (IWB) holsters enable you to better conceal your handgun, but they can be uncomfortable to wear, particularly when you first start using them. You'll still need an overgarment, but in most cases even a T-shirt will do because the bulk of the gun and holster is inside your pants. Drawing from an IWB holster is a little more

Photo by Alfredo Rico

Small-of-the-back carry has its advantages, but it may be uncomfortable if you're going to be seated.

This Galco SOB (Small Of the Back) holster enables you to easily conceal a wide array of guns. Shown here is a Springfield Armory EMP.

difficult because the grip of your gun is less exposed.

WHAT SUPPLEMENTAL GEAR?

I've known police officers who, while off duty, carry two guns, spare magazines, two sets of handcuffs, pepper spray, a knife, a flashlight and other tactical swag. I'm all for being prepared, but come on...

At a minimum, you should carry a compact flashlight in addition to your firearm. The light can be secreted in your pants pocket and accessed in a hurry when clipped to your pants. A light is required equipment because in a darkened environment you may have to illuminate a subject to ascertain whether he poses a threat. If you're going to make the decision to use deadly force against someone, you better be certain that you see what you think you see.

If you carry a 5-shot revolver, having an additional 5 rounds in a speedloader or Speedstrip makes perfect sense. However, if you carry a semiautomatic pistol that holds 17 rounds, having a spare magazine isn't as critical.

HOW TO DRESS?

If you carry a concealed handgun, dress around the gun. If your jeans are too tight to accommodate your IWB holster, you have a tough decision to make. Wear your skinny jeans and go unarmed, or check your ego and buy a pair of pants that are

Photos by Alfredo Rico

Using your gun hand to lift your closed garment may not be ideal, but it's probably doable.

The Tuck This II holster has a pouch to store a spare magazine. This is a convenient way to double your ammunition capacity.

The author prefers a closed garment for concealed carry.

"IF YOU LIVE IN A RELATIVELY COLD CLIMATE AND TYPICALLY WEAR A JACKET, CONCEALING YOUR 1911 MAY BE NO BIG DEAL, BUT THAT 1911 MIGHT STICK OUT LIKE A SORE THUMB IF YOU LIVE IN A BEACH COMMUNITY WHERE A T-SHIRT, SHORTS AND FLIP-FLOPS ARE THE NORM."

a couple of sizes bigger in the waist so you have room for your gun and IWB holster. Choose wisely.

As mentioned, IWB holsters can usually be concealed by something as simple as a dark-colored, loose-fitting T-shirt. In addition to the shirt that covers your gun, you'll probably want to wear a T-shirt between your body and the gun to prevent the gun from rubbing against your bare skin.

A T-shirt, like a pullover, button-up or zippered shirt, is a closed garment. Closed garments are a little better at concealing your gun, especially when they are dark-colored and slightly oversize. In order to draw from a closed garment, you'll have to lift up your shirt to get to your gun. This is best accomplished with your off-hand, but it could be done with your shooting hand if necessary.

As the name implies, an open garment is open in the front, as would be the case with an unbuttoned or unzipped shirt. Open garments are easier to draw from, requiring only that you sweep the outer garment out of the way to access your firearm. However, when the wind is gusting or you bend down for some reason, your outer garment is more apt to move, possibly exposing your gun.

WHEN TO DRAW?

Being set up to properly carry a concealed handgun is the easy part. You must consider under what circumstances you would draw your gun. Remember that just because you're armed when a crime occurs doesn't mean that trying to intervene is the best idea.

In most cases, your goal should be to be a good witness. In other words, take note of what the suspects looked like, their mannerisms, the type of vehicle they fled in, maybe even the license plate number. Carrying a gun doesn't make you a police officer. You don't have the training, equipment or resources (including backup) that police do.

If while standing in line at a convenience store, a man wearing a ski mask barges in and sticks a gun in the clerk's face, you may be tempted to take action because you reasonably believe that the clerk and everyone in the store are in imminent danger. You would be right in your assumption, but if you draw and issue a verbal command for the robber to drop the gun, he might shoot the clerk, turn to shoot you or even take the clerk hostage. Then what?

What if you shoot the robber, and his partner (the guy you didn't see because you were so focused on the masked gunman) shot you or your family member who was in the store with you? Taking action to prevent crime is admirable, but it's risky business that takes more than a couple of hours at the range a few times a year to be prepared for.

If you carry a concealed firearm, you better be familiar with the laws related to use of force and self-defense in your area. And you need to learn sound tactics for deploying your gun in the real world because there's more to winning a gunfight than marksmanship.

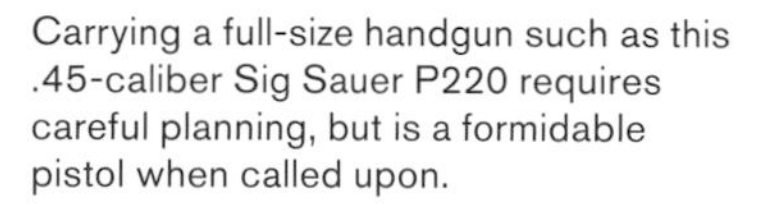

Carrying a full-size handgun such as this .45-caliber Sig Sauer P220 requires careful planning, but is a formidable pistol when called upon.

Photo by Alfredo Rico

Photo by Alfredo Rico

PACKIN' HEAT

Choosing the right gun, holster and garment for concealed carry.

BY RICHARD NANCE
PHOTOS BY ALFREDO RICO

In the police academy, my Recruit Training Officer (RTO) relayed a story to my class that had a profound influence on my life. He was in a restaurant with his fiancée when armed gunmen decided the establishment would make a good location for a robbery. As a police officer, the RTO was certainly authorized to carry a concealed firearm, but on this day, he left home without it. One thing led to another, and the RTO and his fiancée found themselves literally running for their lives out the back door of the restaurant. He recounted that with each step, he promised himself (and God) that if he and his fiancée made it through that harrowing ordeal, he would never again be caught without his gun. Fortunately, the robbers decided not to shoot them. My RTO made good on his promise and carries a concealed handgun religiously. I could imagine how helpless he must have felt, unable to protect himself or his fiancée and at the mercy of armed robbers.

Photos by Alfredo Rico

LEFT - Wearing an outside-the-waist (OWB) holster in the 3 o'clock position requires a better choice of cover garment. Here the gun creates an unnatural bulge.

RIGHT - This jacket conceals the OWB holster much more effectively.

Several of my fellow officers leave their one and only gun (their issued duty pistol) in their locker at the station and live their off-duty lives unarmed, presumably carefree. Some have asked why I choose to carry a gun when I'm not working. The short answer is that I refuse to experience the feeling of helplessness that my RTO felt as he and his fiancée ran for dear life, praying they wouldn't be shot in the back. Long ago, I resolved to carry a concealed firearm every day.

While carrying a concealed handgun will always be somewhat burdensome, choosing the right gun and gear can make being discreetly armed much more tolerable. Keep in mind that the more comfortable it is to carry a concealed handgun, the more likely you are to have it within reach when you need it most.

CHOOSE YOUR GUN

When considering a concealed carry handgun, it's probably best to stick to a "middle-of-the-road" approach. That .44 Magnum made famous by "Dirty Harry" might be a tempting option considering its ballistic capability and off-the-charts coolness factor. That is until you realize you'll need to wear a parka to conceal it. On the other hand, while a .380 pocket pistol or a snubnose revolver might be convenient to carry, they can be difficult to shoot and they typically hold precious few rounds.

Selecting a concealed carry handgun is a very personal decision. Just because the guy behind the counter at the gun shop advocates a particular gun doesn't mean it will work for you. The right gun for you is dependent on your perceived need for carrying a gun, your typical attire, the types of activities you routinely engage in, your allotted training time and your physicality. Is your hand large enough to establish a proper shooting grip on that full-size .45-caliber pistol? Do you have sufficient upper-body strength to rack the slide? Do you practice enough to accurately shoot that compact pistol or revolver with its miniscule sights and reduced sight radius?

When you achieve a proper shooting grip, with the barrel aligned with your forearm, can you comfortably reach the trigger? Are you able to manipulate all the bells and whistles on the gun while maintaining a shooting grip? If not, the gun is too big for your hand.

Is the gun well balanced, and does it seem to point naturally for you? Can you manage the pistol's recoil? Of course, the best way to tell if a firearm is right for you is to actually shoot it. Find a range that rents guns, and give several a try before making a purchase.

Although caliber is obviously a factor when considering a concealed carry gun, a hit with a smaller caliber always beats a miss with a larger one. Unless the shot from your handgun is precisely placed (or you're very lucky), it's not likely to result in immediate physiological incapacitation regardless of caliber, which is all the more reason to choose a caliber that you can control. It's often said that every bullet that leaves the barrel of your gun has a lawyer attached to it. Remember that in the real world, you are accountable for every round you send downrange.

Ammunition capacity is another important factor when selecting a concealed carry gun. In theory, the more rounds your gun holds, the less likely you are to have to reload during a life-and-death encounter. However, a skilled shooter might resolve a deadly force encounter without having to reload his 5-shot revolver, while a novice shooter, who is reliant on the spray-and-pray technique, could easily burn through an entire 15-round magazine without registering a single hit.

Once you've decided on a concealed carry handgun, it's time to decide the manner in which you intend to carry it, then pair your gun with an appropriate, high-quality holster. Avoid the inclination

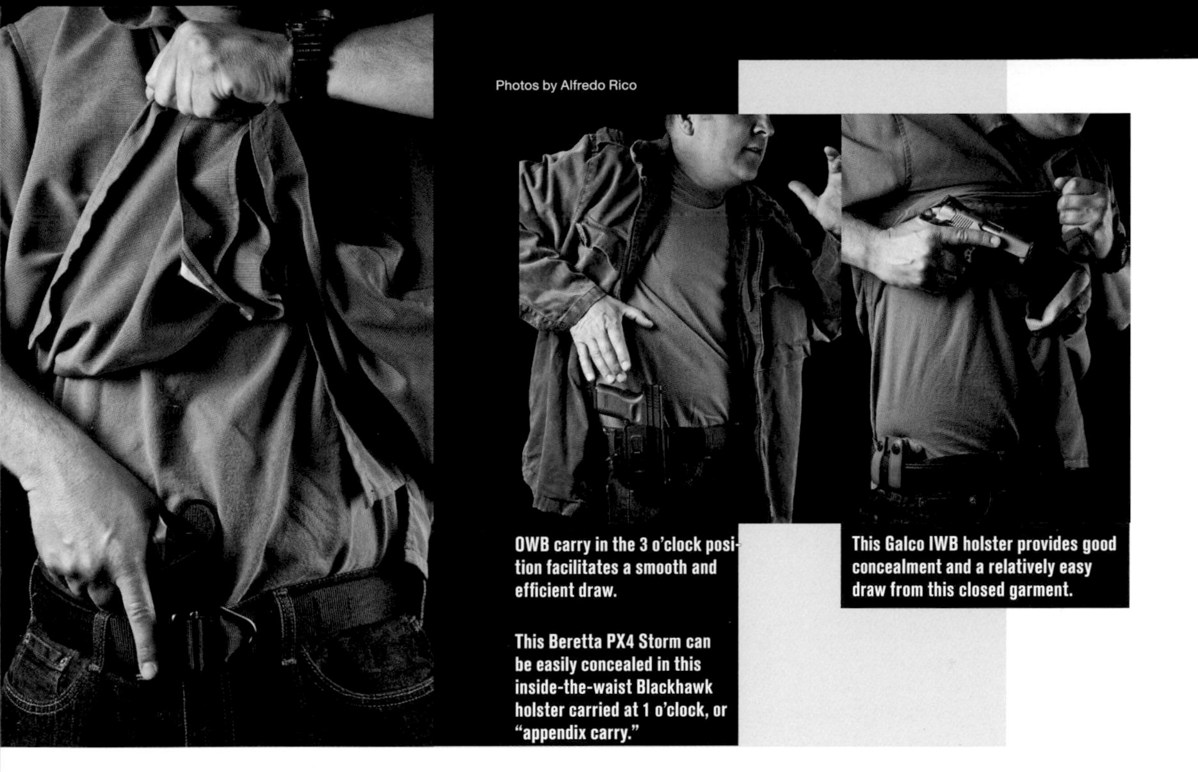

Photos by Alfredo Rico

OWB carry in the 3 o'clock position facilitates a smooth and efficient draw.

This Beretta PX4 Storm can be easily concealed in this inside-the-waist Blackhawk holster carried at 1 o'clock, or "appendix carry."

This Galco IWB holster provides good concealment and a relatively easy draw from this closed garment.

of many concealed carry newbies to spend so much on their gun that they purchase a discount holster to carry it in. If you skimp on your holster, it won't take long to realize you screwed up. You'll either stop carrying your gun altogether, or you will foot the bill for a quality holster.

HOLSTER SELECTION

These days, there's certainly no shortage of well-made, highly concealable holsters on the market. In fact, with so many options, choosing one can be quite difficult. The first consideration when selecting a holster for your handgun is to determine where on your body you will wear the gun. For most of us, the waist is probably the most appropriate location.

Waistline carry lends itself to a natural draw and is readily accessible in most circumstances. The accessibility of carrying a gun along your waist is critical in extreme close-quarter engagements, where you might be clenched with an adversary. In this most precarious fighting distance, getting to a gun carried on your ankle, under your shoulder, in the small of your back, in a fanny pack or, worse yet, in a purse would be all but impossible.

Pocket carry is immensely popular these days. With today's technologically advanced ammunition, the once underpowered .380 cartridge is now a legitimate option for personal defense. A pocket gun is easy to tote but tough to draw quickly under circumstances that preclude you from covertly gripping your gun prior to deployment. Also, as a rule of thumb, the smaller the gun, the more difficult it is to shoot, especially at distances beyond a few feet.

If you elect to carry a gun along your waist, you need to consider whether inside-the-waistband (IWB) or outside-the-waistband (OWB) is right for you. IWB holsters are easier to conceal because they keep the gun closer to your body, but they are slightly harder to draw for that very same reason. OWB holsters stick out farther, making concealment more of a challenge, but they provide an ideal platform for expediently drawing your handgun. Since they are not secreted in the waistband of your pants, OWB holsters also tend to be a little more comfortable to wear than IWB holsters, so if you're going to carry for hours, keep this in mind.

Another consideration with waistline carry is where along your waist you will carry your gun. For a right-handed shooter, carrying in the 1 o'clock position is considered appendix carry. This carry method facilitates a relatively fast draw but requires the muzzle point in close proximity to a portion of your anatomy that makes some a bit squeamish. It can also be uncomfortable to carry a gun in the appendix position when you're seated, since the muzzle tends to dig into your thigh.

The 3 o'clock position is probably the most common location for concealed carry. From here, you have a very natural path to the gun, and it tends to be quite comfortable, even when seated. However, the comfort of the 3 o'clock position carries with it the burden of more difficult concealment. When worn on the hip, your gun will protrude farther from your body than any other waistline carry location.

In the 4 o'clock position, your gun rests just behind your dominant-side hip. This carry location makes it easier to conceal your handgun because your body helps mask its shape and your gun is not as susceptible to being revealed should a gust of wind blow open your garment. For these reasons, as well as the fact that drawing from the 4 o'clock position is essentially the same as from the 3 o'clock position, it is a favorite among many who carry concealed.

Carrying in the 6 o'clock position is commonly referred to as "small-of-the-back carry." Since there is a natural hollow in the small of the back, concealing a handgun here is relatively easy. It's also unexpected to carry a gun in this position, which could give you the drop on a bad guy who demands your wallet. However, since drawing from the 6 o'clock position is somewhat awkward and generally requires you to momentarily place both hands behind your back, it is not the most advantageous position from which to draw at extreme close quarters.

Another drawback to 6 o'clock carry is having to sit with a gun between your back and the seat. If you'll be seated for long periods, this method is probably not for you. An additional concern surrounding the 6 o'clock position is that if you are knocked to the ground and land on your back, you could sustain serious injury.

As the saying goes, you don't get something for nothing, and the downsides to waist carry are that it can be uncomfortable and it requires an overgarment to conceal. Additionally, if you're seated in a vehicle, with the seatbelt secured around your lap and shoulder, getting to your waistline-carried handgun could be problematic. In such a case, an ankle holster or shoulder holster, which are impractical in extreme close quarters, are sensible alternatives.

Some prefer to carry their gun in a purse, briefcase, disguised day-planner or other off-body location. While perhaps a more comfortable option, off-body carry presents myriad potential problems. Off-body carry will typically be significantly slower than other carry methods, and gun retention becomes a very real concern. You are basically relegated to carrying around your purse, briefcase or other off-body "holster" with you at all times. If you set down your purse and someone swipes it, financial loss could be the least of your problems. If you opt for off-body carry, be sure the device you choose is specifically designed to carry a handgun, that you're well

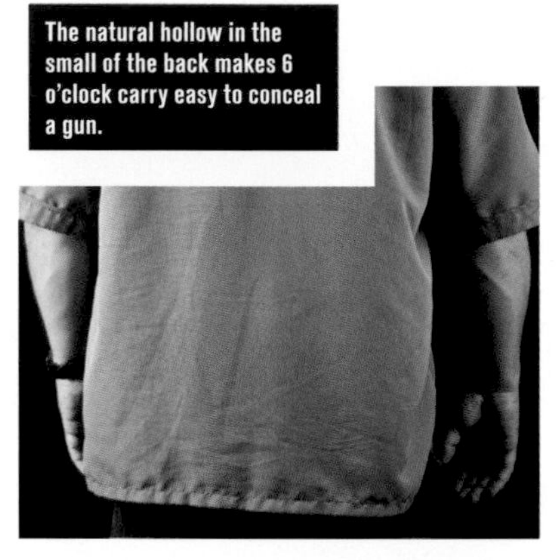

The natural hollow in the small of the back makes 6 o'clock carry easy to conceal a gun.

Here, the author is carrying a Springfield EMP in a Galco OWB small-of-the-back holster.

Photos by Alfredo Rico

Although caliber is obviously a factor when considering a concealed carry gun, **a hit with a smaller caliber always beats a miss with a larger one.**

versed in drawing from the device and that you don't carry other items in the immediate vicinity of your gun, which could potentially foul your draw.

DRESS FOR SUCCESS

Carrying a concealed firearm is a serious commitment. You must ensure that your attire is consistent with concealing a handgun. If you can't pass up those skinny jeans and size "extra medium" shirt to show off your figure, you might need to resort to off-body carry. A more reasonable solution would be to dress around your gun. In other words, if you opt to carry IWB, you'll need to buy pants that are a couple inches larger in the waist to accommodate your holstered gun. If you carry a gun on your waist, you'll want to invest in a sturdy, purpose-designed gun belt to help evenly distribute the weight of your gun and keep it securely in place. If you plan to carry a gun in your pocket, make sure the pocket and the opening to the pocket are large enough to allow quick access to your gun.

Waistline carry requires you to cover your gun with either an open or closed garment. An open garment could be an unbuttoned shirt or unzipped sweatshirt or jacket. On the other hand, a T-shirt or a zipped or buttoned shirt would be considered a closed garment. Open garments make concealing your gun a little more difficult, but since drawing from an open garment requires only that you sweep the clothing away from your gun, it's easier than drawing from a closed garment, in which you need to lift up your clothing to access your handgun.

CONCLUSION

Successful concealed carry is based on several factors. The first step is to find a gun that you feel comfortable with and can shoot well. Then you must decide what carry location and method are most conducive to your lifestyle. Pick your holster based on these criteria. If you carry a gun along your waist, employ a sturdy belt. Dress around your gun to give yourself every advantage. There isn't one best way to carry a concealed handgun. Find what works for you, and practice drawing from your chosen concealed carry location. In order to secure a tactical advantage, your gun must remain concealed until the moment you bring it to bear on your adversary.

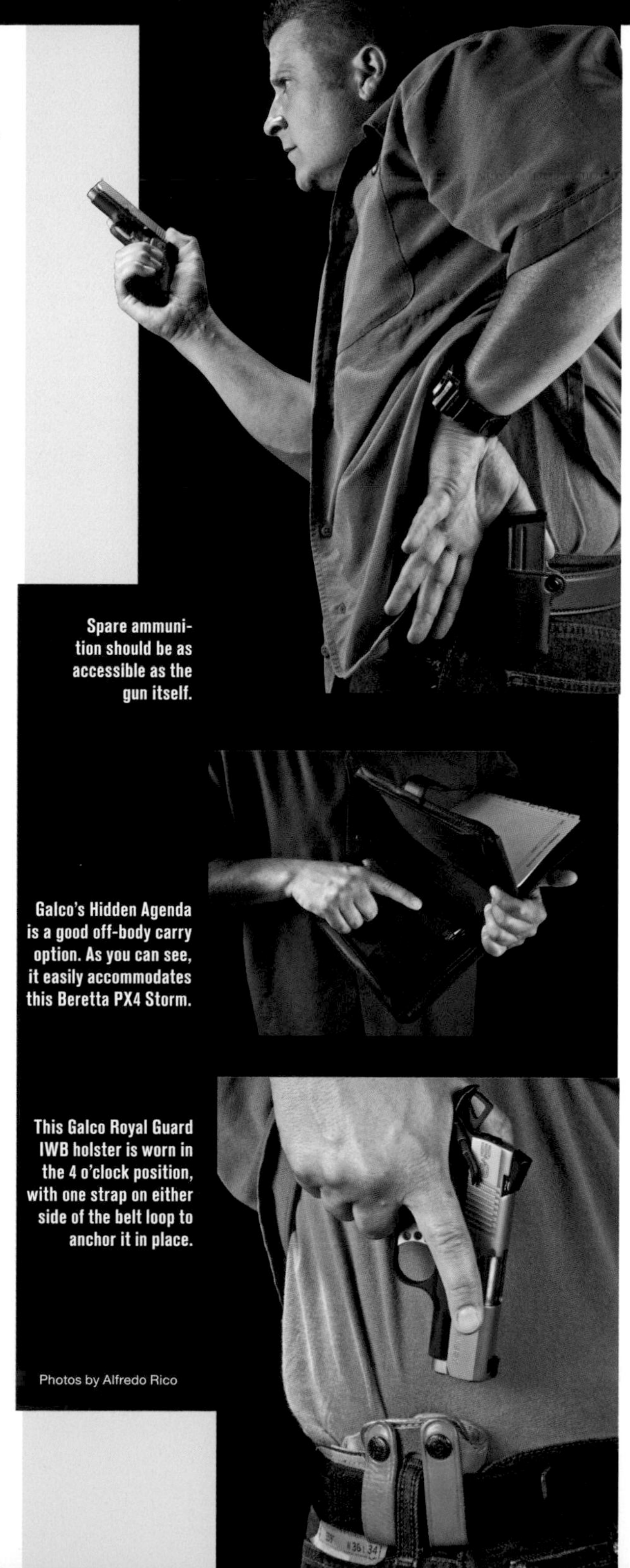

Spare ammunition should be as accessible as the gun itself.

Galco's Hidden Agenda is a good off-body carry option. As you can see, it easily accommodates this Beretta PX4 Storm.

This Galco Royal Guard IWB holster is worn in the 4 o'clock position, with one strap on either side of the belt loop to anchor it in place.

Photos by Alfredo Rico

APPENDIX CARRY

The fastest and most secure way to carry concealed.

Concealed carry is a huge component of personal defense, effectively becoming its own industry. There is no shortage of carrying techniques, all of which offer varying degrees of firearms security, easy access to the weapon and comfort. The method that offers the best balance of the three criteria listed above is appendix carry, inside the waistband (AIWB).

AIWB has been around for a long time but has become a topic of debate in concealed carry circles over the past couple years. The appendix carry I grew up hearing about involved all the sophistication of shoving one's pistol down the front of one's pants. This is not recommended, as it makes the pistol both prone to negligent discharge and liable to drop out the bottom of your pant's leg at an inopportune moment.

Fortunately for us, the firearms industry will almost always move to fill market voids and a fair amount of holster manufacturers now turn out quality products that make AIWB a strong contender for concealed carry purposes. There are a number of holsters and some quality guns that work well for AIWB. Tucking a loaded pistol into a holster just to the left or right of our navel is no casual act, so before jumping into AIWB it's best to think through appropriate training as well as pistol and gear selection to help ensure a successful transition to this carry technique.

BY TOM BECKSTRAND
PHOTOS BY MARK FINGAR

OWNERSHIP DOES NOT GUARANTEE PROFICIENCY

Many new adult shooters come to firearms ownership through a desire to carry concealed. I have several friends who got a concealed carry permit before even owning a gun. I would hesitate to recommend AIWB to a new shooter unless he demonstrated a commitment to study and train to become a proficient shooter.

For the purposes of this piece I'll define a proficient shooter as one who can consistently obey the four rules of firearm safety throughout the loading, training and unloading sequence. Some might chuckle at the "low standard," but experience has shown me that many shooters are way too casual about firearms safety to carry AIWB. Such an attitude can easily prove fatal with this carry discipline. Guns are nothing to fear, but they command respect.

Without belaboring firearms safety, the most dangerous aspect of AIWB comes during the reholstering sequence. It's easy to point the pistol directly at our femoral artery while holstering if we don't take a second to push our hips slightly forward and if we don't watch our muzzle until it's in the holster. Also, we've likely just been firing our pistol, and some shooters are slower than others to remove their finger from the trigger after the festivities have ended. If we try to holster with our finger on the trigger, the gun will fire. It will also likely be pointed at something important.

Failure to do any and all of the above sets the conditions for a catastrophic accident that can easily end in death. Before deciding on whether to carry AIWB, it's necessary to become a proficient shooter. We accomplish this first by instruction, then by practice. An NRA basic pistol course from an NRA-certified instructor is a wise first step. If you can't find online reviews of an instructor, or course, keep looking until you can. Getting instruction from "a gun guy" can be hit or miss. Also, just because someone is a cop or a member of the military is no guarantee of proficiency. Sometimes we stumble upon a jewel, sometimes we find only incompetence and bravado.

PISTOL SELECTION

Once we are adequately trained and proficient in firearms safety, our next consideration is which pistol to carry. Friends and family members ask me often for pistol recommendations, frequently for new shooters. Most often my response is to get a Smith and Wesson M&P or Glock in 9mm. Both are quality pistols that are easy to find and don't cost too much. They also don't have much recoil and hold a bunch of rounds, certainly advantageous. However, my recommendation changes when discussing concealed carry.

For AIWB carry I recommend pistols with external hammers and long, deliberate trigger pulls, but the pull doesn't have to be heavy. Glocks and M&Ps are striker-fired guns that usually have short and light pulls, so I don't think they're a good choice for newer shooters and AIWB. Pistols with longer trigger pulls like double action/single action (DA/SA) autos are a good choice, as are double-action-only (DAO) guns. The longer pull requires a more deliberate action than any striker-fired gun and offers an additional measure of safety.

Some will argue that the pistol isn't the liability with AIWB and that any problems that might arise stem from operator error. This is absolutely true. However, even the most highly trained people can make mistakes under stress when we have an almost overpowering desire to check the trigger to make sure we can find it. We should use all means available to our advantage to mitigate this risk. That's why it's a good idea to pick a pistol that

Photos by Mark Fingar

From left to right are the Custom Carry Concepts Looper, Shaggy with leather snap retention and the Shaggy with the clip retention. The Shaggy is the more refined model, and the clip retention system is the easiest to conceal.

requires simple, yet deliberate action to make it fire. DA/SA and DAO pistols fall into this category.

There is another hybrid pistol type that I prefer for AIWB. It's only available from HK and is called Law Enforcement Modification (LEM). While the "LE" in "LEM" might stand for Law Enforcement, LEM is an excellent choice for civilian use, as the trigger pull is both light and deliberate. It is also consistent from shot to shot.

The LEM trigger works by having two hammers, one internal and one external. The internal "hammer" gets cocked when we cycle the slide, but the external hammer rests in the down position. Pulling the trigger only requires the external hammer to move to the fully cocked position before both hammers drop and the pistol fires.

By requiring the external hammer to swing through its full range of motion before firing, the pistol becomes very safe for concealed carry because we can positively control the hammer with our thumb when we holster the pistol. Being able to control the hammer is an additional safety feature that I encourage new shooters to look for when researching which pistol to buy.

Of course, traditional DA/SA and DAO pistols will have this same feature, so I recommend them as well. However, traditional DA pulls usually hover around 10 to 12 pounds while the HK LEM sits around 6 to 7 pounds of pull. The additional weight on the trigger is certainly manageable and many do it well, but heavy trigger pulls make it harder to keep a good sight picture when we're trying to manipulate the trigger quickly.

Likewise, DA/SA pistols have a long, heavy pull on the first stroke and a short, light pull on each remaining stroke. This is not a hugely difficult transition to make, but it will require some additional practice. If a new shooter knows ahead of time that he is willing to work to get to know his pistol well, then don't worry about it and go ahead with a good DA/SA.

THE HOLSTER IS A BIG DEAL

Holsters play a more significant role in AIWB than they do in other forms of concealed carry. The pistol sits inside our pants near the navel, and every time we bend over there is potential for discomfort. The term "soft" and "underbelly" get used together frequently for a reason.

Getting a good holster for AIWB will require some work and possibly some waiting, but the security and speed that AIWB offers makes the effort worth it. AIWB holsters can be made out of either Kydex or leather, Kydex being cheaper and leather being

Photos by Mark Fingar

The Cadillac of leather AIWB holsters is the 5-Shot Leather's SME, which resulted from three years of testing and evaluation. Each is handmade from the finest materials by a true craftsman.

Each of the Custom Carry Concepts Shaggy models is available with a leather comfort layer or heat shield. Products from CCC are very high quality, yet still inexpensive. Get the leather layer, though. It makes the holster more comfortable.

more durable and comfortable. The holsters I tested in preparation of this piece are the Custom Carry Concepts "Looper" and "Shaggy" models and the 5-Shot Leather "SME."

Custom Carry Concepts turns out well-made Kydex holsters at an affordable price point. I've purchased and used their Looper and Shaggy models for my HK P2000 and their Shaggy model for my HK P30. The Looper is the simplest of the two, offering a straight drop with the pistol's grip protruding slightly away from the body. The Looper gets its name from a continuous Kydex loop that attaches the holster to our belt.

I like the Looper, but I really like the Shaggy. The Shaggy attaches to our belt with either a Kydex clip, a Kydex loop or two leather strips with snap retention. I have Shaggys with both the Kydex clip and leather loops. The loops are secure and convenient, but they are the bulkiest attachment of the lot. The Kydex clip is superconvenient because it's easy to put the holster on and take it off, but it offers slightly less security. If I had to do it all over again, I'd go with the Kydex loop. It's very low profile and offers great security. It just takes a little more effort to put it on and take it off.

After owning and using the Custom Carry Concepts (CCC) holsters for almost a year, I am glad I made the purchases. I feel like I got my money's worth and that the holsters will last as long as I need them to. Regardless of which CCC IWB holster you buy, I recommend getting the leather backing either for comfort or for a heat shield. Leather feels better against the body than plain Kydex.

Leather is a more expensive but more comfortable option for AIWB, so I did some poking around before laying out the bucks for a good leather holster. A lot of knowledgeable friends of mine spoke highly of John Ralston, owner of 5-Shot Leather, so I stopped by to see his products and talk to him at this year's SHOT Show.

Looking at John's products, it was obvious that he knows his business and takes great pride in producing an heirloom-quality product. He is also very personable and took almost an hour of his time to walk me through what separates good holsters from great ones.

If you take a piece of leather and look at its cross section, the surface exposed to the atmosphere is the oldest and thickest part, while the inner surface is the newer, fattier stuff. John

The SME uses only the oldest and tightest grains of leather to make sure that the holster doesn't lose its shape over time. The reenforced mouth will not collapse when we draw the pistol, so holstering is easy.

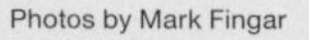
Photos by Mark Fingar

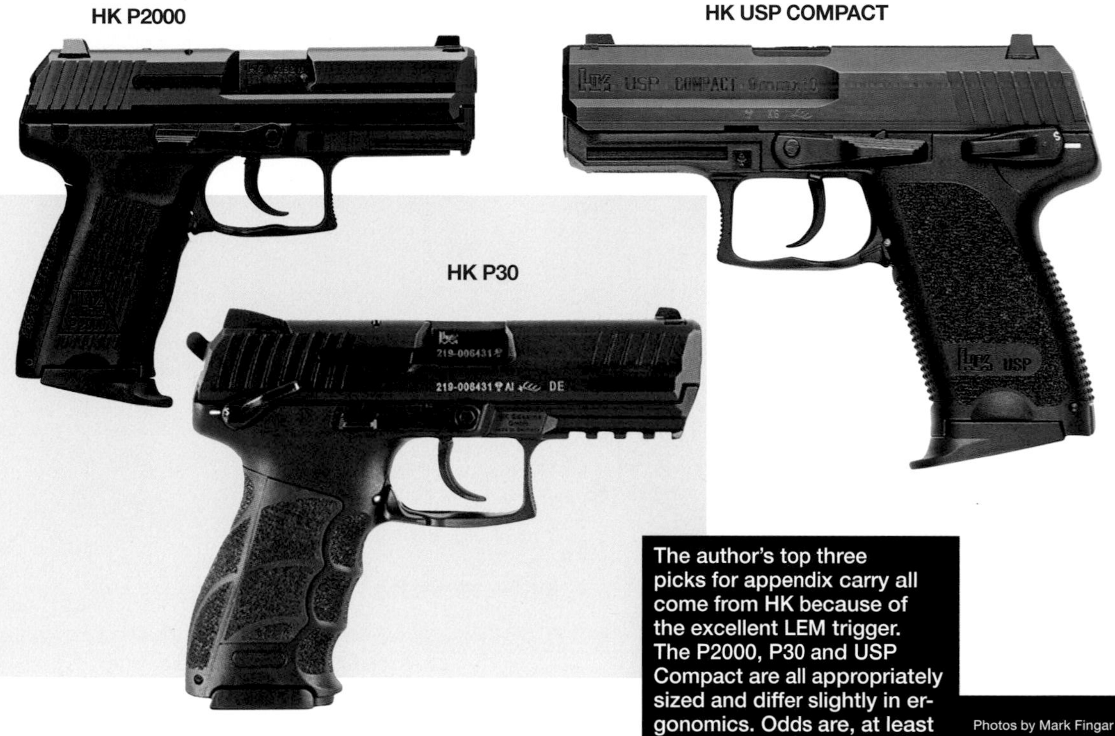

The author's top three picks for appendix carry all come from HK because of the excellent LEM trigger. The P2000, P30 and USP Compact are all appropriately sized and differ slightly in ergonomics. Odds are, at least one will fit your needs well.

Photos by Mark Fingar

separates the outer, older half from the newer, inner half, then discards the newer more porous material and only uses the older skin for his holsters. "The outer half offers the thickest and tightest grain. It won't stretch or lose its shape like the newer skin will."

Only a handful of custom leather guys are fanatical enough about quality to buy only the oldest, thickest leathers and then throw away half their inventory before the first stitch, ensuring that they use only the best material available. John also took three years and countless hours developing the SME. I asked him if he was worried about someone stealing his design. "Nope. An eighth of an inch in the wrong place and [the SME] becomes a much more uncomfortable holster. I know where all those eighths are located."

As you'd expect with a custom leather holster, the stitching is even and straight, and the thick leather looks like it will never lose its shape. If you want one of John's holsters, be prepared to wait. Current lead times run about six months, but the wait is worth it.

IT'S A PACKAGE DEAL

AIWB is a great choice for concealed carry, but it's not going to be a good fit for us unless we put some time and effort into building a package that works. Once we're comfortable with our gun-handling skills, it's time to choose a pistol and holster combo that fits.

My top three pistol choices for AIWB are all from HK: the P2000, the USP Compact and the P30. Other pistols that would make a good fit can be found at Sig Sauer and Beretta. I am partial to HK because I think so highly of the LEM trigger.

When deciding which holster to buy, remember that Kydex is cheaper, but is less comfortable than leather and will eventually crack. We'll pay more for leather, but it's also more comfortable and good leather will likely last longer than we will.

With the right training and equipment, AIWB gives us a very concealed and secure way of carrying our pistol. While it is less forgiving of shooter and equipment errors than other styles of carry, it offers us the fastest presentation and can make our pistol disappear like no other method.

IN PLAIN SIGHT

Carrying to keep it concealed.

BY JAMES TARR

One big component to carrying a gun is being proficient in its use. Having a double kidnapping/homicide in the family gave me motivation to practice . . . a lot. My plan was to shoot competitively until I reached a skill level where I was confident that I would likely be a better shooter than a threat I might run into. Skill level aside, all the range time in the world wasn't going to help me if I found myself in the middle of a gunfight armed only with a .25 ACP. So I started carrying what I was using in competition. Those years of trying to hide large-framed autos in a state that has 100-degree temperature swings has provided some unique insights and painful memories. My pain is your gain.

DRESS AROUND THE GUN

Anyone wearing baggy pants or a suit coat can hide a small revolver or auto. As far as I'm concerned, this sacrifices stopping power for style. It's a philosophy that I don't follow. When compared to rifles and shotguns, even the most powerful pistols are weak and ineffective. If you knew you were heading into trouble, who would choose a pistol over a long gun? We'll play the hand we're dealt.

If you want to carry a medium- to large-framed handgun, you're going to have to modify your wardrobe to help conceal it. Picking a gun that won't ruin the lines of slacks is exactly the wrong way to go about it. When possible, pick a coat that conceals the gun you've decided to carry. This is assuming

If you want to carry a medium- to large-framed handgun, you're going to have to modify your wardrobe to help conceal it.

that you have some freedom in choosing the wardrobe. Those limited to a specific wardrobe are much more restricted in what can be carried. But probably not as much as you think. Compact autos are getting ever more compact and hollow point designs have become substantially more effective (even in marginal calibers like .380 ACP).

BE AWARE

"Which police department do you work for?" asked a man in a bookstore. I immediately realized that the 1911 on my hip had shoved my shirt out so far that a legally blind grandmother would've pointed at me with quivering fingers.

It was only luck that the gentleman next to me was firearms friendly.

If you're not sure how much your gun prints when you bend over or sit down, the answer is probably more than you think. When carrying a large pistol on the hip, look into a mirror and act as if you're lifting something heavy.

BRANDISHING

It's not just a word. Brandishing is a state of mind. It only takes one instance of walking when the wind blows open an untucked shirt. The fact that you didn't pull your gun out won't save you when a passing mom sees your gun and starts screaming in terror. I know someone this happened to. How did she know he wasn't a cop? The answer is that she didn't. But in this world

The tactical vest is a victim of its own success—anyone wearing one is immediately assumed by those in the know to be carrying a concealed pistol.

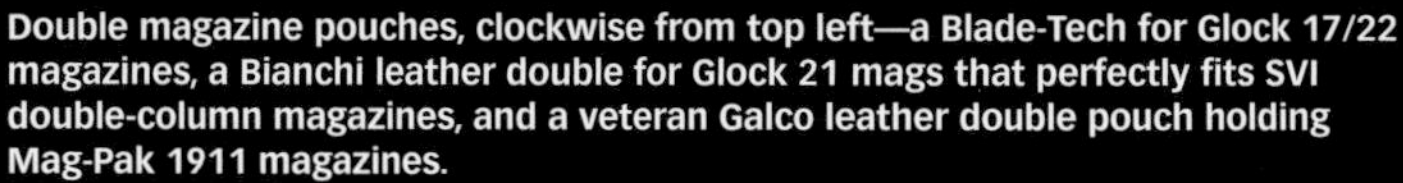

Double magazine pouches, clockwise from top left—a Blade-Tech for Glock 17/22 magazines, a Bianchi leather double for Glock 21 mags that perfectly fits SVI double-column magazines, and a veteran Galco leather double pouch holding Mag-Pak 1911 magazines.

This covert carry pouch from 5.11 offers small arms concealment with a front pouch pistol holder. Tabs can be quickly pulled for rapid deployment and a magazine holder has been added to the front flip down cover. This waste pouch is a $35 CCW solution.

where many people have only seen guns on TV, the accidental flash of a gun in street clothes can end badly. If you're lucky, you'll stay out of jail and pay a few thousand dollars in legal bills. But you might not have a carry permit after everything shakes out.

UNARMED

A friend owns a number of pistols: a Glock 19, a SIG P229, and several full-size 1911s. Depending on the wardrobe or his destination, he'll put the P229 on his hip, keep a 1911 in his briefcase, or the Glock in his glove compartment. Now, while the number one rule of a gunfight is "have a gun," if you can't remember where you put it, how long will it take to get a gun while the bleeding is going on? Jeff Cooper's maxim was "If you can't get a loaded gun in your hand in five seconds you're unarmed." If you don't want to stick with carrying the same type of gun every day, at least keep it (or better yet carry it) in the same place, so you don't have to think about it.

ACCESS

Pocket guns are not only carried by residents of very hot climates but those in cold climes as well, for different reasons. The snubnose in the winter coat pocket is often the backup that's generally used to buy time while accessing the bigger gun hidden underneath the polar fleece. If the gun is covered by bulky outerwear, determine the fastest way to get to it. Practice that. Depending on the type of pocket pistol, a holster designed for the pocket is certainly a good idea.

SUBTLE

Everything that covers a gun is not necessarily a concealment garment. I refer to clothes that scream "I'm carrying a gun!" Tactical vests are a fine piece of equipment and have been worn in sandy hotspots throughout the world in roles of personal protection but when I see someone wearing one on the street, I immediately assume that they're carrying a gun. Those vests are a victim of their own success and sometimes designate the wearer to those in the know as a gun bearer.

Clothes aren't the only thing to be wary of. I knew a U.S. Border Pa-

opposed to the various tactical gun cases that
ny retailers sell, athletic equipment cases
padded and just the ticket for shorter rifles,
ether it be in vehicles or moving through
gested areas.

Sources
5.11, Inc.
866-451-1726
www.511tactical.com

Blade-Tech Industries
253-655-8059
www.blade-tech.com

Galco Gunleather
800-USGALCO
www.usgalco.com

Safariland
800-347-1200
www.safariland.com

Milt Sparks Holsters, Inc.
208-377-5577
www.miltsparks.com

Bianchi International
800-347-1200
www.bianchi-intl.com

Uncle Mike's
Bushnell Outdoor Products
800-423-3537
www.uncle-mikes.com

DeSantis Holster & Leather Goods
800-GUNHIDE
www.desantisholster.com

trol officer and he kept his duty gun concealed in a fanny pack around the waist. I knew that (even though I never saw his pistol) because his service pistol was a large .40-caliber semiauto. With one spare mag, the fanny pack hung like it was loaded with lead. Upon retrospect, I suppose it was.

As a side note, most products marketed as "discreet gun cases" are anything but. Particularly those designed for long guns. That's why so many custom and semicustom shops sell purses and day-planners with hidden holster compartments. If you want a truely concealed carrying case for your long gun, a 16-inch-barreled AR with a 6-position collapsible stock will generally fit inside a sports case like those made for baseball or tennis. Many of these are even padded.

HOLSTERED

It used to be that quality holsters cost money, and lots of it. With the invention of Kydex and other polymers, that's no longer the case. But whether the holster is made of cheap plastic or hand-worked horsehide, if it doesn't keep the gun tucked away and out of sight it's just a waste of money for concealed carry purposes. A holster shouldn't just cover the trigger guard but should also retain the gun in the event of jostling. I've never had my gun fall out of its holster but I can't say the same for spare magazines. Seeing your reload skipping across the concrete while you're running is not a reassuring sight. Just about every holster now has some sort of retention device built into it. Many are just simple tension screws and others are extreme such as the Level 3 retention holsters often utilized by law enforcement.

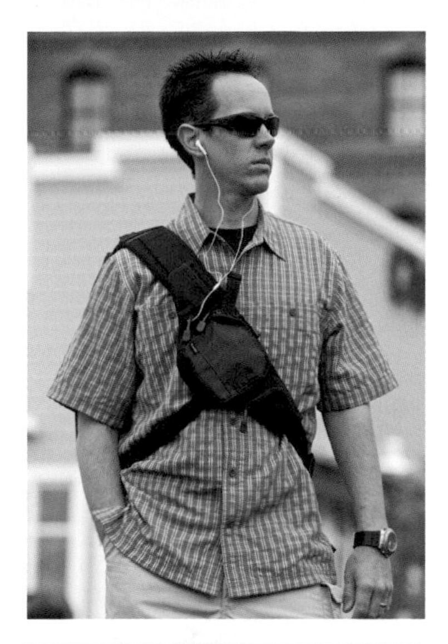

Presenting a wholesome, non-threatening appearance is half the battle. New for 2009, 5.11 introduced the Select Carry Sling Pack for concealed carry that reflects current clothing trends.

Nearly as important as holster choice is belt choice. Size, shape, material, and color doesn't matter as much as making sure that the belt is up to the job of supporting the weight of what you carry. Many custom leather and horsehide holsters are sold as part of a package including a magazine carrier and a matching, fitted belt. There's a reason for this.

BE PREPARED

Forethought, planning, and the proper mix of holster, belt, and clothes can conceal just about any pistol but there's no magic button to make a carry gun invisible. Anyone with a carry permit needs to be just as aware of the image they're presenting to the world as they are of the potential threats around them.

559
W34 L30

GOT YOUR BACK

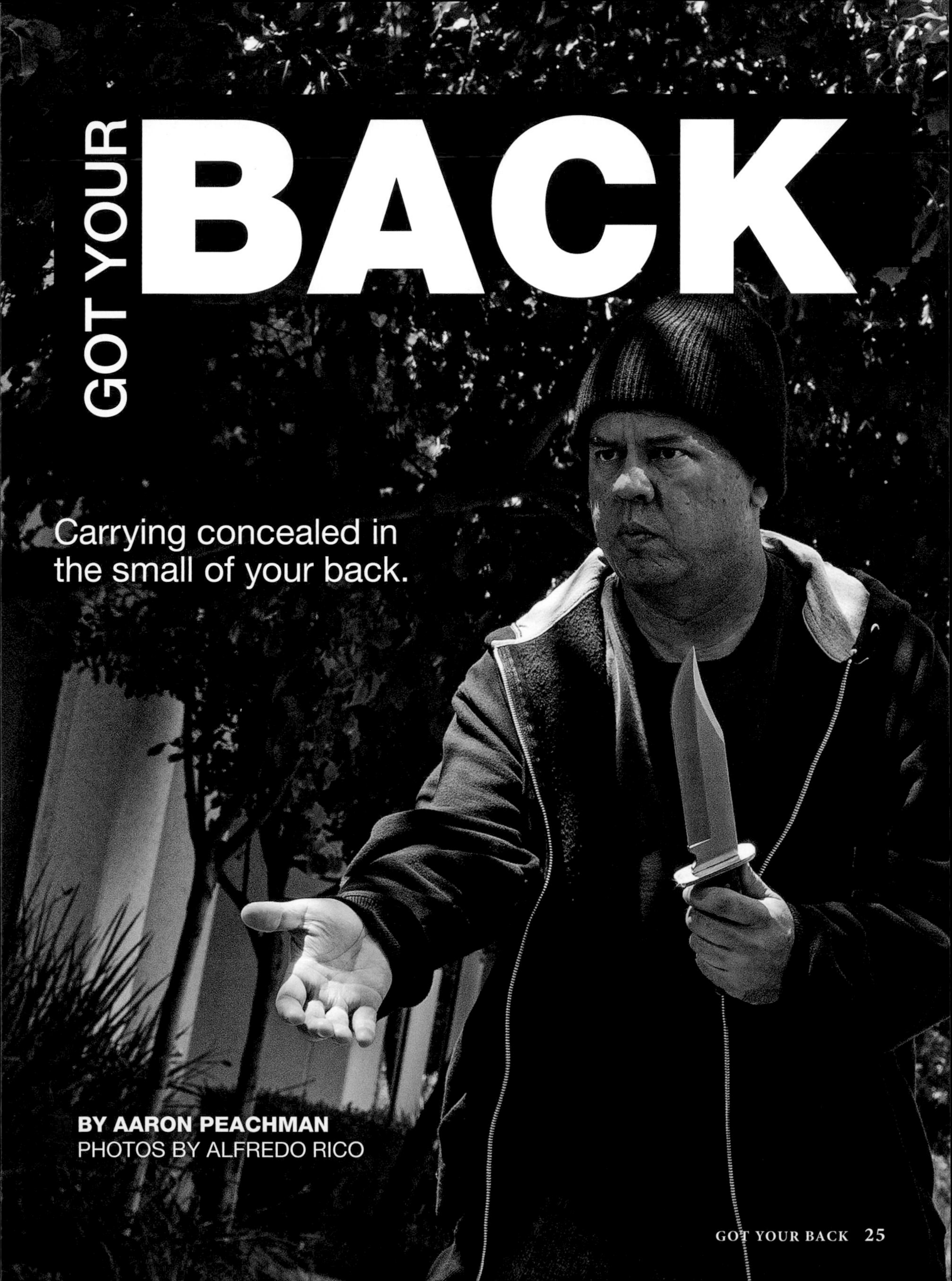

Carrying concealed in the small of your back.

BY AARON PEACHMAN
PHOTOS BY ALFREDO RICO

You return your wallet to your back right pocket and turn away from the ATM only to find yourself confronted by the wicked point and gleaming steel edge of a blade grasped in a sweaty hand. Your eyes travel from the tip of the blade up your attacker's arm to his unshaven face, and you see a look of desperation in his eyes that chills you to the bone. He may leave you be if you give him your wallet, or he may open up your throat to ensure there isn't a witness. You defensively raise your hands and start pleading. You slowly reach behind your back with your right hand, but instead of reaching into your pocket, you wrap your hand around the grip of a pistol. A maneuver you've practiced many times before, you intuitively find a good shooting grip, draw and spring into action. Instead of seeing a wallet fresh filled with cash, he is now staring down the barrel of your .45.

There are a lot of options for locations to carry a concealed handgun, and they all have strengths and weaknesses. Ultimately, the best method is what you find the most comfortable and effective for accomplishing your goals. Body shape, clothing selection, firearm selection and personal preference all factor into selecting a carry location. Small-of-the-back (SOB) carry is often maligned but can be an extremely valid method of firearm concealment.

As a police officer, I have been using SOB carry as my preferred method of concealed carry while off duty for nearly eight years and also utilized it while working plainclothes assignments.

The single biggest benefit of SOB carry is the ability to conceal the most gun with the least clothing. By utilizing the natural contours of your body and placing your pistol in the hollow formed by the small of your back, you are able to conceal a comparatively large handgun with minimal need for special cover garments. I routinely conceal a double-stack-magazine, striker-fired pistol chambered in .45 ACP in the small of my back with only a T-shirt as a cover garment. I typically do this with a subcompact Glock 30 but have, on occasion, when wearing baggy or heavy clothing, even used a full-frame model, a Glock 21.

HOLSTERS

The primary options for SOB holsters can be split into inside-the-waistband (IWB) holsters and outside-the-waistband (OWB) holsters.

The main attraction for OWB holsters is that many people find them to be more comfortable than IWB options. However, there is a significant loss of concealability and options for cover garments, since no portion of the handgun is covered by your pants.

IWB holsters are my holsters of choice for SOB carry because they offer superior concealment. There is a wide selection of pistols and cover garments that are compatible with them as well.

When choosing a holster for SOB carry, I recommend one that has snap-closure loops to secure the holster to a belt. Holsters that are held in place by friction, or those held in place with clips or hooks, do not offer the level of stability needed for a handgun that is being carried in the small of the back. Handguns concealed in the small of your back are

Photo by Alfredo Rico

Utilize a two-handed garment-clearing technique when speed is more important than surprise.

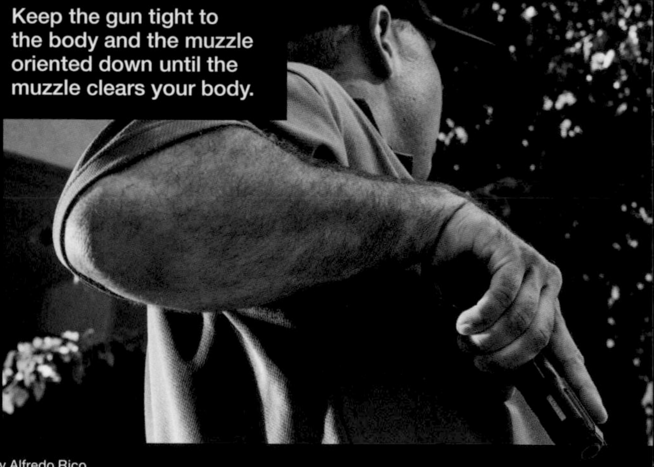

Keep the gun tight to the body and the muzzle oriented down until the muzzle clears your body.

A one-handed garment-clearing technique maximizes the surprise factor and also allows the other hand to be used for pleading or fending.

Photos by Alfredo Rico

exposed to a greater amount of jostling. Just sitting down in most chairs causes the gun to get bumped around, and if it is not firmly anchored, this may cause it to shift.

GETTING THE FIT

Getting the right fit can be a matter of trial and error. Try several different pistol-and-holster combinations to find the best one for you. The most comfortable holsters usually hold the pistol in the center of your back, completely above your tailbone. Usually, single-stack-magazine subcompact semiautomatics are the most comfortable handguns to carry this way. They are often narrower than revolvers, thinner than their double-stack brethren and smaller in every way than full-size semiautomatics. Ultimately, comfort is a personal consideration, but there are several ways you can improve it.

THE DRAW STROKE

SOB carry requires slight modifications to a standard draw stroke. The basic premise of the draw stroke remains the same, but since you are coming from behind your body, you must maneuver the gun around your torso.

Start by clearing your cover garments by either using your support hand to sweep the garment while your dominant hand reaches for your gun or by using your dominant hand to clear the garment. After clearing your cover garment, achieve a one-hand shooting grip while simultaneously breaking any retention features your holster has. Remove the pistol from the holster, and orient the muzzle downward. Keeping the gun close to your body, maneuver it around your torso in a tight semicircle, keeping the muzzle down until it has cleared your body. Use caution when doing this, as the circular motion required to clear your body can easily turn into sweeping the muzzle of your gun across areas and people you don't intend to aim at. That sweeping motion also results in a less efficient draw and may cause you to swing past your target. Once the muzzle has cleared your body, orient it toward your threat in a retention/close-quarter shooting position. At that point you can begin engaging if needed. You can now complete your pistol presentation as you normally would or maintain the close-quarter hold as appropriate.

Utilize the two-hand garment-sweep method when speed is your primary concern and the one-hand method when trying to maintain the element of surprise or when your support hand is needed for other tasks, such as fending off or mock-surrender motions.

If you are seated in a vehicle or chair with a back, you may need to create space for the draw stroke by leaning slightly forward in your seat, allowing room for your handgun. Many modern shooting schools advocate leaning forward aggressively toward the threat as part of the normal draw stroke and shooting position, so this is actually a familiar motion to many experienced shooters.

The SOB draw stroke is awkward while lying supine. To avoid the pistol being pinned by your body, either roll to your support side or sit up at the waist. If those options are not available, plant your feet and elevate your hips, creating enough of a gap to draw.

ADVANTAGES

Aside from being able to conceal a wide range of handguns with nearly any cover garment, another benefit of SOB carry is the opportunity for a sur-

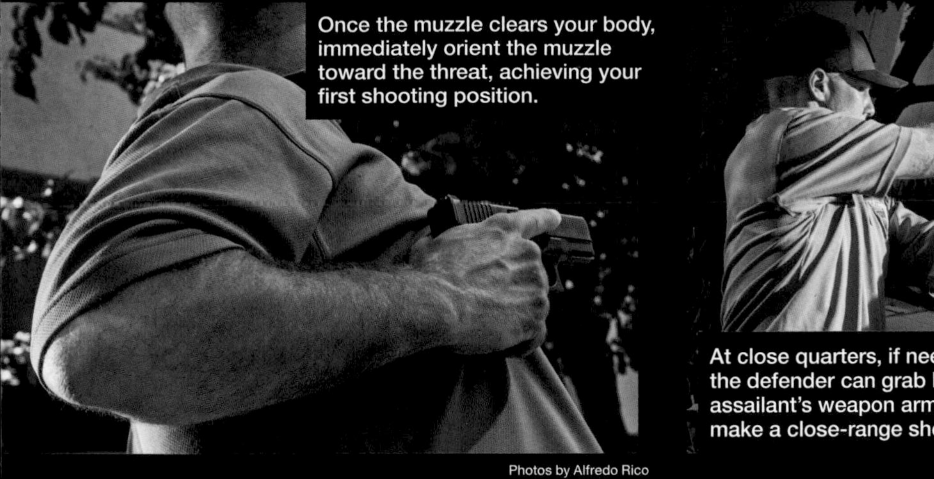
Once the muzzle clears your body, immediately orient the muzzle toward the threat, achieving your first shooting position.

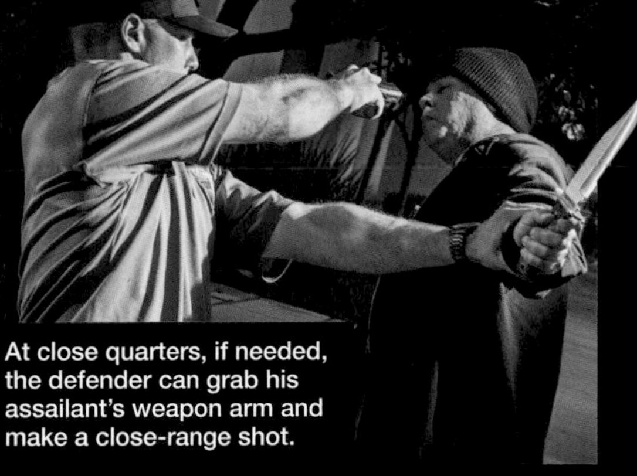
At close quarters, if needed, the defender can grab his assailant's weapon arm and make a close-range shot.

Photos by Alfredo Rico

prise draw stroke while right in front of the bad guy. If he's looking for a wallet, your attacker may expect, or even direct, you to reach into your back pocket. Reaching behind your back is now an anticipated movement. Your attacker will even expect your hand to be returning to the front, but he is planning for a wallet, not a gun. The would-be mugger will not be perceiving the threat, processing it and formulating a response all while you have already committed to action. You have the initiative and a means to defend yourself, which places you at a serious advantage.

DRAWBACKS

The most common complaint about SOB carry is that it is uncomfortable due to the gun constantly pressing against your back. This is very much a function of your own unique physiology as well as weapon and holster selection. My personal tried-and-true combo of a Glock 30 in a Galco Royal Guard holster is very comfortable for me and rarely causes issues, but everyone is different. For me, the barrel of the gun is short enough and held high enough to not be pressed into my tailbone, and the natural hollow of my lower back creates a pocket that is the right size for my gun to be held in place without excessive pressure on my spine.

The other primary concern about SOB carry is the risk of injury to your back if you are knocked over and land on your gun. This is a consideration no matter where you carry your gun. Getting knocked onto your gun-side hip could be very painful and potentially injurious as well. It's true that your lower back has less protected bone structure, and an injury in this area could literally be crippling.

TRAINING

Spend time practicing your SOB draw stroke as you would for any other carry method. Use both one-hand and two-hand garment-clearing techniques, because both have valid tactical applications. Make sure to specifically practice the surprise draw stroke. Acquiring an inert training gun and practicing the surprise draw stroke with a live training partner is highly beneficial since it allows you to incorporate movement off line from the threat and even gives you the opportunity to practice trapping the bad guy's weapon hand or driving it off line while you simultaneously deploy your handgun.

SURPRISE, BIG GUNS AND A T-SHIRT

SOB carry offers tremendous versatility and some real tactical benefits. It is not without drawbacks, but all methods of concealed carry have pros and cons that have to be personally evaluated before deciding on a method. By utilizing the natural contours of your body, SOB carry allows for maximum concealment of relatively bulky handguns with as little as a slightly baggy T-shirt. SOB carry also grants the ability to surprise an attacker and seize the initiative, even when caught flat-footed. A pistol with more ammo capacity, longer sight radius and a more effective caliber, paired with the element of surprise and decisive action, presents a huge advantage on the path to victory in a violent encounter.

IN DEFENSE OF OTHERS

Third-party protection strategies.

In most states, you have a legal right to use deadly force in defense of someone other than yourself as long as you can articulate that the other person faced an imminent threat of death or great bodily injury. It's incumbent upon you to be intimately familiar with the self-defense laws in your state. If you shoot someone who was later deemed not to have posed a deadly threat, you could be subject to civil liability or even criminal prosecution. The bottom line is that if you're going to draw your gun and intervene, you better be damn sure who the bad guy is and that he indeed presents a deadly threat. The focus of this piece is on the tactical aspects of third-party protection.

BY RICHARD NANCE
PHOTOS BY ALFREDO RICO

I'm not a Secret Service agent, schooled in dignitary protection, and chances are neither are you. I don't walk around wearing a dark suit jacket to conceal a submachine gun, and I certainly don't wear sunglasses or the telltale earpiece with the cord running under my collar. While you and I won't be tasked with protecting the president anytime soon, we must understand the dynamics of keeping those around us (our VIPs) safe when a deadly threat emerges.

COVER AND EVACUATE

When you think of a bodyguard protecting his client, you might envision him stepping in front of the client to shield him or her from the threat. This technique, sometimes referred to as "cover and evacuate," requires the bodyguard to intentionally place himself in the line of fire while attempting to direct his client to safety. In essence, the bodyguard is a human shield responsible for protecting the client from harm.

Executive-protection specialists who guard dignitaries, celebrities or any client who would likely be targeted for assassination

SIERRA
Photo by Alfredo Rico

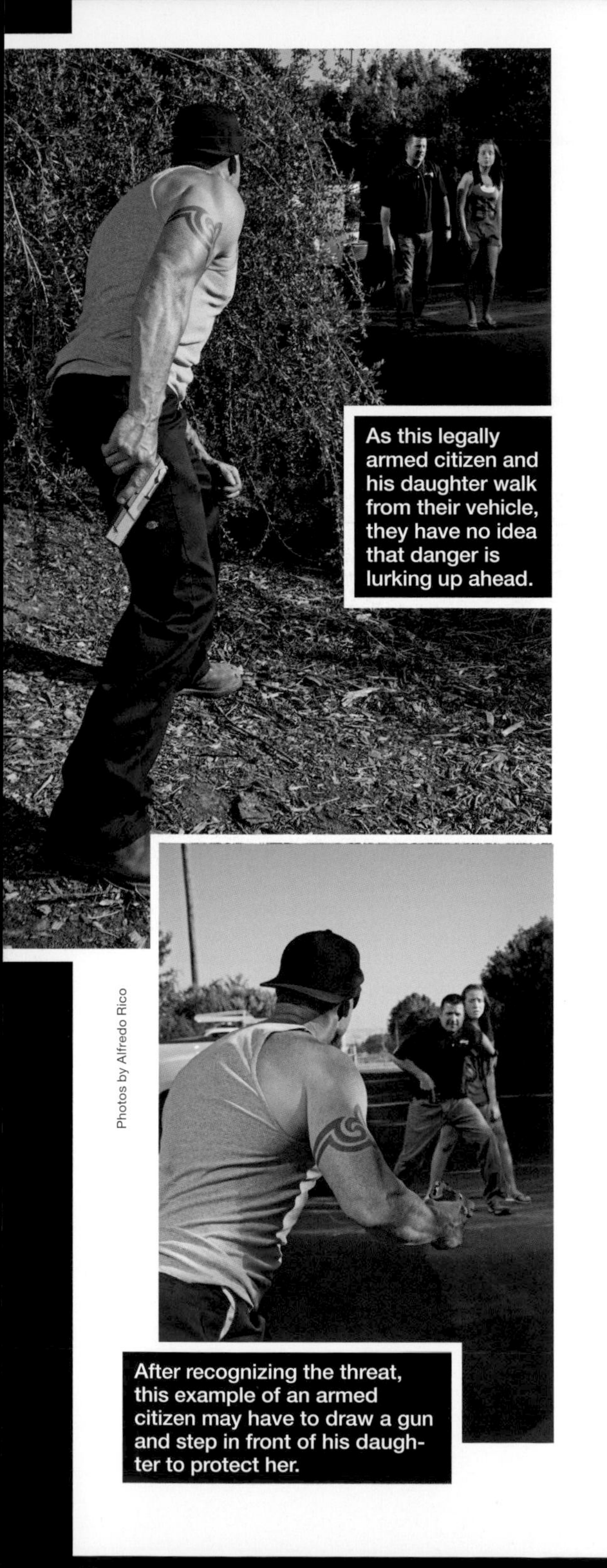
As this legally armed citizen and his daughter walk from their vehicle, they have no idea that danger is lurking up ahead.

After recognizing the threat, this example of an armed citizen may have to draw a gun and step in front of his daughter to protect her.

Photos by Alfredo Rico

must be both mentally and physically prepared to take a bullet. Ideally, the client is aware of his role during an attempted "attack on principal" and acts accordingly. A team of properly trained personnel wearing body armor has a high probability of success using this technique.

But, as you can imagine, many potential problems arise when a minimally trained legally armed citizen attempts to shield a third party while simultaneously delivering accurate fire to stop the threat. One of the most obvious and significant concerns is that protecting someone else while engaging in a gunfight inherently requires you to divide your attention. If you are too focused on the threat, it's quite possible that the one you need to protect could panic and run into the line of fire, trip you or inadvertently bump your arm as you are pressing the trigger. On the other hand, you can't be so concerned with the person you're protecting that you forget about the threat you're protecting against.

If you find yourself having to step in front of another person, you're going to want to communicate what it is the VIP should be doing. You will need to maintain physical contact with the person you're protecting in order to keep the principal directly behind you. This is best accomplished by grabbing hold of the VIP with your support hand as you return fire.

Refrain from blading your body to the threat, since doing so would provide less protection to the person behind you. Keep in mind that unless you're wearing body armor, rounds that strike you could pass through your flesh and into the person you're shielding. A person can only sustain so many rounds and remain standing. When you drop, you are no longer protecting anyone. Therefore, evacuation is a high priority. Your goal is to get the person you're protecting to safety, not necessarily to take out the bad guy.

COVER AND RUN

It's often said that the mission dictates the tactics. Tactics designed to protect a political leader from assassination might not be well suited for protecting your teenage daughter and vice versa. It's highly unlikely that your teenage daughter would be the target of an assassination. She's much more likely to be targeted because you produced a concealed handgun

When the threat emerges, the defender draws and...

...moves between the assailant and the person he's protecting.

Photos by Alfredo Rico

in response to a deadly threat and she just happened to be with you. In such a case, directing your daughter to run behind whatever cover may be available as you move between her and the assailant might be a better option than the cover and evacuate technique.

Since you're not required to keep one hand behind your back to control the person you're protecting, you're able to fire from a more comfortable and accurate two-handed, sighted-fire position. As with the cover and evacuate technique, you want to keep your body squared to the threat to provide as much surface area as possible to shield the person you're protecting. One problem inherent with both the cover and evacuate technique and this technique is that the person you're protecting remains in line with you. Although you are theoretically shielding him from incoming rounds, it's quite possible for a round that misses or passes through you to strike the person you're trying to protect.

DIVIDE AND CONQUER

One tactic that may work very well for a legally armed citizen protecting a friend or family member but would be catastrophic for a Secret Service agent protecting the president is to actually run away from the person you're trying to protect in order to create a diversion. Your movement and gunfire are apt to draw the assailant's attention, which means there's a good chance he will focus on you in order to fight your resistance rather than concern himself with the less threatening person you're trying to protect. In essence, you're putting yourself in harm's way to create a window of opportunity for the third party to gain distance and find cover.

I hadn't really considered this tactic until I was working with Handgun Combatives founder Dave Spaulding on the set of "Personal Defense TV." Dave explained that in all likelihood the person you're protecting is not being specifically targeted and is endangered merely because you have drawn your firearm in

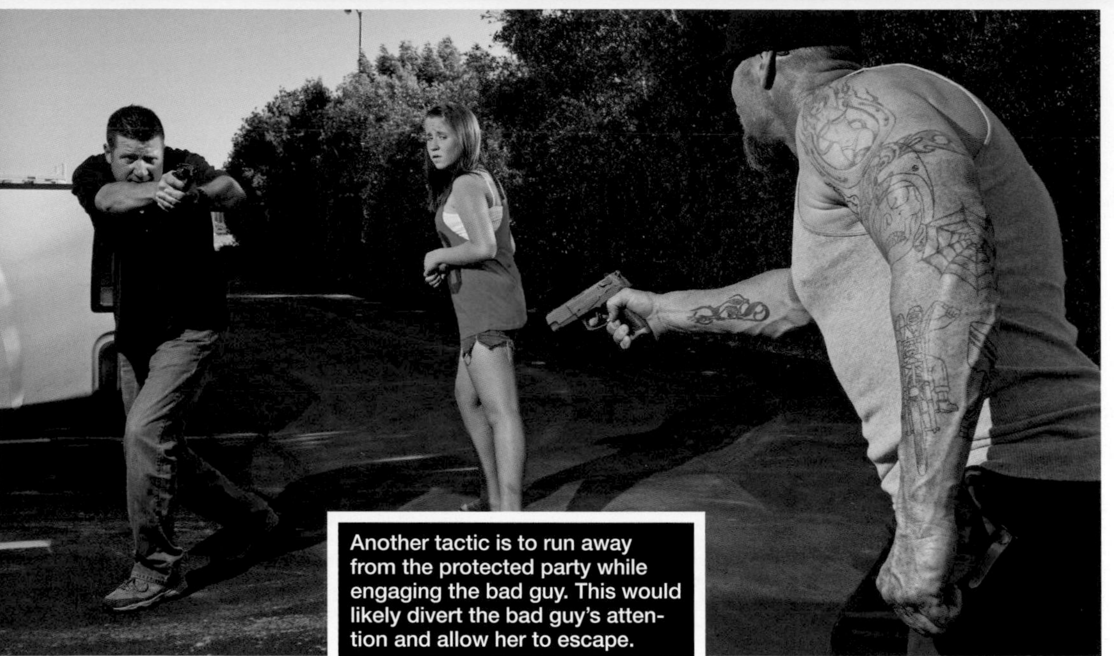

Photos by Alfredo Rico

Another tactic is to run away from the protected party while engaging the bad guy. This would likely divert the bad guy's attention and allow her to escape.

Are you prepared to make this hostage rescue shot?

defense of yourself or others. In such a case the safest place for that person is probably as far away from you as possible. Rather than trying to shield the person you're protecting, run away from him while yelling for him to run to the nearest position of cover. Your movement, yelling and most of all your firearm pointed at the bad guy would tend to cause the bad guy to focus on you instead of the fleeing individual who poses no threat.

If the bad guy did, for some reason, shoot at the person you are trying to protect, he would be forced to shoot a target that was quickly moving farther away. Like the cover and run technique described above, this technique enables you to move freely and fire from a much more accurate two-handed shooting platform.

TAKING THE "HOSTAGE RESCUE SHOT"

SWAT teams typically train for the worst-case scenario, with the rationale being that if you're prepared for that, anything else is much easier to handle. In case you're wondering, the worst-case scenario is a hostage rescue operation. Keep in mind, hostage rescue is the most difficult mission for highly trained SWAT officers armed to the teeth with top-quality rifles and hard-to-miss-with sighting systems.

Understandably, some gun owners dismiss the notion of ever taking a shot with their pistol when an armed criminal has taken a hostage. While it's wise to know your limitations and not attempt a shot that you're not capable of making, the responsible thing to do would be to train to make that precise shot, since it could potentially save the life of a hostage.

Without question, this would be one of the most difficult shots imaginable because missing is not an option. Through frequent and realistic training, you can develop the skills and confidence needed to make the hit at distances from which you're likely to engage a hostage taker. If you're too far away or don't have a clean shot, don't force it.

Photos by Alfredo Rico

When an active shooter is preoccupied, an armed citizen could flank him and deliver a shot that puts an end to the killing.

To make the hostage rescue shot, you may need to position yourself either to the left or right in order to obtain the most advantageous angle from which to fire. Since accuracy is of the utmost importance when making a hostage rescue shot, it's probably best to shoot from a stationary position rather than attempting a shot while moving.

One option is to take several steps to close distance with the hostage taker and afford yourself the best possible angle, then plant your feet as you achieve that perfect sight alignment and sight picture. From there, press the trigger to the rear for that immediately incapacitating T-zone hit that will permanently flip the switch in the bad guy's brain to "off."

PROTECTING A DISTANT THIRD PARTY

I initially wrote this a day after XXXX XXXX entered the Century 16 Movie Theater in Aurora, Colorado, clad in body armor and donning a gas mask during the midnight premiere of the "The Dark Knight Rises." XXXX opened fire inside the packed theater, killing 12 people and injuring 58 others in what has become one of the worst shooting sprees in U.S. history. Can you imagine how dramatically different the outcome may have been had there been a well-trained CCW holder in attendance who could have shot XXXX while he was busy shooting innocent moviegoers?

One of the reasons I choose to carry a concealed firearm every day is that I would not want to live with the regret of having been in a position to save lives if only I'd had my gun. Even a heavily armed criminal wearing body armor is susceptible to a well-placed round to an unprotected area fired from an unanticipated source (a legally armed citizen).

While accuracy is always an important factor in a gunfight, just getting rounds on target in an active-shooter scenario could save the day. The longer it takes to make your hit, the more victims are in danger of being shot. It's true that you can't miss fast enough to win a gunfight, but you could, quite possibly, shoot too slow to save lives.

Ideally, if you were in that theater when XXXX started shooting, you could have drawn your handgun and flanked him. If he didn't see you, you could have taken a breath to steady your nerves and ensure an accurate shot. Even if your round did not immediately incapacitate XXXX, it would, in all likelihood, have slowed his rate of fire and thus potentially saved lives, or it may well have prompted him to leave the theater altogether.

CONCLUSION

Without a doubt, personal defense is the primary reason for carrying a concealed firearm. However, you should prepare for situations in which your shooting skills may be put to the test in defense of others. You don't need to be a Secret Service agent to be able to protect a third party during a sudden attack. All it takes is an understanding of how to best protect that person and the ability to make that criminal-career-ending shot.

STORY BY
PATRICK SWEENEY

PHOTOGRAPHS BY
JEFFREY A. JONES

PAGE
36

Coming to a Cafeteria
Near You !

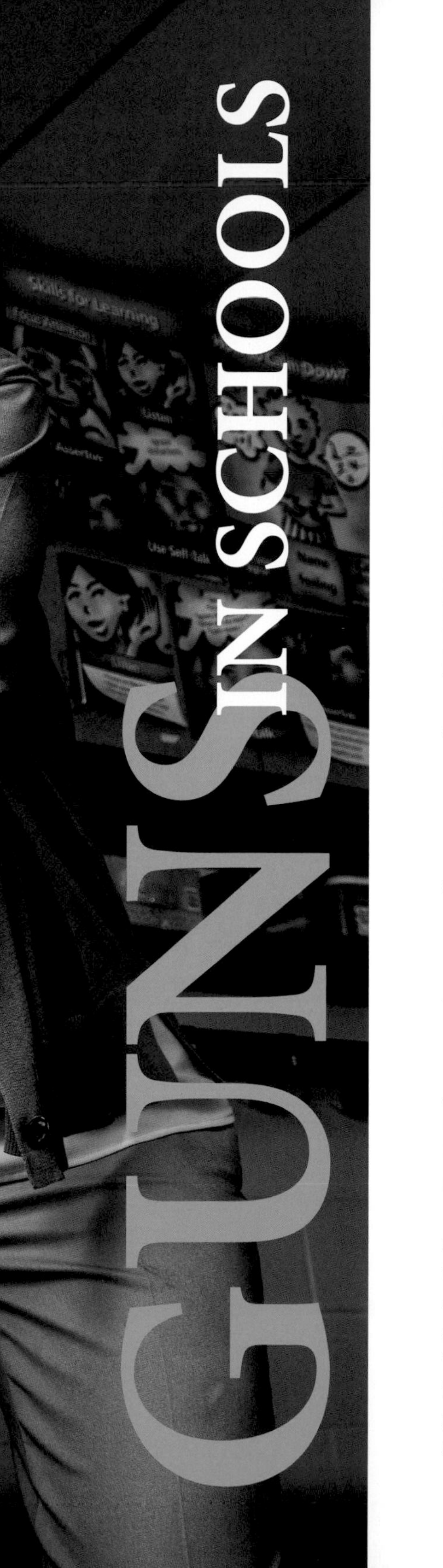

THE DEBATE OVER ARMED TEACHERS.

We all know the quickest way to stop a bad guy with a gun is to have them run into a good guy with a gun. (Or gal; let's not be sexist here.) This is an accepted fact in Israel, where schoolteachers on field trips can be seen herding students with an Uzi slung over their back. But here in the USA? Oh boy.

The NRA has proposed the National Model School Shield Program to train volunteers, including retired police officers, to be low-profile armed guards in schools. Who can object to more training? Or more safety?

How about the American Federation of Teachers (AFT)? As a response, AFT president Randi Weingarten used all the usual buzzwords: bipartisan, commonsense, and heaping blame on firearms, magazines, bullet design and the "lack of background checks."

The problem seems to come down to a matter of trust. Or rather, the lack of it. The NRA and other gun rights organizations feel that teachers can be trusted, retired police officers can be trusted, and that schools can be protected in the same way we protect many other locations and operations. What these people don't trust are the efforts of the traditional gun control groups such as the Brady Campaign or moderate-appearing groups like Moms Demand Action and Sandy Hook Promise.

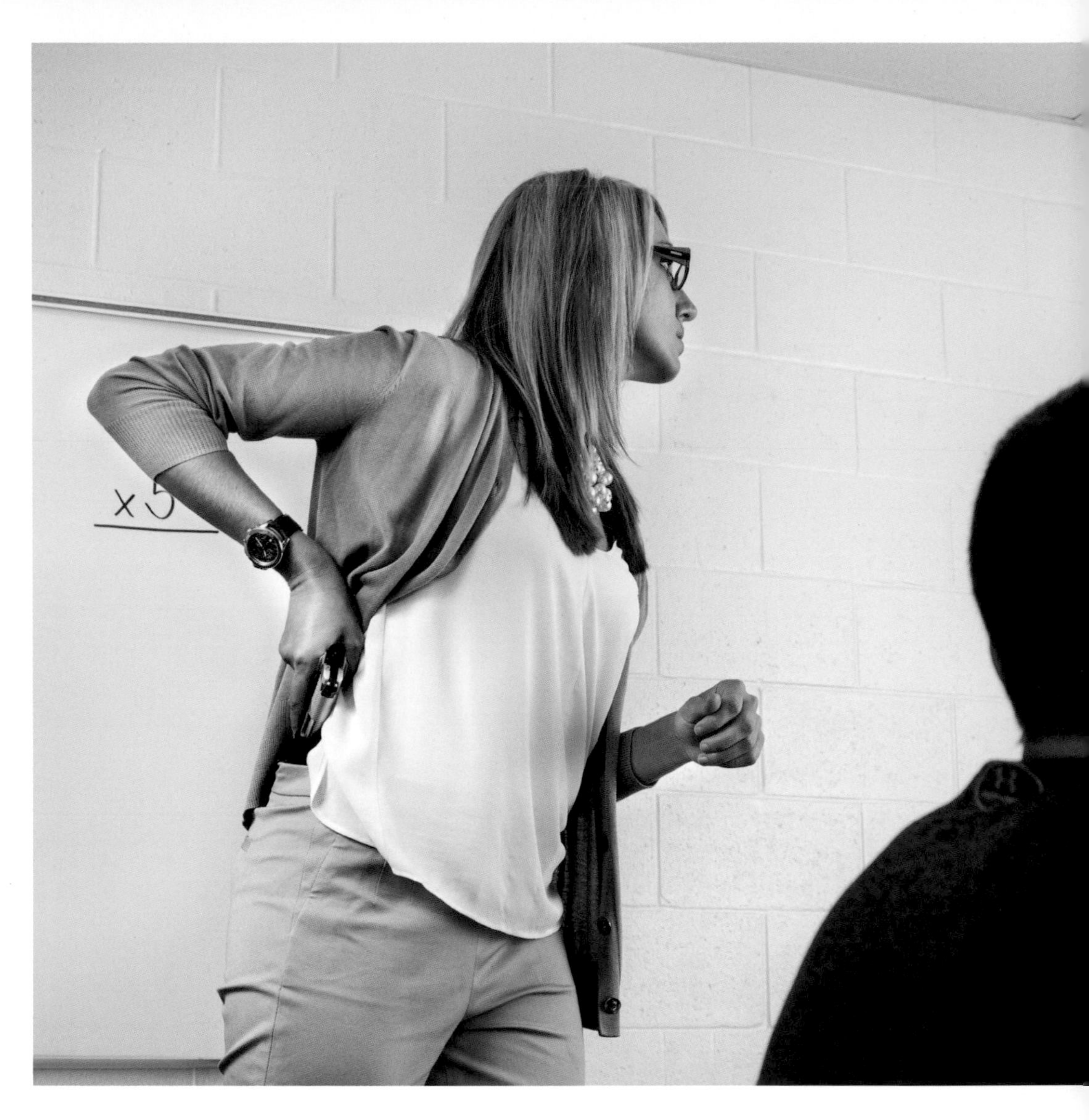

“

**THIS IS AN ACCEPTED FACT IN ISRAEL, WHER
SCHOOLTEACHERS ON FIELD TRIPS CAN BE
SEEN HERDING STUDENTS WITH AN UZI
SLUNG OVER THEIR BACK.”**

Photo by Jeffrey A. Jones

The Brady Campaign has apparently changed their approach. Instead of a firebrand antigun organization, the Brady Campaign is now only interested in "reasonable" approaches to reduce "gun violence." The suspicion on the part of gun owners stems from three areas: 1) the same Brady Campaign is still run by the same people; 2) "reasonable" efforts have not been demonstrated to actually work; and 3) where they have been enacted, the next step has been to decry them as "insufficient" and in need of just a bit more work to be effective while still being "reasonable."

The Brady Campaign on children and "gun violence" states: "Over 18,000 American children and teens are injured or killed each year due to gun violence." Notice the inclusion of teens. That means anyone under the age of 20, which sweeps a lot of gang, drug and other violent crimes into the total. And the neutral and vague "gun violence." Not people being violent, but violence committed by guns.

The entire focus of the Brady Campaign is fixed on how to prevent the bad guns getting into schools and not on such straightforward approaches as teaching kids that "Guns are loud and painful if used wrong. So don't." And not a word about how to prevent "bad guys" from getting into schools or about armed security for schools that might need it.

The Moms Demand Action web page is full of earnest entreaties to improve safety. While it is difficult to argue against greater safety, as an old adage tells us, "The devil is in the details."

They are also sidestepping the issue by focusing on guns as animate actors. Yes, keeping firearms out of the hands of the untrained is good. Their approach is to make guns mysterious, hidden secrets, and as an inadvertent result, alluring. Oh, and proud of their work, to lobby for more gun control "in states like Colorado, Connecticut, Maine, Minnesota, New Hampshire, New York, Oregon and Washington." The connections between them? The usual suspects: bans on high-capacity magazines, requiring background checks and gun storage.

The lack of trust appears to be rooted in a particular frame of reference; are guns inherently evil, or are they simply tools? From the viewpoint of those holding the "tools," trying to get a handle on school shootings by further restricting firearms is merely overlooking the real problem: bad people. Or confused people. Or mentally problemed people. It is like trying to prevent drownings by drying up every lake in the county.

The other side of the argument views guns and any talk of arming or educating people to be safe as the equivalent of air-dropping dime bags of heroin into schoolyards across the country. These are people who state guns are evil, more is bad, and anyone who doesn't agree is also evil, and possibly even part of a conspiracy to expand gun ownership.

Those who are unaware of the minefield they are wandering through can find themselves suffering as a result. Singer Tim McGraw was so moved by the Sandy Hook school shooting that he changed his tour schedule to include a fundraising concert for the Sandy Hook Promise charity. While a heart-warming gesture, raising money for the families, it ran headlong into the buzzsaw of mistrust. The gun-control side saw and touted it as a means of raising money and awareness for the families and their plight, since the "heartless" gun lobby won't. On the other side, the gun rights organizations decried the publicity it gave to the positions of those who would enact more controls, and pointed out that the money won't, in all likelihood, go to the families of the victims.

> "THESE ARE PEOPLE WHO STATE GUNS ARE EVIL, MORE IS BAD, AND ANYONE WHO DOESN'T AGREE IS ALSO EVIL, AND POSSIBLY EVEN PART OF A CONSPIRACY TO EXPAND GUN OWNERSHIP."

The *Hartford Courant* reported that the Sandy Hook Promise is not a charity set up to aid the families, but is instead a national organization that "funds protection and prevention programs." They are not set up to aid the families; it was created to lobby for national changes in gun laws.

Regardless of where you stand on the armed teacher debate, we can all agree that safer children is our goal. The purpose of this piece is to get you thinking, really thinking, about what's best for your children and your community. Get informed and get involved.

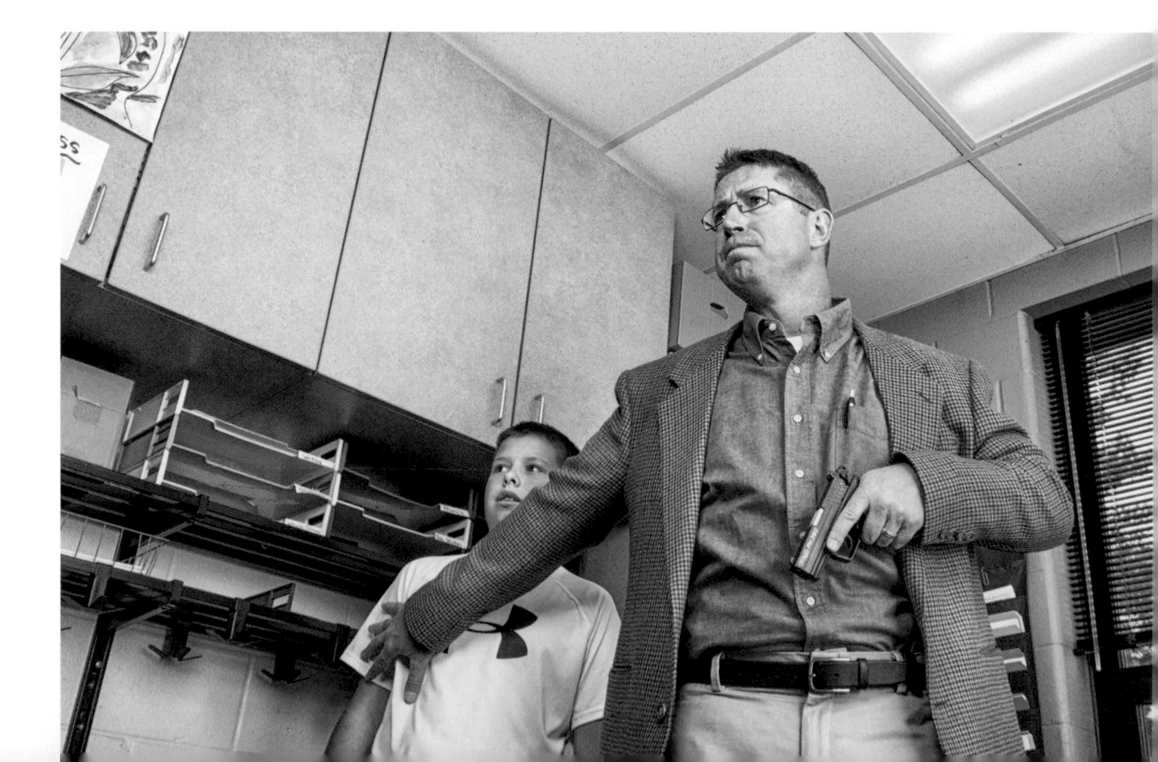

PART II

COMBAT TACTICS

Having a firearm doesn't preclude you from engaging in violent hand-to-hand combat.

IN-HAND GUN RETENTION TACTICS

You must be able to retain possession of your gun during a deadly close-range encounter.

BY RICHARD NANCE
PHOTOS BY ALFREDO RICO

Handgun retention is a critical skill set because what starts out as a shoot scenario could quickly transition to hand-to-hand combat, requiring you to fight with your gun in hand. Even if you shoot your adversary, there's no guarantee that your rounds will immediately incapacitate him. If your gun is grabbed, respond immediately and aggressively until you have fully extracted the gun from the bad guy's hands.

There are myriad handgun retention techniques out there. Some look impressive, but are far too complex to bet your life on. To be effective in the real world, handgun retention techniques must be quickly learned, easily recalled under stress and simple enough to execute under the absolute worst of conditions, such as when you're in a life-or-death tug of war with a larger, stronger adversary who's fully committed to disarming you. When your life is on the line, keep your responses simple and few.

While a critical component, technique is only part of the solution. Perhaps even more important is your willingness to do what must be done to keep the bad guy from getting your gun. Whether this means gouging an assailant's eye, stabbing him or shooting him, you must resolve never to be disarmed.

PREPARATION

If you expect to be able to maintain possession of your gun against an opponent, you should consider what a real disarm attempt would entail. It will probably bear little resemblance to the static, lackadaisical grab that's common in many training sessions.

Using this fully extended shooting position places your firearm dangerously close to your adversary.

Photo by Alfredo Rico

Life or Death

Without question, firearm retention is a matter of life or death. Every year, police officers are disarmed and killed with their own guns. In some cases, inadequate training was undoubtedly a factor. But at least officers receive *some* training in this life-saving skill set. Few civilian shooters receive any sort of firearm retention training.

In the "Keep Your Piece" DVD and workbook set, Wartac CQC cofounders Richard Nance and David Hallford, along with Aaron Peachman, present a simple and effective firearm retention system designed to work under the worst conditions. The 107-minute DVD covers in-hand and in-holster handgun retention while standing, from the ground, against a wall, even while being choked. There is also a segment on long-gun retention, an important but often overlooked topic. If you carry a firearm, you had better know how to maintain it when an assailant is hell-bent on taking it from you.

For more information, contact Paladin Press, 800-392-2400, paladin-press.com.

If someone really wanted to take your gun from you, there's a good chance he would first try to punch you or take you to the ground. One thing you can count on is the bad guy clutching your gun with a death grip. He will probably use both hands, and he will pressure you—full speed, full power. If your techniques don't hold up under these conditions, it's time to find some that will.

GRIP

Not only is grip one of the fundamentals of marksmanship, it is also a critical factor in retaining possession of your firearm. To establish a proper grip on your gun, your shooting hand should be as high on the backstrap as possible, with your thumb pointed forward. Keep your index finger along the frame, and wrap your remaining fingers around the grip. Then your support hand fills the void left by your shooting hand, and the

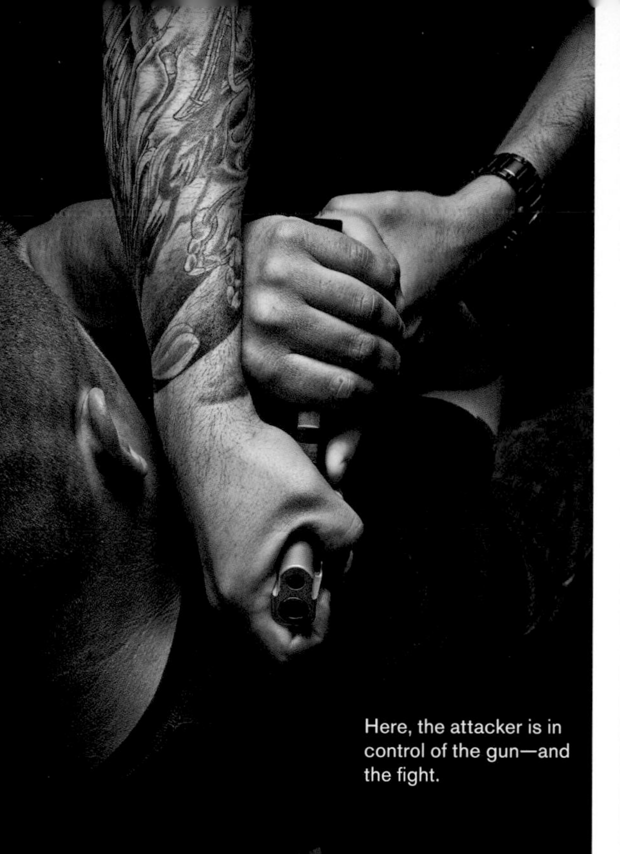

Here, the attacker is in control of the gun—and the fight.

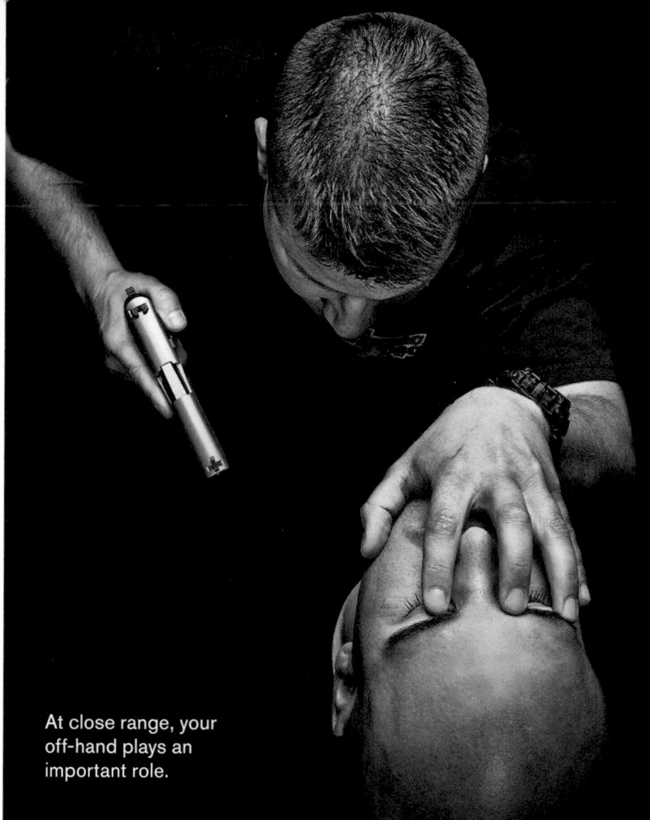

At close range, your off-hand plays an important role.

fingers of your support hand wrap around the fingers of your shooting hand.

This is the most secure grip you can achieve, because your hands are completely enveloping the grip of your gun. No matter how an opponent may grab your gun, he will be working with an inferior grip. While it could be argued that your adversary could gain a leverage advantage by grabbing the slide, the fact remains that you are reaping the retention benefits of holding the gun the way it was designed to be held.

If you were to bend the thumb of your shooting hand downward and wrap your support-hand thumb over it, there would be a gap because your thumbs prevent the palm of your support hand from fitting flush against the grip. This gap allows the gun to move slightly within your hands and could ultimately lead to you being disarmed.

"WHEN YOUR LIFE IS ON THE LINE, KEEP YOUR RESPONSES SIMPLE AND FEW."

DEFAULT RESPONSE (PUSH/PULL)

When your gun is grabbed, you must respond as though your life depends on it, because it does. Your default response should be to employ the push/pull methodology. This is a simple, gross-motor-based response that has a high probability of success when executed with vigor. To execute the push/pull technique, take a lunging step toward your adversary with your support-side leg, and try to drive the muzzle into his chest. Immediately step back with your gun-side leg, then your support-side leg as you pull the gun with all your might.

To further tilt the odds in your favor, add a twist as you pull the gun toward you. The twisting motion helps to break that assailant's grip, and if you're lucky, the front sight will tear into his flesh. (If you're a right-handed shooter, twisting counterclockwise will be more natural.)

The reason the push/pull is so effective is that when the bad guy attempts to resist the push by instinctively pushing back, you are then pulling the gun from him. The combination of his push and your pull should be sufficient to extract

If the attacker grabs your handgun, drive the muzzle toward him and attempt to pull the gun from his grasp. If that doesn't work, use your off-hand to pry the weapon from him.

Photo by Alfredo Rico

the gun from his hands. If for some reason the first attempt is unsuccessful, you can simply repeat the process. Chances are it will be even more difficult for the bad guy to hold on the second time around.

> **"IF YOUR GUN IS GRABBED, RESPOND IMMEDIATELY AND AGGRESSIVELY UNTIL YOU HAVE FULLY EXTRACTED THE GUN FROM THE BAD GUY'S HANDS."**

A variant of the push/pull technique could come into play when you are clinched with an assailant and unable to perform the lunging steps necessary to execute the standard technique. As an alternative, you could place your support hand under the assailant's chin and push his head away while pulling the gun to your chest. This variation adheres to the push/pull concept and is a viable option in close quarters where your mobility is restricted.

PLAN B (PRY)

Of course, no technique is foolproof. If the push/pull technique is not effective, transition to plan B, which in this case involves releasing your support hand from the gun and using it to pry the gun from the assailant's hands. The pry concept is effective while standing and, with slight modification, from the ground. Like the push/pull technique, the pry is both simple and reliable.

In order to exert maximum leverage and reduce the odds of the muzzle crossing your support-side arm, step at an approximately 45-degree angle to your gun side as you position the exterior portion of your support-side forearm against the assailant's wrist. Then pivot on the balls of your feet to face the assailant. To pry the gun from the assailant's grasp, simultaneously push against the assailant's wrist with your arm and pull the gun toward your chest.

As you strip the assailant's hands from the gun, take hold

If the attacker has gained control of your hands and the gun, you risk being disarmed and/or taken to the ground.

The closer the threat, the closer to your body you must position your firearm.

Photos by Alfredo Rico

of his wrist if possible. With your gun in the one-handed close-quarter hold (retention position), pivot at the waist to orient the muzzle to the threat. From there you could deliver accurate rounds to the torso and/or shove the assailant away to create distance and achieve a sighted fire position.

As mentioned, a real disarm attempt is sure to be dynamic. During the struggle, you could end up on your back with the assailant on top of you, clutching your gun. In such a case, thrust your arms to one side to negate the assailant's leverage advantage. From there, use your arm to pry your gun free as though you were executing the standing version of the technique. Use your support hand to push the assailant away from your gun. Fire as needed to escape.

"USE YOUR SUPPORT HAND TO PUSH THE ASSAILANT AWAY FROM YOUR GUN. FIRE AS NEEDED TO ESCAPE."

FOLLOW UP

Anytime you're involved in a struggle over a semiautomatic handgun, it's likely that the weapon has been rendered out of battery. In other words, the weapon will not cycle properly. If there was a round in the chamber, that round could fire, but subsequent rounds would not until the malfunction was cleared. When you rip your gun from the bad guy's clutches, you should tap the bottom of the magazine to ensure it is properly seated, rack the slide to chamber a round and assess the situation to see if you need to pull the trigger.

CONCLUSION

If you own a firearm, you owe it to yourself and those who depend on you to be capable of preventing being disarmed. If you're not willing to do whatever it takes to maintain control of your firearm, you have no business carrying one to begin with.

The best way to prepare is to engage in realistic scenarios using inert training guns and appropriate protective gear to see which techniques work under stress. Make sure your techniques are simple enough to recall and execute under real-world conditions. When it comes to handgun retention, you need to enforce a strict "hands off" policy.

CLOSE-QUARTER GUNFIGHT

Preparing for a shootout at arm's length.

BY RICHARD NANCE // PHOTOS BY ALFREDO RICO

There is a common misconception that the closer you are to your adversary in a gunfight, the easier it is to deliver rounds on target to stop the threat.

While hitting a paper target is considerably easier from a distance of 5 to 10 feet than 25 yards, the same isn't necessarily true for a living, breathing adversary who is trying to kill you. In an arm's-length showdown, a new set of challenges emerge as contact-distance weapons including knives, clubs, even fists come into play.

From this distance, you must be proficient at fighting with your gun. Proximity to your adversary may preclude you from achieving a proper stance or extending your arms to assume an eye-level shooting position. As such, close-quarter shooting, shooting from unconventional positions, striking, fending and gun retention are critical factors in determining the outcome of the gunfight.

CLOSE-QUARTER SHOOTING

When your adversary is close enough to grab your gun or shove your arms to redirect the muzzle, pull the gun in close to your body. This can be accomplished using either the one-handed or two-handed close-quarter hold. It's important that you're proficient with both positions because the situation will dictate which would be most effective.

The one-handed close-quarter hold affords you a relatively secure gun retention position while freeing up your nongun hand to strike or fend, depending on the circumstance. The drawback to the one-handed close-quarter hold is that you only have one hand on your gun. It does not provide the same level of retention against a gun grab as the two-handed version. However, since the one-handed close-quarter hold enables you to keep your gun farther from your adversary, it's harder for him to grab it.

To assume the one-handed close-quarter hold, pull the gun to your chest while canting it slightly outward. Canting the weapon prevents the slide from impacting your body or becoming entangled in your clothing, either of which could induce a malfunction. Be sure to anchor your thumb, the heel of your hand or the bottom

The one-handed close-quarter hold enables you to keep your gun away from your adversary. Anchoring the gun to your body allows you to orient the muzzle to the threat using body alignment rather than using the sight for alignment.

Shooting from a kneeling position could thwart a violent assault, preventing you from having to grapple with your adversary on the ground.

of your magazine to your chest as a reference. This is vitally important because it ensures that your wrist does not extend beyond your torso, which would make it hard to know where your muzzle is oriented and leave you susceptible to a disarm. Ideally, you could use your nongun hand to strike under your adversary's chin and drive him backward as you engage with your gun. If needed, your nongun hand could be used defensively to fend incoming strikes.

The two-handed close-quarter hold affords maximum gun retention, since your natural two-handed shooting grip should completely envelope the grip of your gun. You could strike in a thrusting motion with the muzzle of your gun rather than shoot, when appropriate. However, since both hands are on your gun, the two-

If your gun is grabbed, you can use your forearm to pry it from your adversary.

Photos by Alfredo Rico

handed close-quarter hold offers little in the way of defense.

To transition to the two-handed close-quarter hold from an eye-level shooting position, simply draw in both arms until the rear of the slide is a few inches from your chest. Anchor the inner portion of your elbows to your sides to ensure consistent muzzle orientation. To track left or right, simply turn your entire upper body like a turret on a tank. The two-handed close-quarter hold enables you to aim using body alignment, which is important considering that you will only have a peripheral view of your sights from this position.

UNCONVENTIONAL SHOOTING POSITIONS

The dynamics of a close-quarter gunfight might require you to fire from unorthodox positions, such as while clinched with your adversary, from your knees or even from your back. It's a good idea to experiment to determine what it takes to draw, shoot or fight from these and other unconventional shooting positions. While you can live-fire most of these positions, shooting while clinched or on the ground with your adversary will require the use of Simunition or Airsoft guns. Even non-firing training guns are beneficial for this type of training in that they at least allow you to practice achieving a viable shooting position while having to deal with an adversary who's in your face.

If you're having a hard time grasping how you might end up in a clinch, on your knees or fighting on the ground, you probably haven't been in many fights. Imagine shooting an adversary who suddenly charged with a knife. The fact that you shoot him most likely will not preclude him from grabbing hold of you or stabbing you. There's a good chance you'll find yourself in some form of a clinch. Unless you are well versed in fighting from the clinch, you might be taken down in a deadly ground fight. If you don't have at least a basic knowledge of how to fight while on the ground, you could be in serious trouble.

Here's another scenario you may not have considered. What if you were literally beaten to the ground by a bigger, stronger adversary who ambushed you? Maybe there are multiple adversaries who are clearly trying to severely injure or kill you. You're armed but haven't had an opportunity to draw your gun. You feel as though you might lose consciousness as you are hit with blow after blow. How can you get to your gun from here?

Photo by Alfredo Rico

At close range, your handgun can be employed as a bludgeon should you experience a malfunction or run out of ammunition.

One option is to shield your head with your elbow while drawing and firing from a kneeling position, using the one-handed close-quarter hold. Another choice would be to draw and intentionally roll onto your back. Retract your legs and firmly plant your feet on the ground. With your head up, extend your arms into a two-handed eye-level shooting position. Although lying on your back significantly limits your mobility, it might help you separate from your adversary and create an opportunity for you to bring your gun into play.

STRIKING

People tend to forget that a gunfight is still a fight. Chances are that if you are involved in a gunfight, it will be a close-quarter engagement where fists and feet can change the course of the fight just as easily as a gun. Keep in mind that your nongun hand plays a critical role in the fight. Since shooting your adversary with a handgun is not likely to drop him, you need to be ready to control him physically to prevent being taken down or disarmed.

One of the best strikes you could employ is to drive the palm of your nongun hand under your adversary's chin. Drive forward to throw him off balance while continuing to force his head back. From there you could fire from the one-handed close-quarter hold or disengage to create distance and assess the situation.

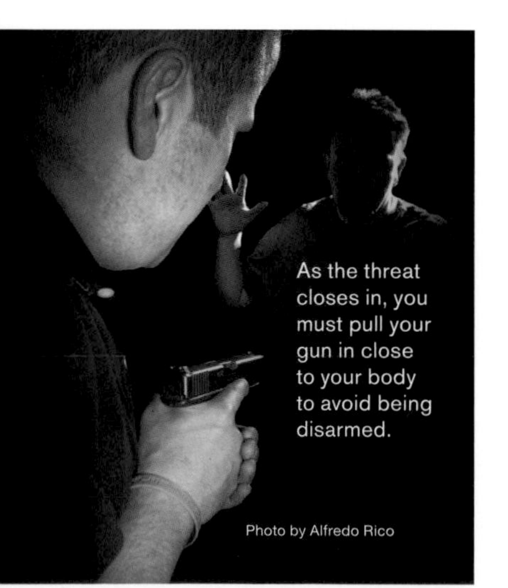

As the threat closes in, you must pull your gun in close to your body to avoid being disarmed.

Photo by Alfredo Rico

Using your gun as a striking implement is another viable option. Some are opposed to this type of strike because they worry about damaging the gun or, even worse, unintentionally firing during the strike. While these are valid concerns, they are not sufficient to completely dismiss the notion of striking with your gun.

Oftentimes, a gun malfunction or running out of ammunition is what prompts a gun strike. If your gun stops working, are you going to reload or clear the malfunction while the threat is at arm's length? Are you going to waste time trying to holster a gun that's non-operational? Will you drop this potentially life-saving tool on the ground? The only thing that makes sense in this scenario is to strike your adversary with the gun.

Striking with your gun can be done with one hand or two. If you have a one-handed grip on your gun, you could deliver a downward, diagonal blow from gun side to nongun side to strike with the frame of your gun or the bottom portion of the magazine. The head, neck and collarbone are prime targets for the one-handed gun strike. When striking from a two-handed grip, thrust the muzzle out and back in a motion reminiscent of a boxer's jab. The head and upper chest would probably be the best areas to target. In either case, keeping your finger off of the trigger and out of the triggerguard will help prevent an unintended discharge. After you've diminished your adversary's ability to injure you, you can create distance and get your gun up and running again.

FENDING

There's no guarantee your strikes will be effective or that you will even know you are in a fight until you're already losing; that's why fending is so important. Fending is not about executing a fancy martial arts-style block. Such techniques are slow, impractical and likely to fail miserably during an unscripted violent encounter.

The goal when fending is to avoid being hit by means of parrying and evading or to absorb some of the impact from blows you can't avoid. Against a telegraphed punch, when there is sufficient room to maneuver, stepping off line and parrying the punch in a slapping motion with your open palm might be your best bet. But when the blows are coming in rapid succession and you're in a confined space, parrying isn't going to cut it. In this instance, you can use your nondominant elbow to shield your head from incoming strikes. You can orient your elbow either horizontally or vertically. In either case, be sure to tuck your chin and shrug your shoulders. This helps stabilize your head and neck and reduces the odds of you being knocked out when struck.

Of course, fending is no way to win a fight. It should be viewed as a brief transition from defense or offense.

GUN RETENTION

Obviously, gun retention is a matter of life or death. As such, you've got to have a planned and well-practiced response to negate a disarm attempt. The "push, pull, pry" technique is simple and relies solely on gross-motor skills. Best of all, it works regardless of how your adversary grabs your gun. This prevents you from having to make split-second

Use your elbow to protect your head while assuming the one-handed close-quarter hold.

Photo by Alfredo Rico

decisions as to which technique to employ against various types of grabs such as an over-handed grab, under-handed grab, right-handed grab or two-handed grab.

The moment your gun is grabbed, lower your center of gravity and assume a two-handed grip on your gun. Lunge forward and drive the muzzle of the gun toward your adversary. If possible, strike him with the muzzle to inflict pain and perhaps compromise his grip. Then immediately step back and pull the gun as hard as you can. In most cases, this push/pull action alone will fully extract your gun from your adversary's hands. That's because by the time he starts to resist the push (by pushing the gun toward you), you are already pulling it away from him. Your adversary's push in conjunction with your pull makes this a highly effective technique. However, with something as important as gun retention, you have to have a backup plan. That's where the pry comes in.

If the push/pull methodology doesn't work, simply release your grip on your gun with your nongun hand and use the outer portion of your forearm to assist in prying the gun from your adversary's hand. This is a leverage-based technique that doesn't require a great deal of strength to accomplish. The pry is relatively foolproof, since it works no matter how your adversary grabs or what direction you pry from. In fact, the pry even works while you're on the ground with your adversary on top of you. After extracting the gun, create distance and tap the magazine, rack the slide, then assess the situation.

PARTING BLOW

As your can see, there's more to preparing for a gunfight than shooting a paper target at the range. Firing at paper targets and thinking you're prepared for a gunfight is like shadowboxing and thinking you can defeat the reigning heavyweight boxing champion. Incorporate close-quarter shooting, unconventional shooting positions, striking, fending and gun retention into your training program to add an element of realism that could save your life in a close-quarter gunfight.

ARM'S-LENGTH SHOWDOWN

Employing your handgun when time and distance are scarce.

BY RICHARD NANCE | PHOTOS BY ALFREDO RICO

There's no denying the fact that marksmanship is a critical factor when it comes to using your handgun in self-defense, but there's more to winning a close-range gunfight than being a skilled marksman. In fact, from typical shooting distances, your mindset and your ability to fight with your gun could be even more important than marksmanship. The dynamics of a close-range lethal encounter require a well-trained response, with a razor-thin margin for error.

MINDSET

At close range, you won't have a lot of time to perceive, much less respond to a lethal threat. In most cases, there is not one correct response, but rather several responses that could work if executed with complete commitment. When the threat is staring you in the eye, you don't have the luxury of

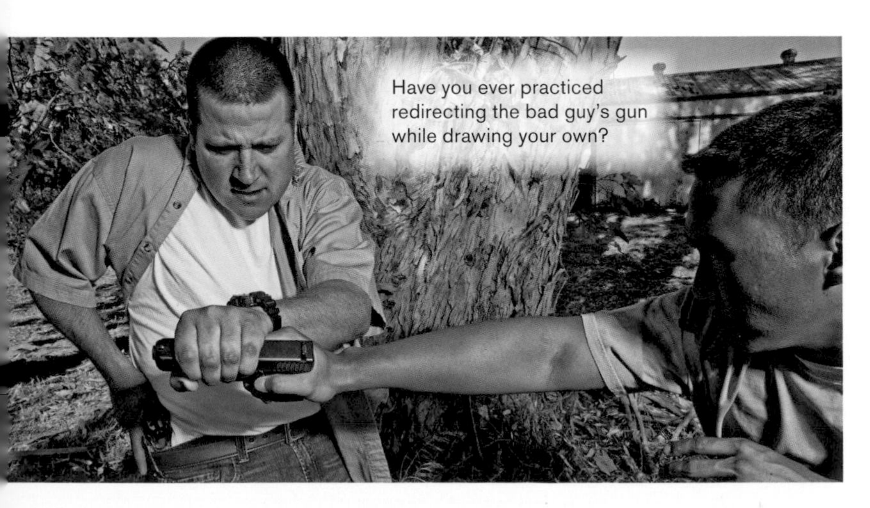

Have you ever practiced redirecting the bad guy's gun while drawing your own?

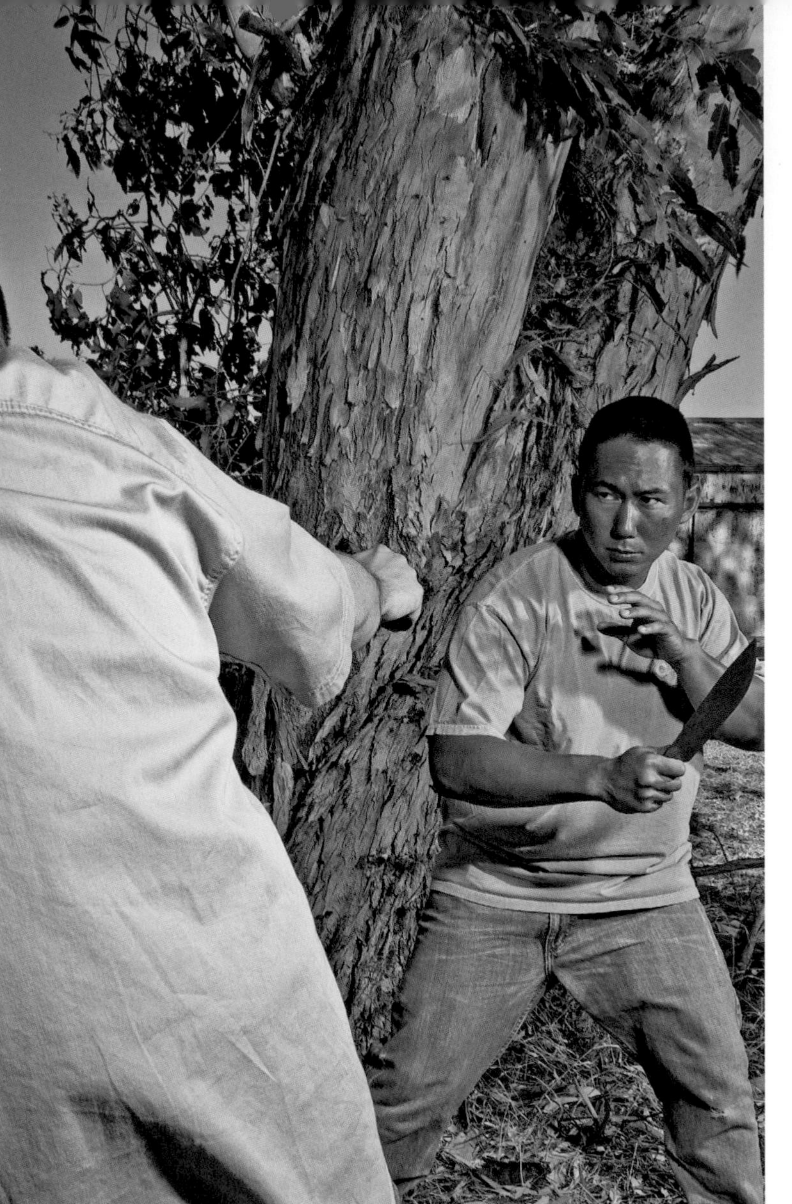

Photos by Alfredo Rico

being overly analytical. The specific tactic you employ probably has far less bearing on the outcome of the encounter than the degree of commitment with which you execute it.

One of the best ways to mentally prepare for a close-range lethal encounter is to rehearse likely scenarios in your mind and envision yourself doing whatever it takes to come out on top. This is nothing too mystical or metaphysical; it's just a common-sense approach to get your mind right before your life is on the line. Of course, mental preparation only goes so far. You still need to possess the physical attributes to get the job done.

OFF-HAND APPLICATIONS

When faced with a lethal threat, reaching for your concealed handgun is a reasonable response. However, at arm's length, that alone isn't good enough. Chances are you'll need both hands to prevail. This can be problematic when you're wearing a closed garment such as a button-up, zip-up or pullover-type shirt, because your off-hand is typically required to pull up your shirt to allow access to your gun. If your off-hand is holding up your shirt, it's not holding your adversary at bay.

An open garment, such as an unbuttoned or unzipped shirt, offers easy one-handed access to your firearm simply by sweeping away your shirt with your gun

When facing an assailant armed with a knife, a tie is not good enough.

Get off the "X"! Whenever possible, incorporate lateral or diagonal movement rather than backing up.

hand prior to drawing. Of course, there are pros and cons to every carry method. While using an open garment is more practical for one-hand draws, it's a little harder to conceal your gun with an open garment, especially when it's windy or you're in an environment where your shirt is likely to snag something, thus exposing your gun.

At close range, you could use your off-hand to strike under your opponent's chin, driving him back. This forces the attacker to backpeddle in an attempt to regain his balance. Using your off-hand in this manner also considerably diminishes your opponent's vision. This combined with the potential psychological impact of being forced backward might make your opponent more concerned with self-preservation than continuing his attack.

You might need to use your off-hand to parry or grab an assailant while your gun is in-hand. This could be as simple as shoving the attacker as you sidestep to flank him, or it could involve you actually redirecting the muzzle of a drawn gun when an assailant has the drop on you. This might occur when you're taken by surprise and don't have an opportunity to draw your gun initially.

When facing a close-range firearm threat, move your body out of the line of fire while simultaneously grabbing the barrel with your off-hand. Direct the barrel down, and orient the muzzle toward your opponent. Meanwhile, you should be drawing your gun with your other hand. This is a relatively simple technique, but it takes practice.

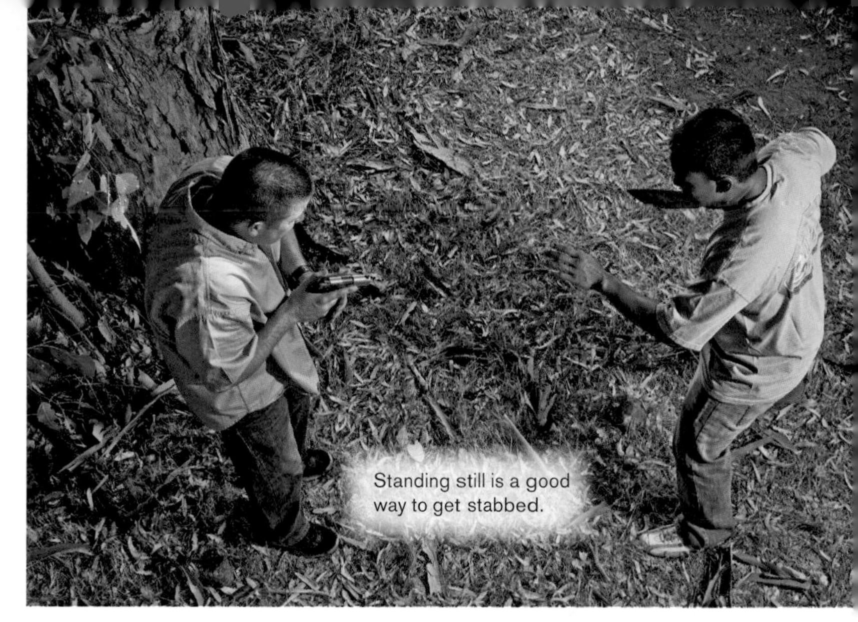
Standing still is a good way to get stabbed.

MOVE OFF-LINE

It's not hard to comprehend that a moving target is harder to hit than a static target. Moving away from a threat is a natural reaction, but at close range, moving back is not a good idea for several reasons. Moving back is retreating and therefore inherently defensive. Being defensive is no way to win a fight of any kind.

Moving back is relatively slow and awkward. If you're not careful, you might end up on the ground. Even if you don't fall, you can't move backward as fast as the average person can move forward.

Statistics tell us that most handgun wounds are survivable, and even a mortal wound might not immediately incapacitate your opponent. In other words, even if your shot was well placed, your adversary may have several seconds of fight left in him before he succumbs to his wounds. Make no mistake that your adversary, although wounded, may still present a lethal threat during this time. When you're facing an armed assailant, a tie is not acceptable. Shooting him and being stabbed or shot in the process is not a good trade. Get off-line and deliver as many rounds as are needed to stop the threat.

Moving straight back doesn't require the assailant to reorient whatever weapon he's armed with to attack you. Let's face it: shooting from 10 feet isn't much harder than shooting from 5

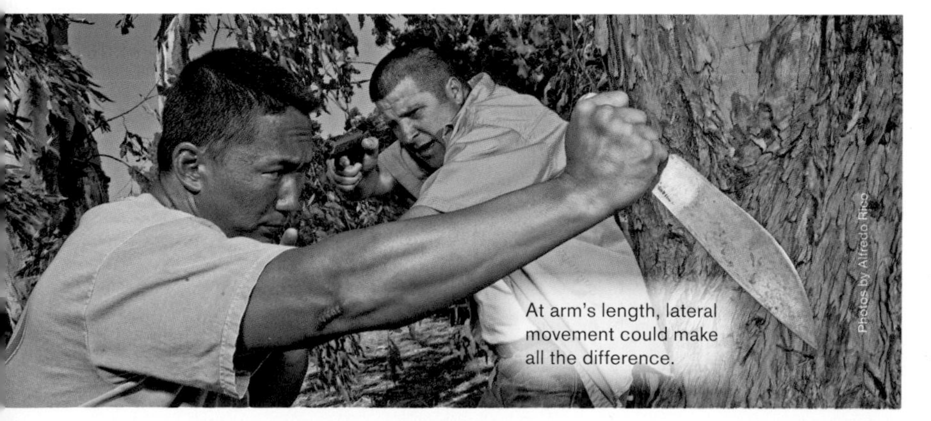
At arm's length, lateral movement could make all the difference.

Photos by Alfredo Rico

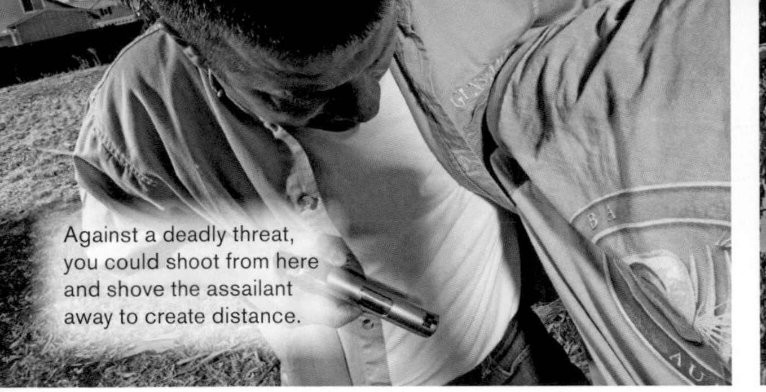
Against a deadly threat, you could shoot from here and shove the assailant away to create distance.

At arm's length, marksmanship is less important than your ability to fight with your gun.

feet. Instead of backing up, get off-line by moving diagonally and/or laterally.

When moving diagonally, think of moving off an imaginary "X." When a step or two is all that is required, take a big step with your near leg, followed by a smaller step with your far leg. This helps you quickly get off-line while maintaining your balance. Moving at an angle affords you a position of relative safety and exposes portions of your opponent's anatomy that you might not have otherwise been able to target.

The importance of lateral movement in a close-range armed encounter cannot be overstated. Moving laterally forces the bad guy to reorient to you, buying you time to assess and engage the threat. If the assailant is charging you, lateral movement requires him to quickly change his direction. This is likely to slow him down and take away a good degree of his power as he struggles to regain his balance. If you're facing an opponent armed with a firearm, he will have to track a fast-moving target that's shooting back at him.

SHOOTING FROM RETENTION

If the assailant is close enough to grab your gun, you need to pull the gun close to your body. When shooting from a retention position, you won't be able to see your sights. To compensate for this, you will need to rely on consistent and reliable physical index or reference points. (This is where you would really benefit from having a laser mounted to your handgun.)

When shooting from the one-handed retention position (close-quarter hold), the bottom of your fist should be in contact with your pectoral muscle. There are several benefits to using a physical index point. First, it ensures consistent muzzle orientation, which leads to predictably accurate rounds. Second, pressing the bottom of your fist against your body tends to cant your gun outward slightly. This minimizes the chance of experiencing a malfunction caused by the slide snagging on your clothing. Finally, when your hand is against your body, it affords you considerable leverage from a firearm retention standpoint.

To achieve a two-handed close-quarter hold from a typical sighted fire position, simply pull in the weapon until your elbows contact your sides. As with the one-handed version, this technique can easily be replicated and facilitates proper muzzle orienta-

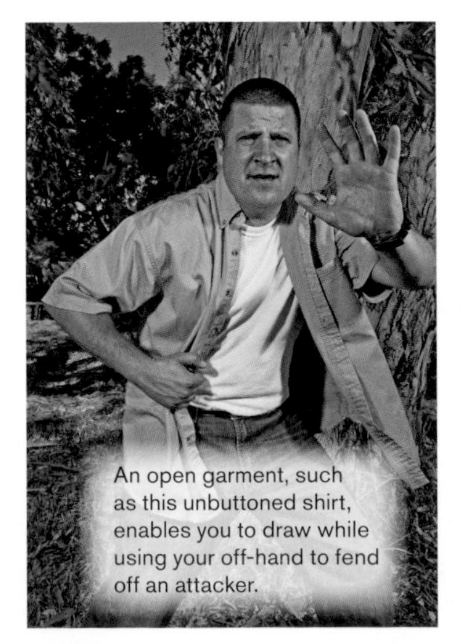
An open garment, such as this unbuttoned shirt, enables you to draw while using your off-hand to fend off an attacker.

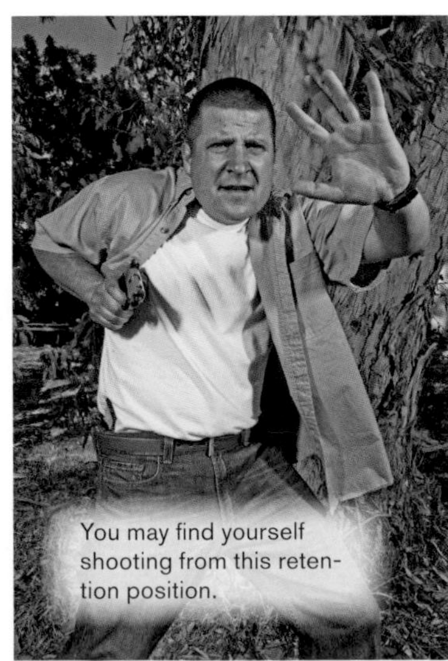
You may find yourself shooting from this retention position.

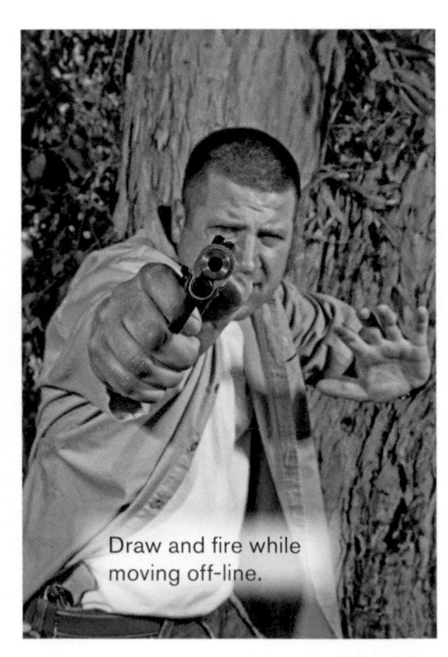
Draw and fire while moving off-line.

Photos by Alfredo Rico

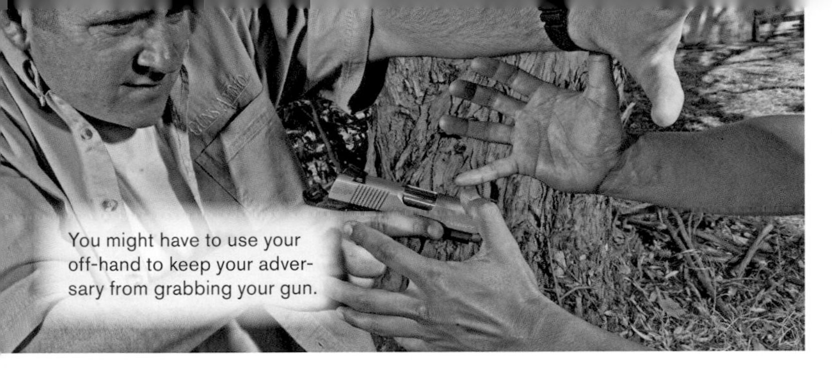

You might have to use your off-hand to keep your adversary from grabbing your gun.

tion. If the assailant were to grab your firearm, you have a position of superior leverage to wrench it from his hands.

SHOOTING ON THE MOVE

Shooting on the move may be a tactic you employ initially, or you may transition to shooting on the move after firing from a retention position. For instance, after firing two quick shots from the close-quarter hold, you might opt to move away from the threat while continuing to engage with gunfire, possibly targeting the head. If two well-placed shots to the torso at close range were ineffective, your opponent might be wearing body armor or under the influence of drugs that enable him to continue to attack despite being wounded.

Shooting on the move involves walking in a particular direction and orienting your upper body to the threat. It is an acquired skill that warrants considerable training time. In training, you'll soon realize that hitting your target while moving is no easy task. However, at close range you don't have to be a world-class marksman to achieve effective hits.

ONE-HANDED SHOOTING

Against a close-range threat, you may have to shoot with one hand for a variety of reasons. The distance between you and your adversary will dictate whether there is sufficient room to extend your shooting arm and achieve a sight picture, shoot from retention or shoot from somewhere in between. One thing you can bet on is that the encounter will be dynamic and unpredictable. If you have an opportunity to shoot one-handed, you need to have the skill to make your shot count.

CONCLUSION

Most gunfights occur at little more than arm's length. In this kind of lethal encounter, you need to possess a unique skill set that includes more than marksmanship. Practice drawing from concealment while using your off-hand proactively. Incorporate diagonal and lateral movement as well as shooting on the move. When the fight is up close and personal, it's going to take more than marksmanship to prevail.

Photos by Alfredo Rico

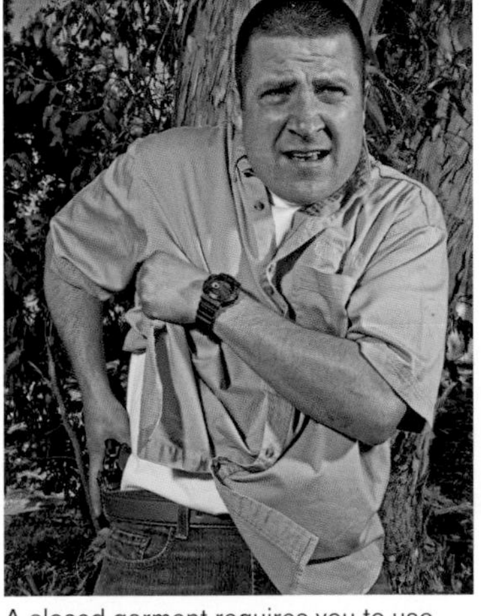

A closed garment requires you to use both hands to draw, one to lift the garment and the other to produce the gun.

At close range, shooting with two hands is a luxury.

Don't assume you will be able to fire from a stable, two-handed shooting position.

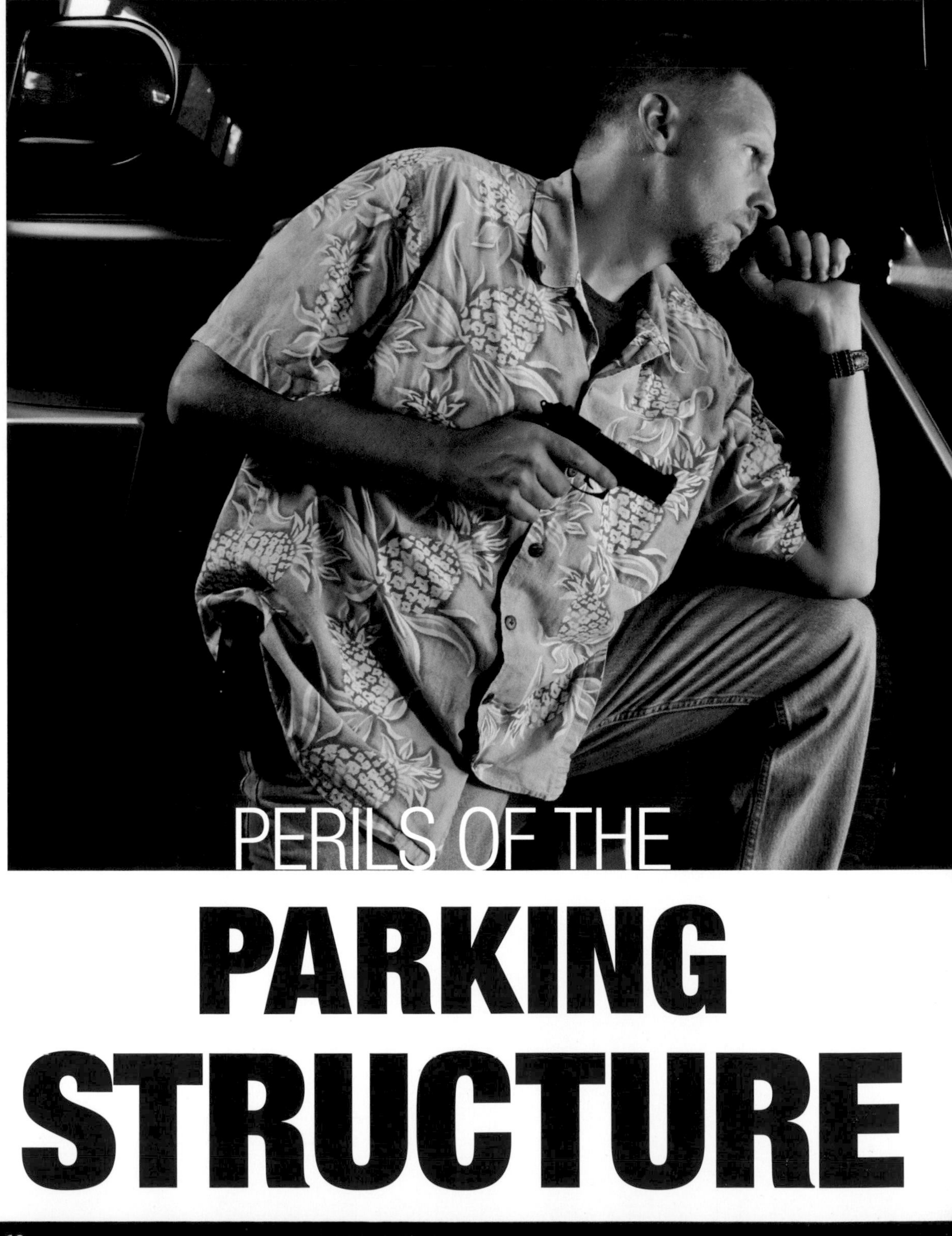

PERILS OF THE PARKING STRUCTURE

If you find yourself in serious trouble, any gun, even a small gun, is better than no gun at all, and the same is true for flashlights. Just remember that flashlights tend to work like tracers—they let people know exactly where you are.

The inside of a newly built parking garage, designed for safety—lots of light, everything painted white and security cameras. However, as long as there are vehicles and support posts, there will always be places for criminals to hide.

How to negotiate an urban terrain that has become the icon of vulnerability.

BY JAMES TARR

What most people know of private investigators is what they've seen on TV, such as *Magnum P.I.* or perhaps one of those reality shows where the PIs are busting cheating spouses. The reality of the job is that 90 percent of it is insurance work, and 90 percent of that is surveillance. I don't even want to think about how many thousands of hours I have spent on surveillance over the last 15 years. An average day of surveillance consists of sitting in a minivan or SUV for 8 to 12 hours, peeing in a bottle, waiting for something to happen. Most of the time, nothing does.

The only bright spots are those days when we actually get to sit in parking lots or parking garages to watch our targets. Why? Because nobody ever sees anything in a parking lot. Other cars are treated like background noise, and all too often other people are as well. It's amazing—if you're in the next row over, it's like you're on the dark side of the moon. You don't exist for someone walking to his car, even though you may be only feet away. This is exactly the opposite of the way it should be, because parking lots and garages are ranked second after residential property for violent crimes. Specifically, in parking garages, dim lighting combined with multiple vehicles make it easy for criminals to hide.

Many people believe that nothing bad will happen to them, ever. Once you get past that point—seeing the world for what it really is and acknowledging the fact that bad things happen to good people—sometimes for no reason at all—you have gone through the looking glass and there is no going back. You see that you are responsible for your own safety, and you begin to be proactive instead of just reactive. There's no way to avoid using parking lots and garages, so the task is to recognize the dangers and take steps to reduce your risk.

Appearances matter. First off, if you look like food, chances are that at some point someone will try and eat you. I'm not talking about sexual attractiveness, I'm talking about whether you look like an easy target. Physical size is a factor here, and it's the one we have the least control over. A woman who is five feet tall will always seem a much more attractive target to predators than a towering, muscular male, even if the fact of the matter is that the former is a well-armed blackbelt with anger issues and the latter is a hybrid-driving vegetarian obsessed with the musical *Cats*.

Physical size, however, is only part of the package. Situational awareness is a huge factor. Ninety percent of self-defense is self-awareness. Walk with a purpose, and look around. Look like you know where you're going, even if you can't remember where you parked your car. Preoccupied or distracted people are easier targets. Talking on a cell phone or digging in a bag or pocket for car keys is a good way to distract yourself from any potential threats that might be present. Get out the car keys before you get to the car. Take out the iPod earbuds so you can hear if someone is walking up behind you. What you should be looking out for are people, especially single males, loitering around your car. Anybody standing still in a parking garage should draw some attention. And just because someone looks and sounds like he's talking on a cell phone as he stands near your vehicle doesn't mean that there has to be anybody on the other end of that conversation. I've used that trick a number of times on surveillance. For all you know, he could be talking to an accomplice.

Most parking lot and garage assaults occur when people are returning to vehicles they've already parked, as the predators have a likely target (or have even watched you arrive). However, don't forget to look around upon arrival as well. If things don't look right, don't get out. Drive away. If someone approaches you while you're still sitting in the car, you don't need to roll down the window to talk to him. He can hear you through the glass just fine. If he thinks you're being rude by talking to him that way, so what? Don't let good manners get you killed.

That vehicle is the best friend you've got. It's a combination flashlight (headlights), alarm (horn) and deadly weapon. Run-

If the guns come out, remember that you can shoot under vehicles, too, most easily from the rollover prone position as demonstrated here. A gun-mounted flashlight will also be invaluable. Shown here is a Smith & Wesson SD40 with an Insight Technologies X2 light mounted on it.

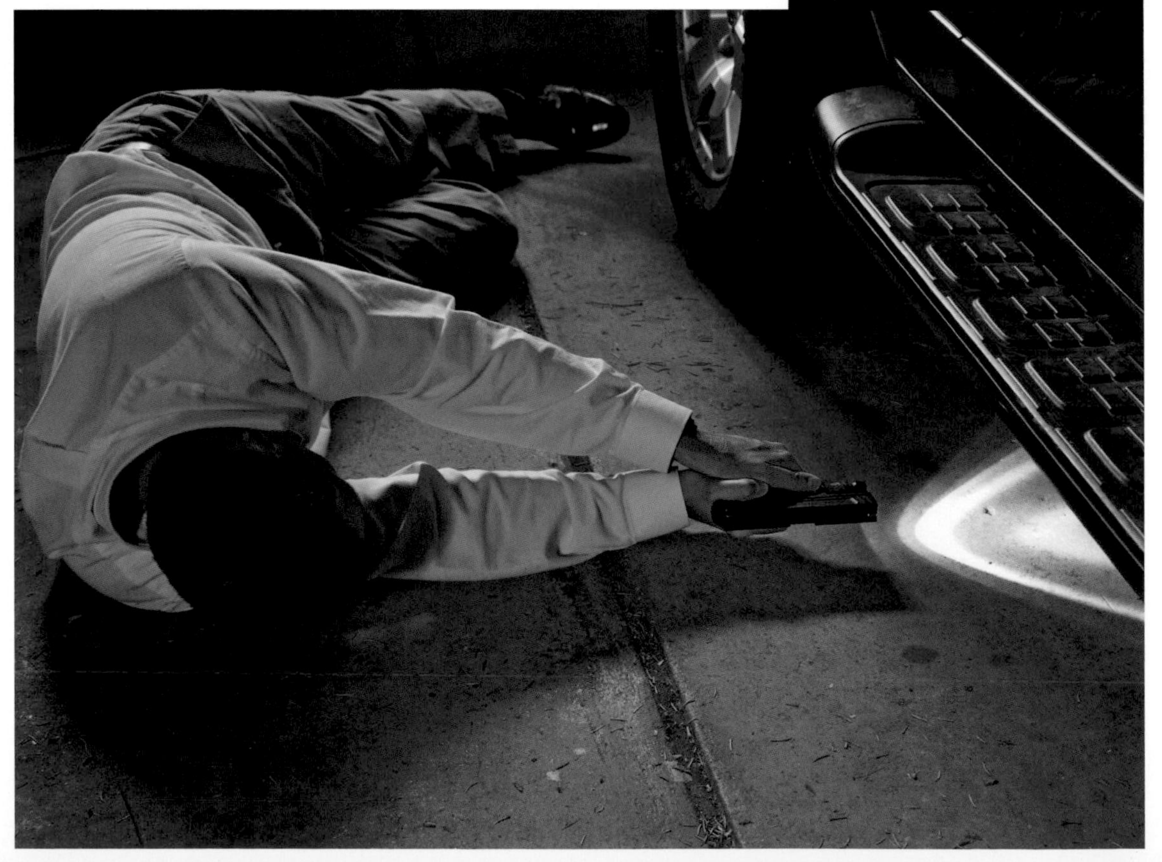

ning over someone or crushing him against the wall with your bumper is always an effective fight-stopper, but you better be able to convince a judge that you were in such fear for your life that you had to hit the suspect with a two-ton hammer. Even if you're taking incoming rounds, driving away is usually the best option.

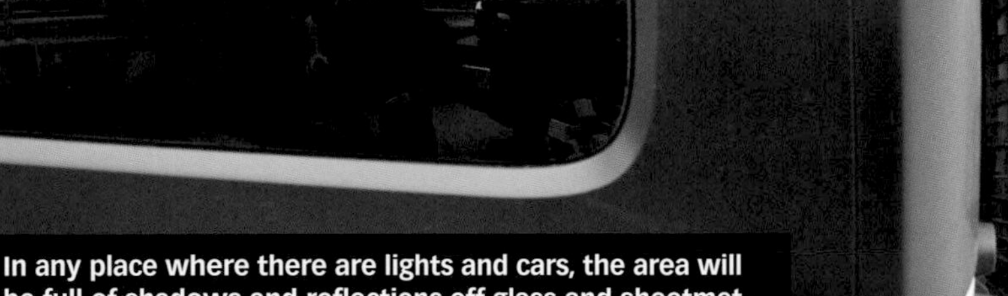

In any place where there are lights and cars, the area will be full of shadows and reflections off glass and sheetmetal. Keep your eyes and ears open as you approach your car.

Years of tactical firearms training have taught me to hug the walls and that anything that stops bullets coming my way is my friend. When it comes to avoiding trouble in parking garages, though, I have to adjust my mindset. Stay away from the walls, dark corners and cars as long as possible. Walk as close to the middle of the traffic lane, in the open and where it's better lit, until you get close to your car.

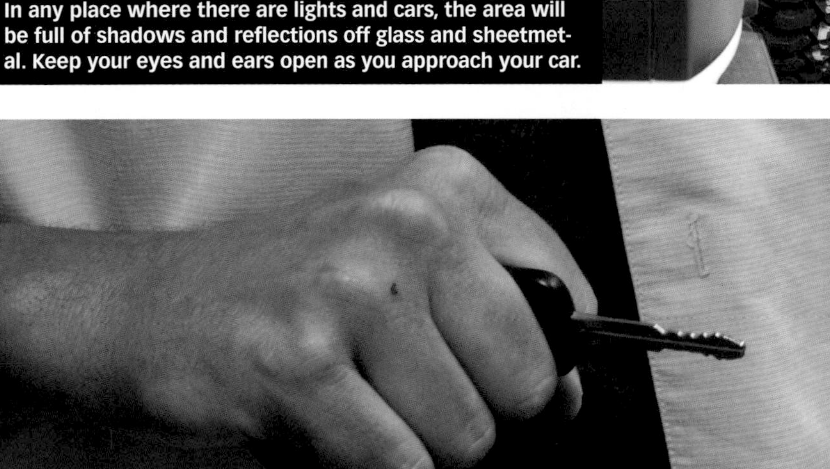

The improvised key punch. If you appear ready and willing to fight back, chances are predators will prey on someone else.

Parking garages are notorious for being poorly lit. I recommend having a small LED light on your key ring just for everyday use, but it can come in very handy when approaching your car in a parking garage after dark. It's better to park in a well-lit section of the lot or garage, but sometimes you have to take what spot you can find.

Vans or large vehicles with tinted windows parked right next to your car should also raise some red flags. If there is someone by your car or there's another vehicle nearby that just doesn't look right, go back. Talk to the parking lot attendant. Chances are that the attendant won't be allowed out of his booth to escort you to your car, but he can call security. I'd rather feel a little foolish as I walked to my car with a grumpy security guard than have to shoot somebody because I didn't want to appear afraid or foolish.

If your parking lot at work is a bit dicey, make it a habit to walk out to your car with several coworkers—predators don't attack groups of animals, they spot one that looks weak or slow and go after it. Some workplaces don't allow you to have a gun on premises, and they reserve the right to search your vehicle at any time because it's parked on their property, so your self-defense might be even more limited than what the law allows. An umbrella is not a self-defense implement by nature, and neither is a nice solid walking stick, but I'd rather have either than go empty-handed. When I fly I always have at least one high-quality, metal-shafted ballpoint pen on my person for personal defense.

Keep your keys ready as you approach your car. Keeping one hand free and on or near your concealed self-defense device, whatever that might be, is not a bad idea. Once you get to your car, unlock it, get in, lock it, then immediately drive away. Sitting in a car in a parking lot is another way to invite trouble.

Make sure that you lock your doors when you get into your vehicle. I learned this the hard way one day long ago while doing surveillance in Detroit. A passing prostitute noticed me sitting there in the front seat and thought I was looking for love. She just jumped right in, but getting her back out of the car was a lot more work. She just as easily could have been armed with a knife and looking to separate me from my jewels. It's funny now, but it wasn't funny then.

Mini LED lights are great for finding keyholes in dim parking garages, but they will also help you see what's in those dark areas near and under your vehicle.

Flat tires are easy to arrange, and you should assume any flat tire you discover in a parking lot/garage is a precursor to an assault. This is especially true if some good Samaritan points out your flat as you approach your car and offers to help you change the tire. Back off, stay in the open, and call someone, whether it's security or 9-1-1.

Any self-defense device, even an improvised one, is better than none at all, but the first thing you'll need to use it is willpower. In doing research for this piece I found numerous references to improvised self-defense tools to use in parking lots, from car keys wedged between fingers for punching to pointy umbrellas for poking. I don't care what it is, if you're not going to use it, don't carry it. Buying something just to show to the bad guys in hopes that it will deter them, without any intent of ever pulling the trigger, is a very bad idea. I regularly carry a handgun, but I don't have anything against mace, pepper spray or Tasers. Every self-defense device, however, has advantages and disadvantages, and if you're going to use it, you need to know what those are.

If the situation does degenerate into gunplay, there are important things to remember. The first is that car bodies will stop just about every kind of pistol round out there, so get behind their cover. Safety glass might slow or deflect a bul-

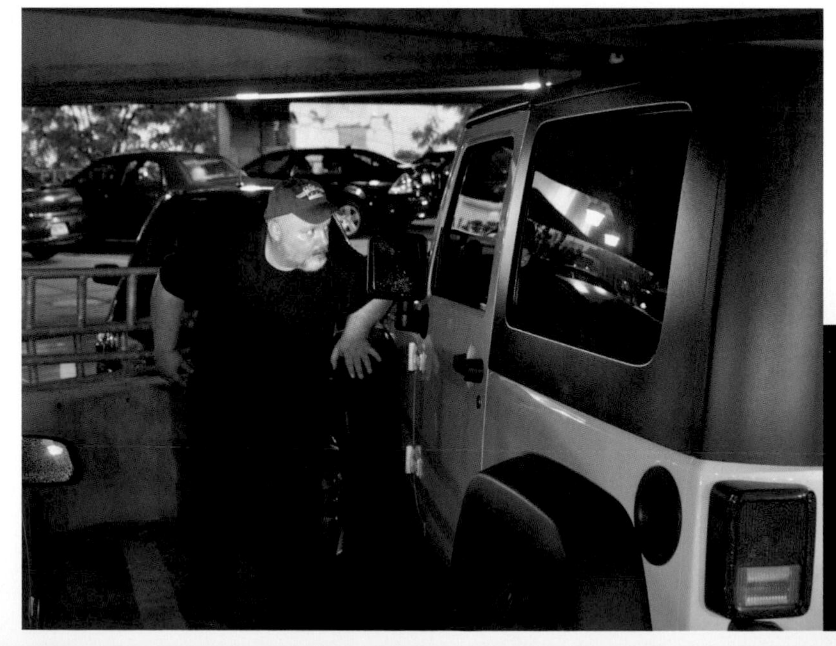

High-intensity LED flashlights are small, cheap and getting ever more powerful. They not only help you see better, they let other people know they've been seen. Lack of a visible gun or knife doesn't necessarily mean anything. It takes only a second to push you down and steal your purse/backpack/laptop.

let, but car doors, wheels and engine blocks will generally stop pistol bullets in many circumstances.

The second thing to remember is that in any place where there are lights and cars, the area will be full of shadows and reflections off glass and sheetmetal. Use that knowledge to your advantage so that you have the upper hand. Keep your head on a swivel, and listen.

While there may not be enough room under most vehicles to hide, there is more than enough space to see and shoot. The best technique for this is rollover prone, which is best described as lying on your side with your arms extended from your body in a firing position. Most often rollover prone is done with the strong side on the ground and the head resting on the biceps, but it can be done on either side. This is a very easy and quick position to get into and is stable to shoot from, but I would only recommend it if you had nowhere left to retreat. Lying on the ground reduces your ability to move quickly, and while shooting someone in the lower leg or foot will ruin his whole day, rollover prone exposes nearly your whole body underneath the car. If a predator sees you before you see him, skipping rounds across the pavement into you won't be tough.

I am not a big proponent of lasers on pistols, as I believe they encourage bad technique, but in a dimly lit parking garage the deterrent effect of that red dot on your assailant may be all he needs to reconsider his actions. Modern high-intensity flashlights will also come into their own in these cave-like arenas, and if temporarily blinding your adversary means that you don't have to shoot him, better for everyone.

No matter what happens, a gunfight in a parking lot or garage will probably be quick and involve a lot of movement and, if you're lucky enough to get some vehicles in between you and the bad guy, improvised shooting positions. If you don't practice all of that regularly, you should, and you can practice at nearly any USPSA or IDPA pistol match.

Remember, while some police officials are more concerned with controlling people or consolidating their power, authority might tell you not to fight back and to just give the criminal what he wants. Scientific studies have shown that people (including women) who resist their attackers are actually less likely to get hurt and/or killed. Personally, I have philosophical issues with letting the bad guy make the decision about whether I get hurt. The main thing to remember is that if you look and act like you're paying attention and ready for trouble, chances are you won't have any. Predators don't like noise, lights or pain and will choose other prey if that's what they encounter when they go after you. If the time comes, yell, scream and fight like your life depends on it, because it may.

VEHICULAR GUNFIGHTING

BY RICHARD NANCE
PHOTOS BY ALFREDO RICO

Tips for deploying your handgun in and around a vehicle.

You're stopped behind a line of cars at an intersection, waiting for the signal light to turn green, when suddenly, out of the corner of your eye, you glimpse a man walking toward your vehicle. Your intuition tells you something's just not right, then you see it. The metallic object in his right hand isn't a cell phone—it's a pistol. Before you know it, the man's pistol is pointed directly at you, and he orders you to move to the passenger seat as he reaches for the driver door handle. What are you going to do?

If you carry a firearm for personal defense, you know (or should know) that your vehicle could well be the setting of a nightmarish scenario requiring you to use your gun to stop a lethal threat. Considering the amount of time Americans spend in vehicles, it's odd that more training time is not devoted to winning a gunfight that erupts in or around a vehicle.

WHERE DOES YOUR GUN RIDE?

If you legally carry a concealed handgun on your person, keep it on when you're in a vehicle. You might be tempted to take your gun off and secure it in your glovebox or other more "tactical" location, such as wedged between your seat and the center console, under your seat or in some other nook or cranny. Some instructors advocate these off-body carry locations while seated in a vehicle, but you'd be well served to dismiss the notion of separating yourself from your gun just because you're inside a vehicle.

In the infamous FBI Miami Shootout that occurred on April 11, 1986, an FBI agent placed his service revolver on his seat in anticipation of a gunfight with two armed bank robbery suspects, but when the agent's vehicle crashed, his revolver went flying and was inaccessible to him during the ensuing gun battle that tragically led to the deaths of two FBI agents. Fortunately, the agent who lost his primary revolver was carrying a backup gun.

Photos by Alfredo Rico

It may not be a crash that keeps you from getting to your gun. It may be that you exit your vehicle so quickly that you forget to arm yourself. Think it can't happen to you? Stranger things have happened during the stress inherent in a life-and-death encounter.

Another reason to avoid leaving your gun in your glovebox, wedged between your seat or otherwise accessible is the possibility of someone else, namely a child, finding the gun when you leave the vehicle "just for a minute." In such a case, a gunshot might be the beginning of your worst nightmare.

1 When exiting the vehicle in response to a threat, shift into park, then open the door. The placement of the foot on the door keeps it open.

2 Next comes the seatbelt. You won't get far if you forget to unbuckle.

3 As your left hand clears the seatbelt, your right hand reaches for your gun.

4 From this position, you can simply punch the gun out in the direction of the threat—no need to sweep the gun around the steering wheel.

5 When you exit the vehicle, keep the muzzle oriented toward the threat.

DEFENSIVE DRIVING

"Stay back far enough from the pickup when waiting behind it so that you can see where its tires contact the road." This was my Field Training Officer (FTO's) way of teaching me, the rookie driving his patrol car, to leave enough space between our car and the vehicle in front of us so that I could maneuver around the vehicle should we come under fire or, more likely, be required to respond to a more mundane emergency such as a burglary in progress or a 9-1-1 call. My FTO's sage advice is not restricted to policework. Leaving sufficient distance between your car and the car in front of you affords you the option of remaining in your vehicle and getting the heck out of Dodge rather than being forced into hastily exiting in response to an unforeseen threat.

If you're paying attention, with your head scanning for potential hazards (as you should be when you are driving), you may very well spot danger in time to evade it. Maybe you make an unexpected turn at an intersection, make a U-turn or simply back up to avoid crossing paths with a perceived threat. Or perhaps accelerating past the threat is your best bet. The bottom line is that if you are aware of your environment and leave a gap between your car and the one in front of you, you have options.

USING YOUR VEHICLE AS A WEAPON

If, while in your vehicle, you observe a bad guy on foot who presents a deadly threat, get low in the driver's seat to make yourself a smaller target and reap the full benefit of the protective cover provided by the engine block. If the bad guy is shooting at you, it's probably safer to put the pedal to the metal and shoot him with the 4,000-pound bullet you're driving than to stop and engage in a gunfight.

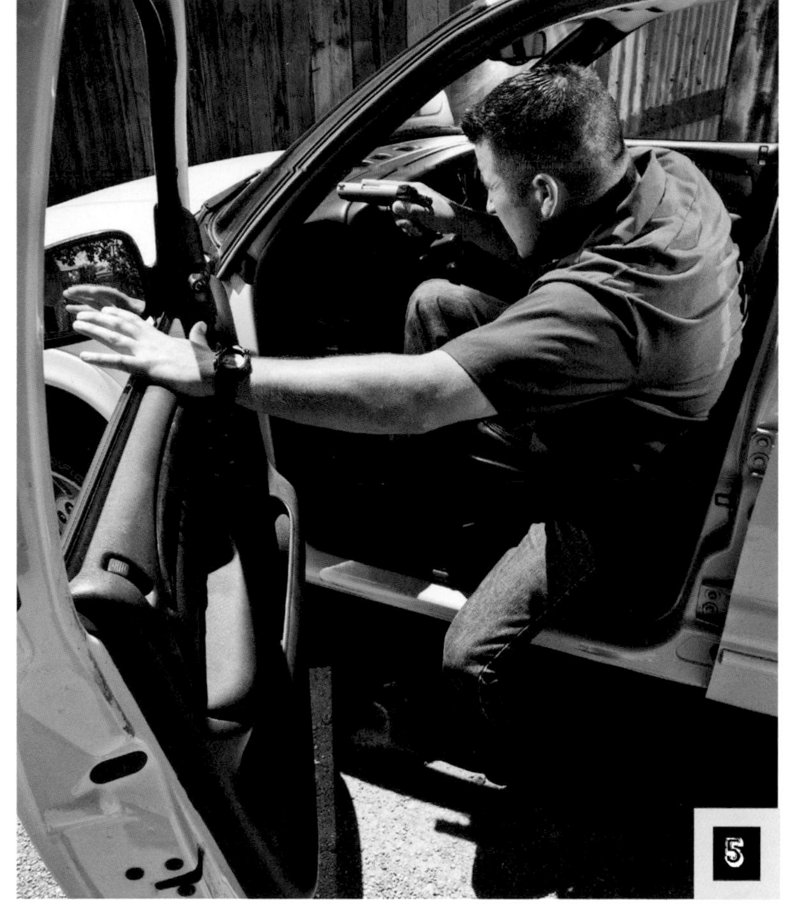

Photos by Alfredo Rico

DEPLOYING YOUR GUN FROM A VEHICLE

There may be a situation where driving away from a deadly threat or exiting your vehicle is not an option. In such cases, you may be required to shoot the bad guy from your vehicle. When shooting from your vehicle, there are a few things to keep in mind. Since being able to shoot is predicated on being able to draw your gun from its holster, let's start there.

While removing your seatbelt is an important step to exiting your vehicle (I've tried to skip this step a time or two, with little success), you may not have time to worry about the seatbelt if an armed criminal rapidly approaches your vehicle. In such a case, forget about your passive restraint device and focus on bringing your "proactive threat-stopping device" into play.

If, while seated in your vehicle, you encounter a deadly threat that warrants attention, simply draw, then orient the muzzle to the threat. If you're in the driver's seat and an armed assailant approaches from the driver's side, don't draw and make a circular motion around the steering wheel to bring your gun to bear on the threat as many firearms instructors advocate. By the time you get on target, you will be playing a potentially deadly game of catch-up. Not to mention the fact that raising the gun in this manner is likely to result in the gun striking the steering wheel, gear shift or other gadgetry and tumbling to the floorboard.

To keep things simple, execute your normal draw, and, with your gun held close to your torso, turn in the direction of the threat, then punch out to the extent necessary to make the shot you're presented with. Be careful about extending your arms too far through an open window, as your gun could be susceptible to being grabbed.

If you have a passenger in your vehicle, you need to make sure you extend your gun past him or her whenever possible before shooting. It's your responsibility to control your passenger either verbally, physically or both. The last thing you want is for the passenger to move in front of your muzzle as you press the trigger intending to shoot an assailant. Give this some thought, and practice controlling a passenger while engaging from various directions using a designated training gun.

GLASS PENETRATION

When you're shooting through glass, a bullet's trajectory will be affected. To what degree is dependent on the bullet's construction, the window glass itself, the distance from the muzzle to the window and the distance from the window to the bad guy, among other factors. There is a significant difference between how a vehicle window reacts to handgun rounds and how a windshield reacts. The former is likely to shatter, since that's what windows are designed to do during a crash. This prevents large glass shards from flying through the passenger compartment and causing significant injury or death. The windshield, on the other hand, is typically made of laminated safety glass and is designed to stay intact to prevent occupants from being ejected from the vehicle during a major collision. A handgun round fired through a vehicle windshield is likely to cause little more than a hole slightly larger than the bullet that penetrated it. Vision through the windshield should remain relatively clear after having been shot, while a window could spiderweb upon the bullet's impact, significantly hindering your ability to see through it.

In general, rounds fired through a windshield from inside a vehicle tend to impact higher than the shooter's point of aim. This can be attributed to the angle of the windshield, which causes the top portion of the bullet to impact first. When the top of the round digs into the glass, it directs the bullet upward.

As you might have guessed, shooting through a windshield from outside a vehicle has the exact opposite effect, resulting in rounds impacting lower than the shooter intended. How much variance will there be between point of aim and point of impact when shooting through a windshield? That depends on velocity, bullet construction, the slope of the windshield, the distance the bullet travels and numerous other factors.

Keep in mind that when you're shooting from a vehicle through a window or windshield, tiny glass particles will circulate through the interior of the vehicle. While this could potentially be detrimental to your health, it's much less so than incoming fire. Common sense dictates wearing appropriate eye and face protection such as a paintball mask to keep the glass from entering your eyes, nose or mouth. Likewise, in training, ear protection is always important, but perhaps even more so when firing from a vehicle, which amplifies the sound of gunfire. Of course, during a real-world deadly force encounter, sustaining a degree of hearing loss would be the least of your worries.

EXITING THE VEHICLE

In many cases, when faced with a deadly threat, driving away is your best bet. But your vehicle may be inoperable, or you may decide to exit the vehicle for some other reason. If you deem exiting the vehicle to be your safest alternative, remember the following, "Door, Belt, Gun." This sequence will allow you to most efficiently disembark from the vehicle.

After shifting into park, open the door and use your foot to prevent it from closing on you. Reach

Photos by Alfredo Rico

Guide the seatbelt away to clear a path for your gun.

The driver's right leg is oriented to the left to stay clear of the muzzle.

over with your left hand (assuming you are in the driver's seat), and hook your thumb under the shoulder harness as you press the button to disengage the seat belt. Guide the belt away from your body as you access your gun in the manner previously described. Now you're prepared to exit the vehicle, gun in hand.

VEHICLE AS COVER

When it comes to stopping incoming rounds, not all parts of a vehicle are created equally. On several occasions at the range, I've fired a wide array of bullets at various portions of vehicles. In most cases, handgun, rifle and shotgun rounds easily penetrated vehicle doors. So if you consider a door to be cover, you could be in for a rude and painful awakening. Don't get me wrong—poor cover may be better than no cover, but I sure wouldn't want to bet my life on the ballistic resistance of a car door. If you're behind the engine block or even a tire, you're probably much better off. The trunk, depending on what's in it, could also be a good bullet stop.

The defender is prepared to shoot as he creates distance in order to use the vehicle as cover. Don't linger here. The door may be incapable of stopping incoming rounds.

Keep in mind that when a round impacts a solid object, it is likely to travel in a direction a few inches away from but relatively parallel to the object. That means if you're resting your handgun over the hood of the car to steady your shot, you are in danger of a skipped round hitting you in the head. To reduce your odds of absorbing a round with your noggin, stay a few feet back from the vehicle. Coincidentally, this position will also afford you a wider field of view, which could help keep you from getting flanked by your adversary.

CONCLUSION

Deploying a firearm in and around a vehicle isn't rocket science, but it is a very specific skill set that requires practice. Given the amount of time most of us spend in our vehicles, it's probably a topic deserving of considerable contemplation and training time. You'd be wise to add this component to your training regimen. By doing so, you can greatly enhance your odds of winning a vehicular gunfight.

Photos by Alfredo Rico

You can shoot effectively even while wearing your seatbelt.

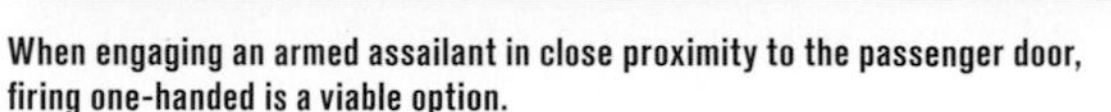

When engaging an armed assailant in close proximity to the passenger door, firing one-handed is a viable option.

DON'T BLOW YOUR COVER

Are you prepared to make the most of available cover?

BY RICHARD NANCE // PHOTOS BY ALFREDO RICO

Unavailable cover is a recurring theme in law enforcement line-of-duty deaths. Despite the fact that officers are trained from the earliest stages of the police academy that cover is critical to their survival in a gunfight, there's still a tendency to remain exposed when shots ring out. If you've never trained to use cover, how can you expect to find yourself behind cover in a gunfight? Only by having a thorough understanding of what constitutes appropriate cover and how to make the most of available cover can you hope to be protected when bullets are flying.

Photos by Alfredo Rico

Here the shooter makes the best o his available cover. Keep in mind tha this metal Dumpster could be mere concealment depending on the type of weapon he's up against.

WHAT IS COVER?

Essentially, anything that is capable of stopping a bullet could be considered cover. Cover is a relative term, since an object that stops a .22-caliber handgun round might not stop a .223 rifle round. Similarly, an interior residential wall might not stop either round, but a brick or concrete exterior wall may easily stop both. Other examples of cover may be a concrete pillar, a metal garbage Dumpster, the engine block of a vehicle or even a large piece of hardwood furniture.

If an object will hide you but not protect you from incoming rounds, it is referred to as concealment. Concealment is better than standing out in the open, but it pales in comparison with cover. If your adversary detects you, concealment is of little value. It's important for you to understand the difference between cover and concealment so you can accurately evaluate which of the two is between you and the bad guy's muzzle.

RECOGNIZING COVER

My driver's education instructor instilled in me the importance of constantly scanning the roadway ahead for potential hazards and always having an avenue of escape. In other words, if an approaching vehicle veers into your lane, you need to have a plan because you won't have time to formulate one in the split second you'll have to take evasive action.

Is there a shoulder to your right toward which you can maneuver to avoid a head-on collision? Is there a lane of traffic to your right that would preclude you from swerving in that direction? Perhaps there were no other vehicles behind the one that veered into your lane. If so, steering to the left

Typically, you want to stay a few feet back from cover to increase your field of view and stay clear of rounds that may skip off the wall.

Photo by Alfredo Rico

might be your best option. The better you are at recognizing an escape route while driving, the safer you (and the occupants of your vehicle) will be.

To apply this same logic to the concept of cover recognition, simply take note of what objects in your immediate environment could be used to stop a bullet. What about the large tree in the parking lot of your bank or the van parked in the stall near the entrance? Would the desks inside the bank stop a round? If you were in line and a man entered with guns blazing, where is your nearest cover? If you've never asked yourself these types of questions, you're not as prepared to survive a shooting as you need to be.

Cover awareness is a really simple concept to grasp. While going through your everyday activities, get in the habit of identifying the nearest and best cover available. I know you're not expecting to be shot at when you go to the bank. I'm not expecting to have an oncoming car veer into my lane while I'm driving down the road either, but I acknowledge the fact that it could happen, and I therefore remain alert for the sake of my safety and that of my passengers.

Photo by Alfredo Rico

MAXIMIZING COVER

Recognizing cover is only half the battle. It's important to know how to make the most of whatever cover you're behind. The value of your cover is based on the orientation of the bad guy in relation to you. If the bad guy moves, your cover might not be as beneficial as it was before he moved.

Generally speaking, people tend to hug cover. This is an instinctive response because we associate cover with safety, which is basically a good thing. However, in most cases cover is just as beneficial if you are back several feet from it. This affords you a much better position with regard to rounds that may skip off the barricade that you're behind, and it affords you a larger field of view.

In certain circumstances, hugging cover is a good idea. For instance, if the bad guy were to flank you, moving closer to cover would make it harder for him to shoot you because he would have to move farther to get you in his sights. If the bad guy is in an elevated position, hugging cover will protect you much more effectively than remaining several feet back. The bottom line is that you must constantly evaluate where you are in relation to the threat and maintain as much of a barrier as possible between you and that threat.

Photo by Alfredo Rico

MOVING TO OR FROM COVER

When you're moving to cover, it's probably because you've identified a deadly threat and are in an open area, which means it's essential that you get behind cover ASAP. Once you're behind cover, don't leave that cover without a damn good reason. A damn good reason may be that the shooter moves so that the cover that was positioned between you and him is no longer protecting you. Or perhaps you're armed and want to move to a closer position to deliver accurate fire.

Whatever the reason, when you move from cover, do so as quickly as possible and stay low to present less of a target. The more time you spend out in the open, the more likely you are to be shot. Keep in mind that although the shortest distance between two points may be a straight line, running in a straight line is not always the best tactic to maximize cover.

For example, if you were hunkered down behind the engine block of a vehicle with a gunman 100 feet directly ahead of you and you needed to move forward 50 feet and to the right 10 feet to get to your next position of cover, running diagonally would leave you exposed much longer than first running to the right and then moving forward to the next position of cover. That's because as soon as you moved 10 feet to the right, you would be protected by the second position of cover.

SHOOTING FROM COVER

If you're a right-handed shooter, shooting around the right side of a barricade is relatively easy, and when executed correctly, it only exposes your hands, your right arm and the right side of your face. However, shooting around a left-hand corner can be problematic. In order to minimize your exposure, many instructors advocate transitioning your gun to your nondominant hand.

While this works well in theory, the fact of the matter is that very few shooters are even close to being as proficient with their nondominant hand as they are with their dominant hand. How practical is it to expect these shooters to shoot with their less coordinated hand when they are taking fire and their life hinges

Photos by Alfredo Rico

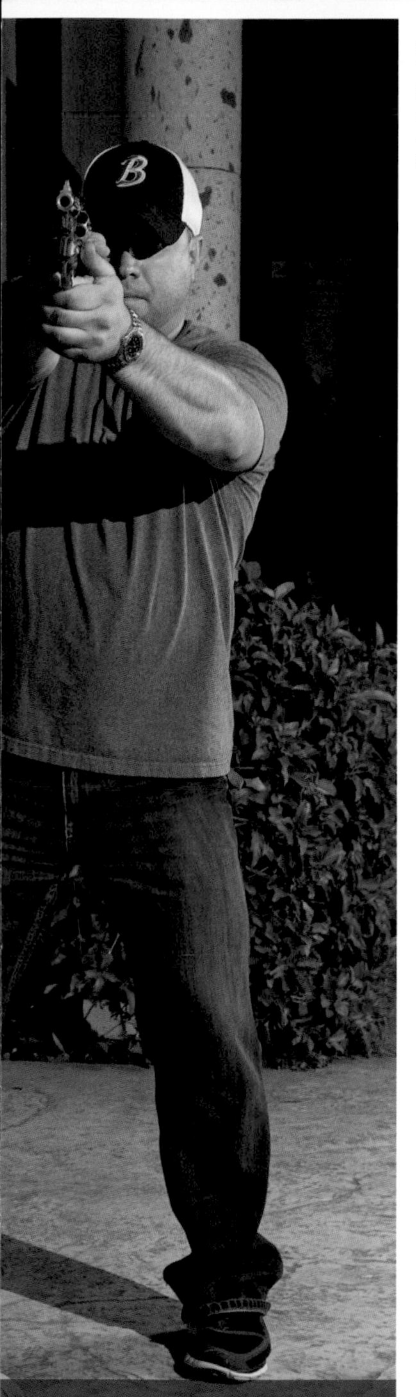

Maintaining a right-handed shooting grip would needlessly expose this shooter to incoming rounds.

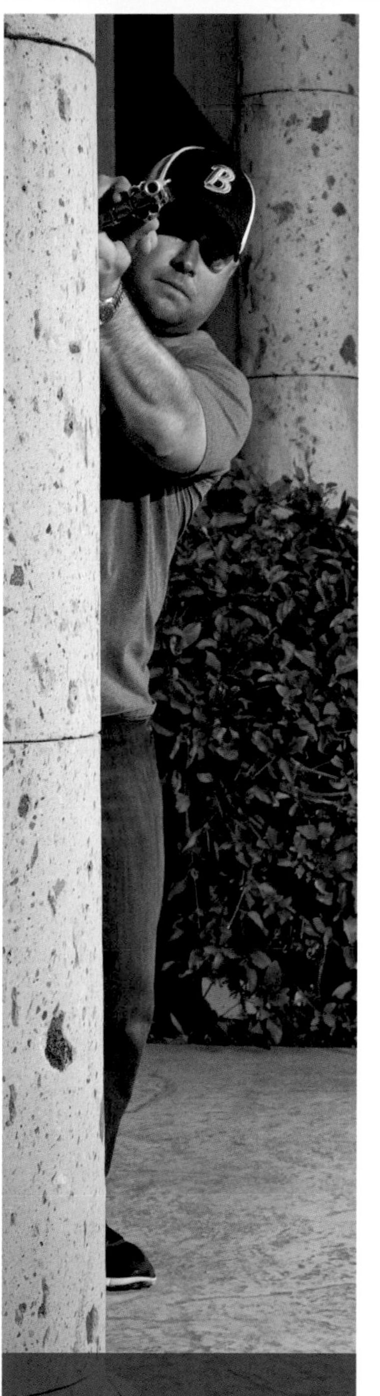

As an alternative, the shooter can keep the gun in his right hand but cant the gun sideways to present less of a target to the bad guy.

Here the shooter is using a left-handed shooting grip to shoot from cover.

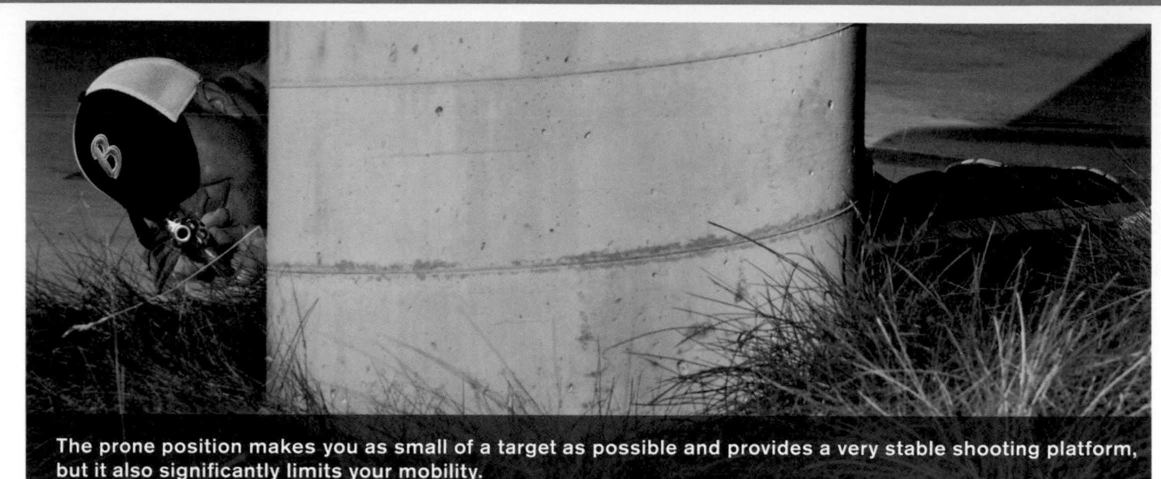

The prone position makes you as small of a target as possible and provides a very stable shooting platform, but it also significantly limits your mobility.

on their ability to make an accurate shot on target?

As an alternative to transitioning your gun from hand to hand depending on whether you're shooting around a left or right corner, why not leave the gun in your dominant hand when shooting around a corner on your nondominant side, but cant the gun to the left so that the sights are in the 9 o'clock position (3 o'clock for left-handed shooters)? Doing so automatically draws your nondominant arm behind cover. This position exposes no more of your body to your adversary than transitioning the gun to your nondominant hand. This sight picture may take some getting used to, but it may be better than having to constantly transition your gun from one hand to the other or attempting to make a precise shot with your nondominant hand.

Many shooters like to brace their firearm or hand against cover to achieve a more accurate shot. When your adversary is at an extended distance, this tactic might be a valid option. While this technique certainly has merit, it is not without flaw. To rest your gun or body on a barricade means you have to be right up on that barricade. As mentioned previously, being this close to cover leaves you susceptible to skipped rounds.

When you're shooting from behind cover, it's possible to be looking through your sights at the threat without your muzzle being clear of the barricade. This is due to the offset of the muzzle and sights. If you were to fire your gun without accounting for muzzle offset, your round could impact the barricade directly in front of you as opposed to hitting your intended target.

CONCLUSION

Cover will save you in a gunfight. If you don't practice recognizing and effectively using cover to shield you from gunfire, you will probably not have the presence of mind to seek cover during a real shooting. Once you're behind cover, know how to fire accurately while minimizing your exposure to incoming rounds. Cover is the only thing between you and the bad guy's bullets. Don't blow it!

PART III
GEAR GUIDE

BY DAVID KENIK

Holster Guide

Choosing a holster can be overwhelming. Here's how to pick the right one for your needs.

Nighthawk Custom's Ostrich Companion holster is comfortable, secure and carefully made—all features shared by quality carry rigs.

Photo by Lynne McCready

PRACTICAL CARRY Holsters & Belts

What good is advice without choices? Here are a selection of holsters and belts built by some of the top makers in the United States.

Belt Holsters

Safariland Model 0701
- Dual-layer polymer
- Level 2 retention

$75

Galco Paddle Lite
- Polymer/leather
- Level 1 retention
- Medium cant

$40

Bianchi Model 120 Covert Option
- Leather

$82

Blackhawk CQC 3-Slot
- Leather
- Thumb-break retention

$74

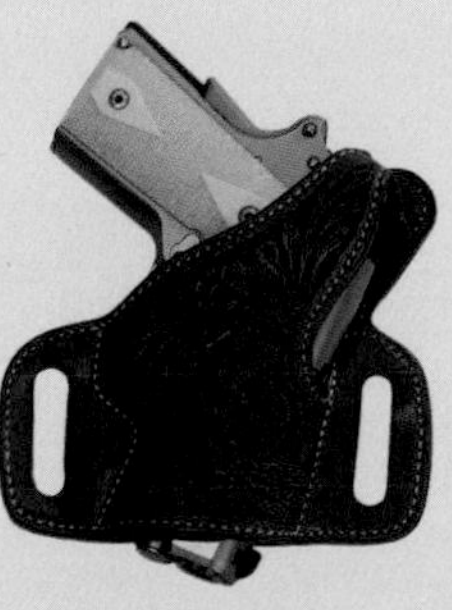

El Paso Sky Six
- Leather
- Thumb-break retention

$79

High Noon Need For Speed
- Rough-out leather

$170

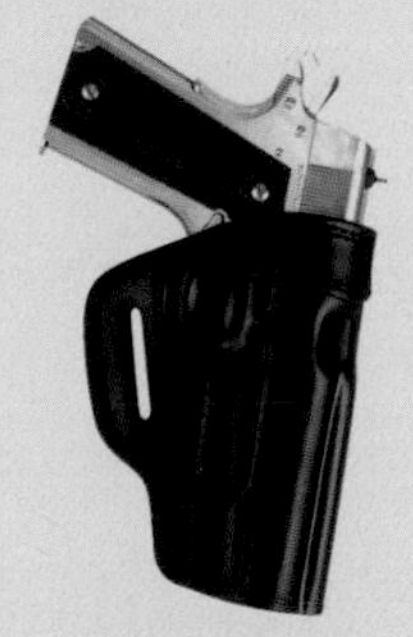

Kirkpatrick Texas Strong Side
- Leather

$68

Holster choice is as important as your selection of firearm because a good gun in a bad holster is like having a fast car with lousy tires. There are a lot of factors that come into play when you're looking at holster performance, and it all starts with gun fit.

Gun Fit

Obviously, a holster holds a gun but it needs to do so properly. If your gun is too loose, it can move and be in a bad position when you need to draw. At worst, the gun can actually fall out. I don't want to be put in the position of trying to explain to someone at the checkout counter that there's no need to worry as I pick up my gun from the floor—not to mention trying to figure out what to say to the responding police officer.

Conversely, a holster that is too tight could foul your grip, throw off your draw and derail your shooting. I have tried some holsters that were so tight that it was nearly impossible to retrieve the firearm.

The better the boning of a leather holster the less tight the holster needs to be. Boning

is the process by which quality leather holsters are fitted to a specific model of handgun, and it entails forming the leather—when wet—to the contours of the gun with a smooth tool or "bone." A properly boned holster will adhere to the trigger guard, slide stop and other physical features detailed into the leather, eliminating the need for a strap to hold the gun in.

The best way to tell whether your gun fits a holster properly is to insert the unloaded pistol or revolver and then run hard and jump up and down. The gun should remain firmly in the holster during these vigorous

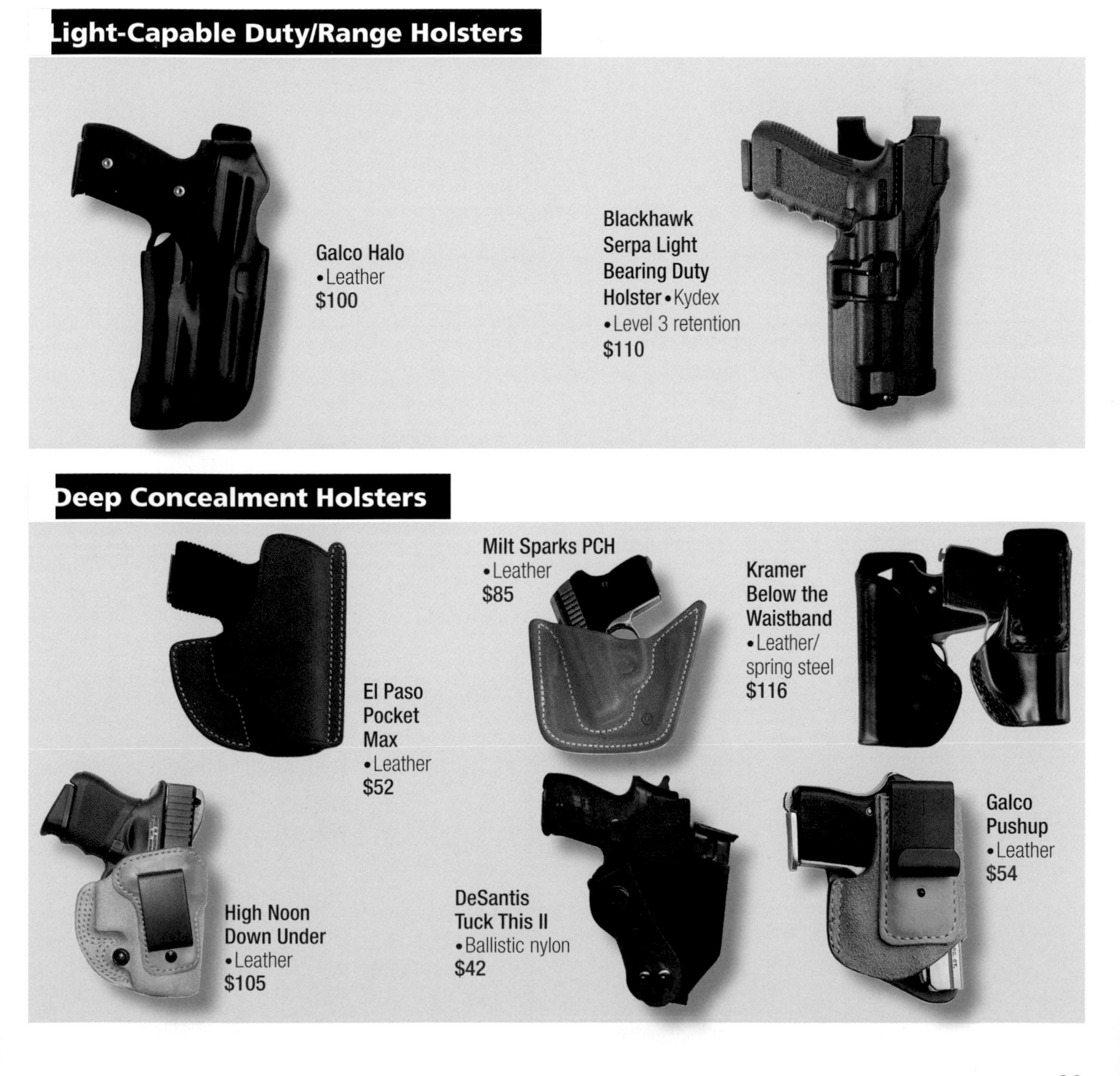

actions, but it shouldn't be so tight that it impedes the draw. If you find yourself tugging hard to lift your gun from the holster, you need to loosen it. If you have an adjustable holster, the adjustment screw will change the tension easily. Leather holsters can usually be broken in by simply wearing them around the house.

Comfort & Support

If you're going to carry for extended periods of time, a holster needs be comfortable. Comfort has a lot to do with how well the holster fits the contours of your body and how well the holster and belt support the weight of the gun. The key to proper support is

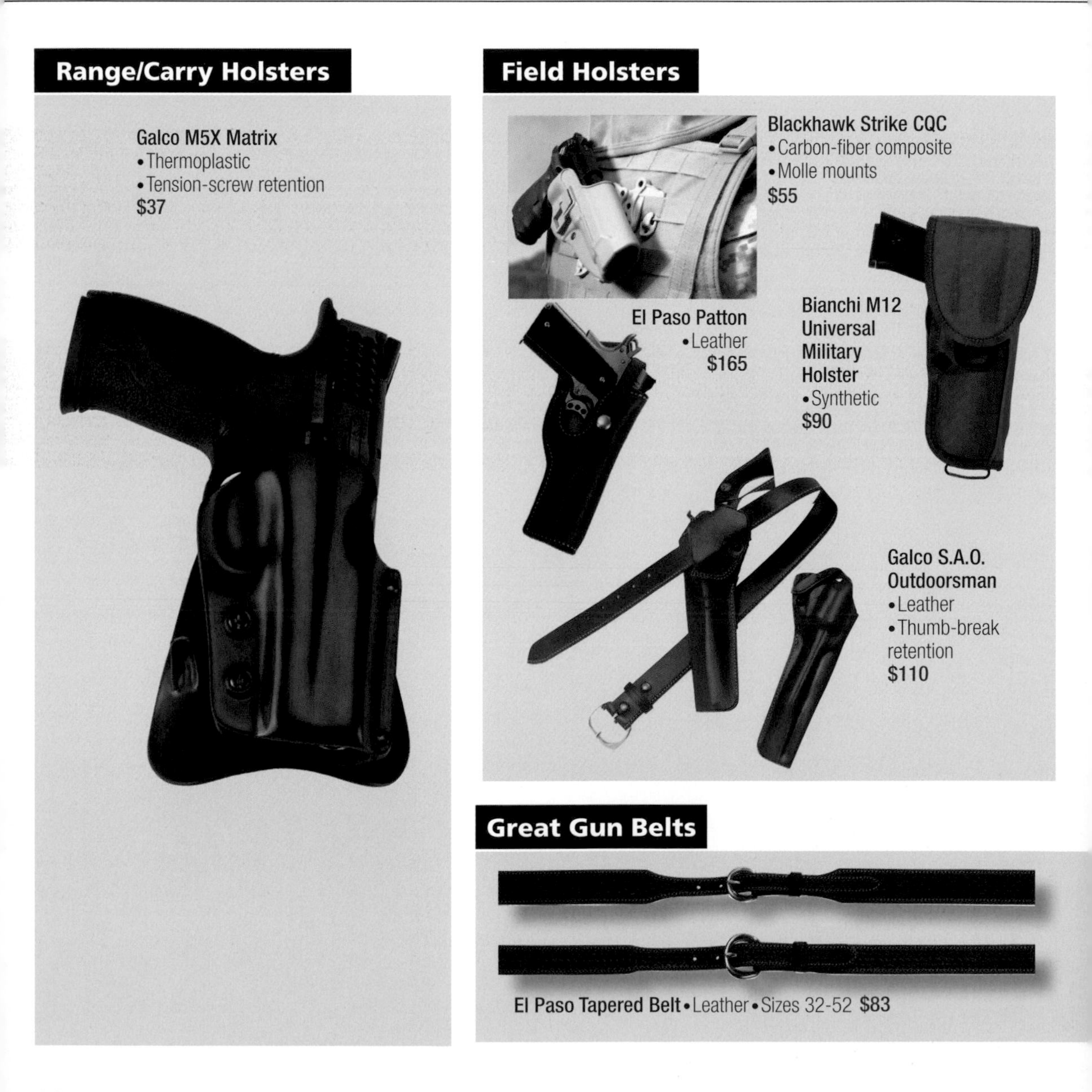

thick, high-quality leather in the holster and especially the belt.

Police officers are far more prone to attempted gun grabs than private citizens.

While frequently overlooked, gun belts are extremely important. They contribute to both comfort and security of your carry rig. The belt is what keeps the holster positioned upright and prevents it from flopping around.

Don't use a common casual or dress belt. For maximum support, the belt should be made of thick two-ply leather to help support and

Alternate Carry Options

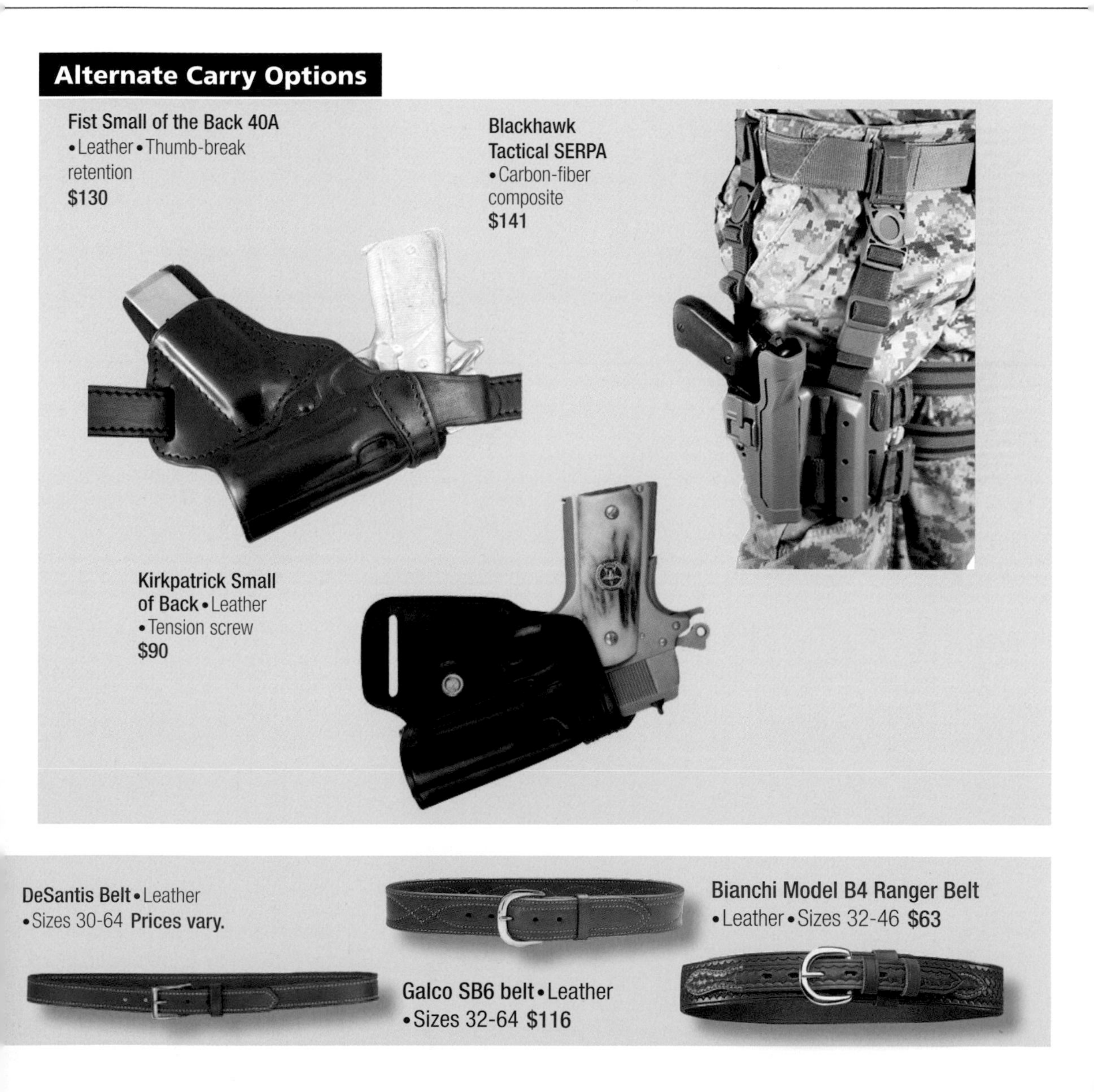

Fist Small of the Back 40A • Leather • Thumb-break retention **$130**

Blackhawk Tactical SERPA • Carbon-fiber composite **$141**

Kirkpatrick Small of Back • Leather • Tension screw **$90**

DeSantis Belt • Leather • Sizes 30-64 **Prices vary.**

Galco SB6 belt • Leather • Sizes 32-64 **$116**

Bianchi Model B4 Ranger Belt • Leather • Sizes 32-46 **$63**

distribute the weight of the gun.

If you intend on using your belt with an IWB (inside the waistband) holster, order the belt 2 inches longer than normal. Whichever belt you choose, be sure that it is properly sized for the belt loops of your holster. If you have a 1.5-inch belt opening in your holster, use a 1.5-inch wide belt. Many shooters struggle with draws and reholstering because of ill-fitting belts and holsters.

Cant

Cant is the angle at which the holster sits on the belt. Holsters are variously designed for a "straight drop," "cant forward" or what some call a "radical cant." Some holster designs offer adjustable cants.

The forward cant, used for strong-side carry, pushes the butt of the gun upward and reduces the amount of the grip that sticks out the back. The greater the cant, the more concealable the gun, but if it's too far forward, getting a proper grip becomes difficult. Cross draw and center carry rigs usually use a rear cant, which pushes the butt of the gun downward.

For strong-side carry, I find a radical cant, which angles the gun forward about 20 degrees, to be a good combination of concealability and accessibility. It's enough angle to keep the butt of a full-size gun from sticking out the back but still allows a good grip.

Rise

Another design element is the rise, or how high the gun sits in relationship to the belt. For taller folks, a high rise works well. I find I get better concealability and less flip-flop motion with standard-rise designs. Those of short stature may find that a low-rise holster makes drawing easier.

Retention Devices

While they may appear to be essential to hold a gun in the holster, retention devices are in fact often not necessary. Quality holsters retain the gun quite efficiently by their fit and boning.

The true intent of a retention device is to deter a gun grab. A retention device reduces the ability of others to grab your pistol from its holster.

Retention devices add time to the draw and may foul a draw if the user is not sufficiently practiced. With lots of continuing practice, the use of a retention device adds only a fraction of a second, but it is yet one more thing to work on.

Another argument against a retention device is that if your dominant hand is injured, using your nondominant hand to draw from a dominant-side holster may be difficult.

Police officers are far more prone to attempted gun grabs than private citizens, and that's why they use security holsters—often with several security layers. The average person may rarely come into direct contact with the criminal element and is often better served with a nonretention holster.

Holster Materials

While leather once dominated the market, Kydex—a plastic-type material that has good molding and machining qualities—has become quite popular. Kydex is relatively inexpensive to manufacture, provides low friction inside the holster and can be designed to be easily adjustable. It's also low maintenance and much less expensive than quality leather.

A great feature of Kydex is that it can be designed so it can be adjusted in terms of tension, cant, rise and types of belt loops.

Kydex has two great disadvantages: it's noisy and lacks flexibility. Also, because the material is hard plastic, it will not mold to your body with use like leather does.

Design Features

Holsters, regardless of material, should feature certain characteristics.

They should cover the entire length of a handgun's barrel or slide. For IWB carry, full coverage eliminates skin burns. For belt carry, it protects the gun and the front sight. In both cases, full coverage also prevents the front sight from catching on the holster during a draw. In most instances, a short gun can be used in a long holster, but not the other way around.

An indispensable feature for an IWB holster is the ability to stay open while the gun is out of the holster. This is vital to one-handed reholstering.

Another must-have feature is the ability to get a full grip while the gun is holstered. A good draw starts with a good grip. Be sure that you can reach around the entire grip and place your hand properly up against the bottom of the trigger guard without the holster or belt getting in your way.

I like holsters with body shields. The shield extends upward between the gun and your body and offers significant advantages. It makes for easy reholstering and helps to keep shirts from being pushed down into the holster. These shields also protect a gun from body oils, sweat and salt.

Body shields also provide an additional advantage for guns with external safeties, helping to prevent the safety from being deactivated accidentally by rubbing against the body.

There is no exact formula for putting all of these elements together. What is comfortable for one person may not be for another. Unfortunately, it's trial-and-error. The good news is that many quality holster manufacturers accept returns if you're not satisfied. It's worth buying from those companies just for that opportunity, even if you have to pay a little more.

FREEDOM OF CHOICE

MAKING SENSE OF MODERN HOLSTERS.

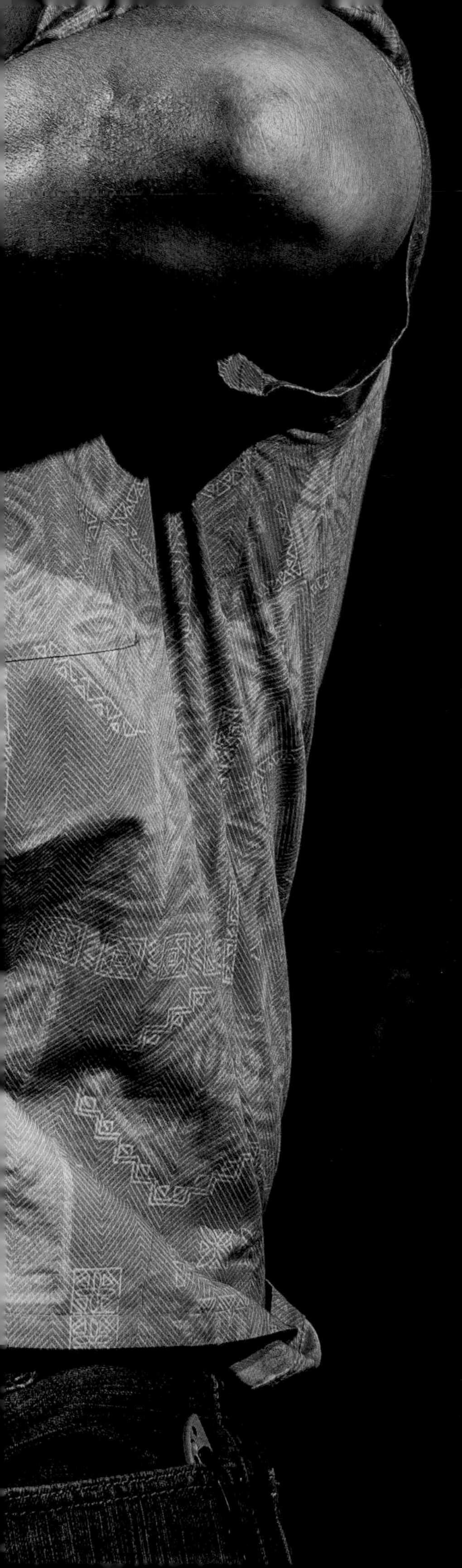

STORY BY
AARON PEACHMAN

PHOTOGRAPHS BY
ALFREDO RICO

Not long ago holster selection consisted of only a few options based upon carry location. For outside the waistband (OWB), the choice was pancake or paddle. For inside the waistband (IWB), the choice was hook or belt loop. All other carry methods (ankle holster, shoulder rig, etc.) were largely based on whatever happened to be available for the pistol.

Nowadays, in the age of modern polymers, manufacturing techniques and Internet sales, manufacturers are able to bring quality products to market more easily, which means consumers have an unprecedented freedom of choice.

Among the biggest advancements in recent holster technologies is the variety of materials. They fall into three major categories: leather, hard polymers and fabrics.

HIDE

The material of choice since people began carrying firearms, leather is durable, shapeable and, because of friction, offers a small degree of ability to hold a gun in the holster in addition to what gravity and straps will do. Drawing a gun from a leather holster is quiet, especially if the holster doesn't have snaps.

Depending on how rigid the construction is, reholstering can range from easy to difficult. Leather is also somewhat pliable, and even slightly breathable, making it comfortable to wear against the body. Porous, it will soak up sweat and water, which will then be in contact with your firearm. Leather will eventually wear out, but that takes quite a while. I have carried the same leather IWB holster every day for over nine years and, although visibly worn, it has not shown any signs of diminished functionality. The wear stages of leather are incremental. In other words, the holster won't just fail without warning. Wear signs lead up to the failure, giving you ample opportunity to repair or replace the holster before it's totally kaput.

PLASTICS

Hard polymers include materials like Kydex and a range of plastics. They are durable and easy to shape, and since polymer holsters are often molded to the specific weapon, they "grab" onto parts of the weapon such as the triggerguard. Depending on design, this locking will often give an audible click when the weapon is properly seated. This clicking also occurs when drawing the pistol. Combine this with the scraping of metal against polymer and you see why polymer is the loudest holster material. Polymers are rigid and do not breath, which can make them uncomfortable, especially if a sharp edge or corner is digging in. Being nonporous, polymers do shield the handgun from moisture, and they are durable, especially the minimal designs. Due to rigid construction, polymer holster failure often manifests with little to no warning. Fine one day, cracked the next. Of the polymer holsters I have used, simple Kydex sheath-style holsters seem to be the least prone to breaking and will probably last just as long

HIDE

The DeSantis Mini Scabbard is simple and affordable.

MSRP:

$62

Photo

Photos by Alfredo Rico

HIDE

The Galco Push Up Inside The Pant Holster is small, simple and pairs well with many different cover garments.

MSRP:

$45

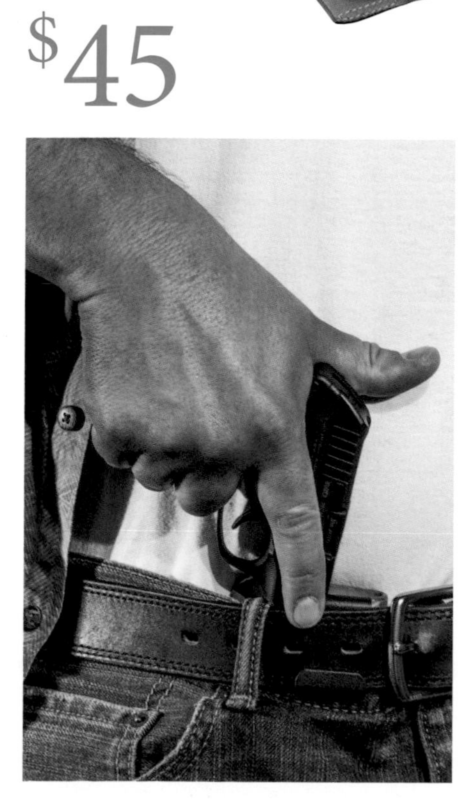

PLASTICS

The 5.11/Blade-Tech/VTAC Thumb Drive Holster provides a positive locking retention feature.

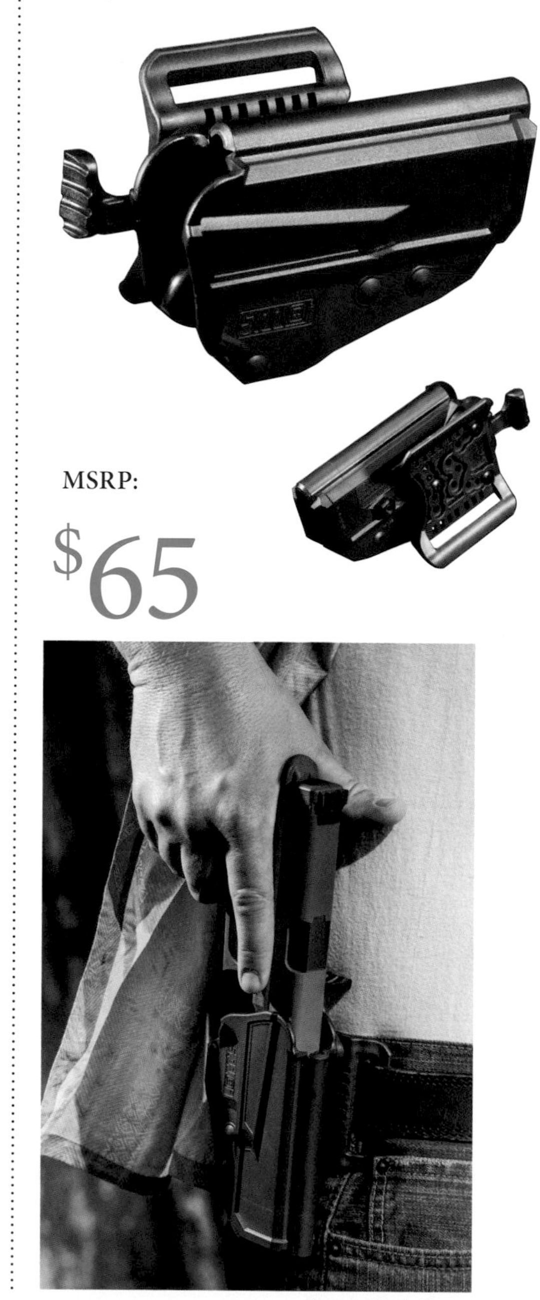

MSRP:

$65

Photos by Alfredo Rico

or longer than their leather counterparts under normal use.

CLOTH

Fabric holsters include holsters made of materials like flexible nylon. Fabric is not especially durable when compared to leather or hard polymers, but it still lasts for quite some time. The good news regarding fabrics and durability is there will almost always be noticeable incremental wear, so you should know well in advance if it's time to look for a new holster. The main strength of fabric holsters is their flexibility that conforms to both gun and body contours better than other materials. This makes it well suited to pocket holsters. Fabric is breathable and slick against gunmetal, allowing for quick and easy drawing. Because of this, it doesn't work so well for retention, but fabric draws silently. Rubberized coatings are sometimes applied to the outside of fabric holsters (especially pocket holsters) to help keep them in place. Fabric is completely permeable to moisture, which means water and sweat will easily pass both into and out of the holster.

"

WE ARE LIVING IN A TIME OF UNPARALLELED HOLSTER SELECTION. THAT'S TERRIFIC, BUT TO THE UNINFORMED IT CAN MAKE THE PROCESS OF SELECTING THE RIGHT HOLSTER A DAUNTING TASK.

PLASTICS

The hard polymer back of the Raven Concealment Systems Appendix Carry Rig – ACR provides a nonporous moisture barrier.

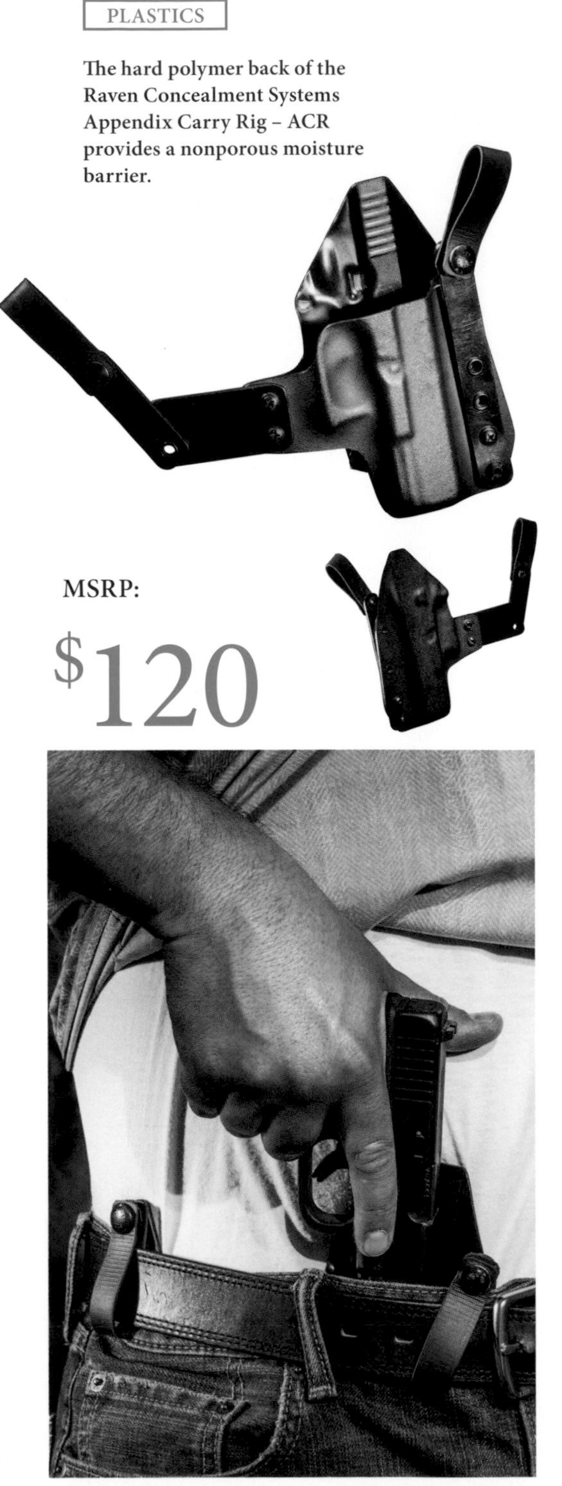

MSRP:

$120

Photos by Alfredo Rico

HYBRID

Hard polymer combined with padded, vented fabric gives the StealthGear USA ONYX a thin profile as well as making it a comfortable rig.

MSRP:

$99

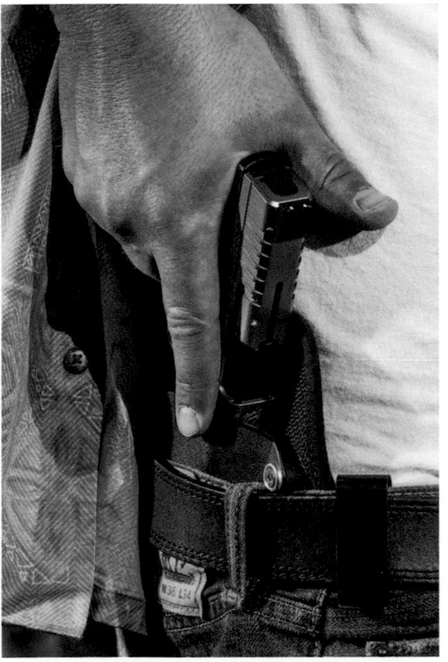

Photos by Alfredo Rico

HYBRIDS

Aside from these major materials, hybrid holsters are an increasingly available holster option. These holsters combine different materials in an effort to meld the benefits of both materials. Most are either leather/polymer hybrids or fabric/polymer hybrids. Most strive to achieve the comfort of a fabric or leather holster by placing those materials against the body while having the ease of reholstering and positive feedback of clicking in and out of the holster that hard polymer holsters offer.

SELECTION AND TRENDS

We are living in a time of unparalleled holster selection. That's terrific, but to the uninformed it can make the process of selecting the right holster a daunting task. Being armed with a little knowledge will assist in making your best choice.

A major trend is the move toward flatter, wider holsters that spread the weight of the weapon over a larger area, much like the Appendix Carry Rig (ACR) by Raven Concealment Systems, or nearly the entire line offered by CrossBreed Holsters. A unique offering is also being manufactured by StealthGear USA. These wide, fabric/polymer hybrids have padding and a breathable layer built in.

At the extreme end of the compact-holster spectrum are options like the Minimal Inside Carry (MIC) holster and VanGuard by Raven Concealment Systems. These holsters consist of a small piece of hard polymer that fits over the triggerguard of your handgun. They are held in place with a lanyard or a single belt loop. Combined with ultra-compact handguns such as the Ruger LCP and LC9 or the Glock 42 and 43, these minimalist holsters offer the ultimate in concealment.

THE SHOULDER RIG

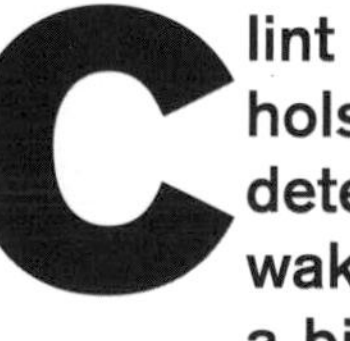**lint Eastwood wore a shoulder holster as the most iconic police detective in "Dirty Harry." In the wake of that cult classic, carrying a bigbore in a shoulder holster was undeniably symbolic for a character possessing cunning wit and unyielding power.**

BY RICHARD NANCE
PHOTOS BY ALFREDO RICO

But in the last two decades, the shoulder holster seems to have plummeted to obscurity. Is the shoulder holster merely a relic or is it a legitimate concealed carry alternative?

WHAT GIVES?

According to Mike Barham, media liaison for Galco Gunleather, the Miami Classic shoulder holster system remains one of the company's top 10 best-selling products. A bit surprising perhaps considering that shoulder holsters get almost zero coverage in the gun media. Yet, despite this obvious lack of attention, the shoulder holster continues to thrive. Barham indicated that while the shoulder holster is still very popular with police detectives, it's also a favorite of many citizens who carry a concealed handgun in cooler environments. "When you're wearing several layers of clothing, including a heavy jacket, it's easier to reach across your torso than behind your hip to access your gun," he explained.

THE TASK

Recently, I decided to test and evaluate several of Galco's popular shoulder holster systems. This proved to be an interesting process, one that gave me a newfound appreciation for this nostalgic carry option. As I soon discovered, in

Relic or modern-day concealed carry option?

certain circumstances the shoulder holster is more practical than waistline carry.

GALCO RIGS

Since Galco set the standard for shoulder holsters with the Original Jackass Rig back in 1969, I decided to base this evaluation on Galco's comprehensive lineup. I ordered the entire family of shoulder systems including the Classic Lite shoulder system, a VHS shoulder system (aka Vertical Holster System), an Executive, a Jackass Rig shoulder system and a Miami Classic II. Each rig is fully adjustable and can accommodate any of Galco's shoulder holsters. These systems are the definition of modularity in that they work with a wide selection of practical accessories.

Except for the economically priced Classic Lite, all of Galco's shoulder rigs are made of only the top 2 percent of domestic steerhide. Interesting. When you consider that your holster's job is to keep your handgun secure and immediately accessible, the advantage of top-quality leather construction should be a given.

Yet another Galco-specific feature is the trademarked Flexalon swivel plate, which, incidentally, is the inspiration behind Galco's new logo. The Flexalon swivel plate enables the harness straps to swivel for added comfort and better concealment. While other holster manufacturers have adopted similar devices, the Flexalon lays flatter and is, therefore, more concealable than any other version. Barham said the biggest advantage Galco has over its competitors is the fact that Richard Gallagher, Galco president and CEO, has overseen more than four decades of design improvements.

BREAK-IN PERIOD

As a little leaguer, I can remember getting a new baseball glove several weeks before the start of the season. I'd place a baseball carefully in the pocket of the glove and tie it tight with shoestrings, then place it under my mattress. After

Photo by Alfredo Rico

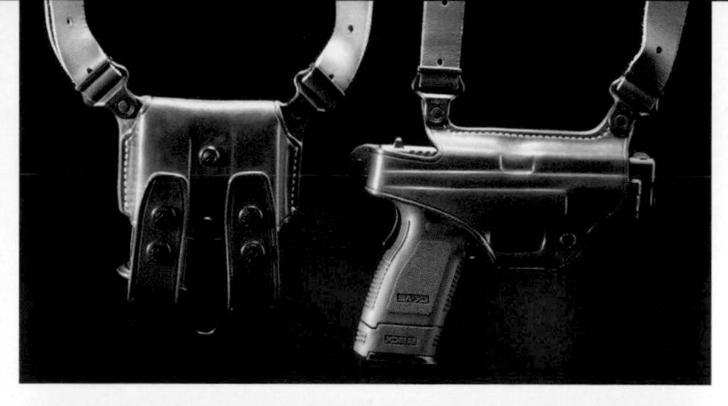

Photos by Alfredo Rico

TOP - The Miami Classic is configured for a horizontal holster and a vertical magazine pouch. The holster was initially very tight for this Springfield XD Compact.

BOTTOM - The Executive shoulder holster system was lightweight, comfortable and conducive to a surprisingly fast draw stroke for this Smith & Wesson Air Weight revolver.

several nights of sleeping on the glove, it would form to the shape of the ball. Like a new baseball glove, a leather shoulder holster needs to be broken in properly for best results.

You won't need to sleep with your holster under the mattress, but you may need to do a little prep work to ensure that your gun fits properly. Unless you've selected the wrong holster for your gun, you will not need to worry about the holster being too loose. However, depending on the particular model of your gun in the holster you selected, it might take every ounce of strength you can muster to seat the gun deeply enough into the holster to snap the retention strap.

If you have a hard time fitting your gun into its holster, don't panic. Galco engineers its holsters to fit tightly initially to allow for the fact that the leather fibers will relax to the perfect shape with use. The product information guide that accompanies each shoulder holster explains in detail Galco's recommended break-in procedure.

For this piece, I reviewed more than a half dozen different Galco holsters. I found that the holsters designed for the Taurus Model 605 .357 Magnum and the Smith & Wesson Air Weight .38 Special fit perfectly into their respective holsters, as did the Smith & Wesson Model 586 .357 Magnum. Both the Nighthawk Talon Model 1911 and the Ruger SR1911 chambered in .45 ACP fit well into a holster designed to accommodate 1911s with 5-inch barrels. The holster designed for the SIG Sauer P220 was a little tighter, but I was able to secure the snap with little difficulty. However, the holster for the Glock 21 and the Springfield Armory XD Compact required significant effort.

If you can't get the gun into the holster, your first step should be to loosen the holster's tension screw, which is typically located at the bottom of the holster, where the front of the triggerguard will rest. If this still doesn't allow you to fully insert your gun into the holster, Galco recommends placing the unloaded firearm in a plastic freezer bag or wrapping it in two to three layers of plastic kitchen wrap, then inserting the gun into the holster slowly and gently

For a more efficient draw, step back with your gun side leg and blade your upper body to the threat.

twisting it from side to side until it's fully seated. At that point, twist the firearm back and forth about 1/16 inch several times. Leave the gun in the holster for 15 minutes. When you remove the pistol from the holster and peel the plastic bag or wrap, reinsert the gun into the holster. If it's still too tight, repeat this process as needed.

Admittedly, I resorted to brute force to make the guns fit into their respective holsters, and fortunately things worked out OK. But if I had it to do over, I would've followed Galco's recommendations to the letter and saved myself the extra effort and upper-body workout.

Don't expect to place your gun in your new Galco shoulder holster, strap it on and walk out the door. A holster is too important a piece of equipment to choose or carry on a whim. It's good that there's a break-in period for the Galco line of shoulder holsters because this process gives you ample opportunity to properly adjust the shoulder harness for your own comfort and functionality. Maybe even more important, you'll get practice drawing your unloaded firearm numerous times before ever having to do so in a real-world encounter.

COMFORT

While comfort is certainly subjective, many find carrying a gun in a shoulder holster to be more comfortable than the more popular method of carrying along the waist. This is particularly true of those who are seated for long periods of time (including those confined to a wheelchair) or who suffer from lower back or shoulder injuries that make waistline carry painfully impractical.

Shoulder holsters may be far more comfortable for individuals with lower back problems than belt-mounted holsters. Anatomically, a shoulder holster won't press against your lower back when seated as would be the case with a holster worn along your waist, between the 3 o'clock and 9 o'clock positions. Similarly, those with shoulder problems often find reaching across their body to draw from a shoulder holster much easier than trying to reach behind their hip to draw.

"Women often find shoulder holsters more comfortable than belt-mounted holsters because of their body type and flexibility," says Barham. "Also, since women are accustomed to garments with straps over their shoulders, they sometimes make the transition to shoulder carry a little easier than men."

In my experience as a firearms instructor, I've noted that the orientation of a belt-mounted holster on a female is typically quite high as compared with a male, which can make it more difficult for a female to draw from a waistline carry position.

It's important to properly adjust the harness on your shoulder rig. This not only helps ensure comfort, but also helps to anchor the holster in place so that it doesn't move prior to or during the draw stroke. Many of the rigs shown on these pages contain a loop on the magazine pouch so that they can be secured with a Galco "tie down" to your belt.

Another important consideration related to the comfort of your shoulder holster is that the rig is well balanced. A shoulder rig enables its wearer to carry

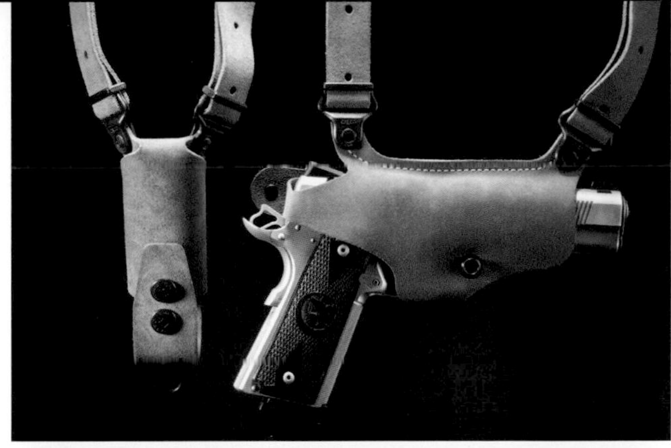

Photos by Alfredo Rico

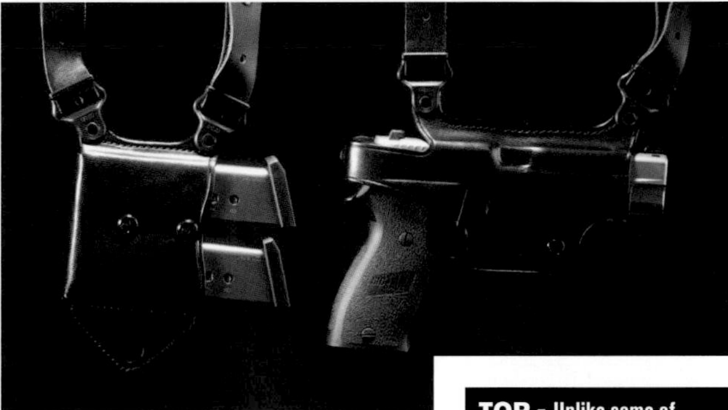

TOP - **Unlike some of their other shoulder rigs, Galco's Classic Lite, shown here with a Nighthawk Talon, required no breaking in.**

BOTTOM - **This Miami Classic II houses a SIG Sauer P220. The spare magazines help to counterbalance the weight of the pistol.**

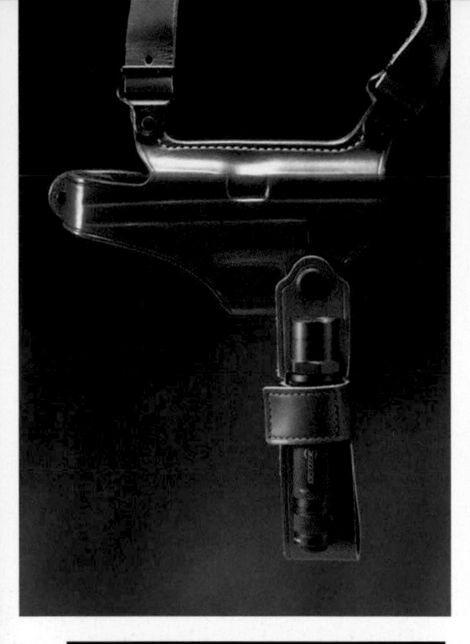

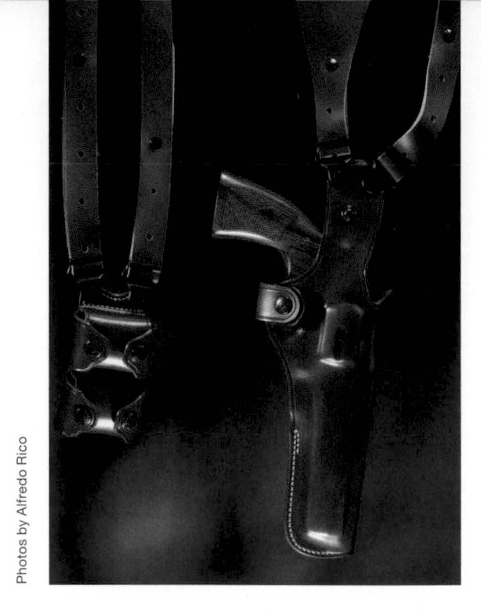

Photos by Alfredo Rico

Galco offers an extensive array of accessories such as a tactical flashlight holder, a handcuff case and a dual speedloader pouch. Tie-downs can be utilized to secure the spare ammo pouch to the wearer's belt.

spare magazines, speedloaders, handcuffs, a tactical light or other items on the nongun side. This creates a win/win situation, because not only do you have access to these potentially lifesaving items, they actually help to counterbalance your gun and evenly distribute the weight of your load.

PRACTICALITY

There's a reason why waistline carry is by far the most popular and preached concealed carry option these days. It provides the most natural draw stroke and offers good gun retention. A hip-mounted holster provides superior access to your firearm in an extreme close-quarter engagement. However, there are times when wearing a gun on your waist can be problematic.

If you're seated in a vehicle with your seatbelt securely fastened, getting to your gun in a belt-mounted holster can be a real challenge. A shoulder holster, on the other hand, provides its user better access to the gun even when seated and wearing his seatbelt.

Several of my fellow police officers routinely ride motorcycles while off-duty. As you can imagine, it's not easy concealing a gun in a belt-mounted holster while riding a motorcycle, since your body position and wind will throw around your leathers, jacket or other garment you'd be wearing for concealment. The last thing you need while riding is other another motorist seeing that you're armed.

DRAWING

A shoulder holster requires its wearer to reach across the body to draw the pistol. Although a cross draw is typically slower than a strong-side waistline draw, I found that with practice it can actually be pretty quick (especially if you cheat by preemptively achieving a shooting grip).

The most efficient way to draw from a shoulder holster is to prestage your hand on the gun. To accomplish this, simply obtain a good grip and fold your other arm atop your gun-side arm. When you decide to draw, step back with your gun-side leg and pivot at the waist to help orient the muzzle toward the target. Simultaneously raise the elbow of your nonshooting arm so that it's out of the line of fire and positioned to offer protection from incoming strikes or attempted gun grabs.

Unfortunately, there is not always sufficient warning that a potentially deadly encounter is about to occur. Therefore you might not have the luxury of covertly achieving a shooting grip prior to drawing. You may also find yourself drawing with your gun-side leg forward. The problem with this technique is that it requires you to sweep the muzzle in a wider arc, which not only takes longer to get on target but offers your adversary an opportunity to intercept your arm to prevent you from bringing your gun into service.

Not surprisingly, the shoulder holsters that orient the gun horizontally facilitate a faster and easier draw than holsters like the VHS, which orient the barrel downward. Of course, if you were to carry a long-barreled handgun like movie-classic Smith & Wesson Model 29, you're also going to need a long torso to conceal it in a horizontally configured shoulder holster. The vertical shoulder holster may be a comfortable option for hunters afield, but for defensive purposes, I'd recommend utilizing a shoulder rig that mounts your carry gun horizontally.

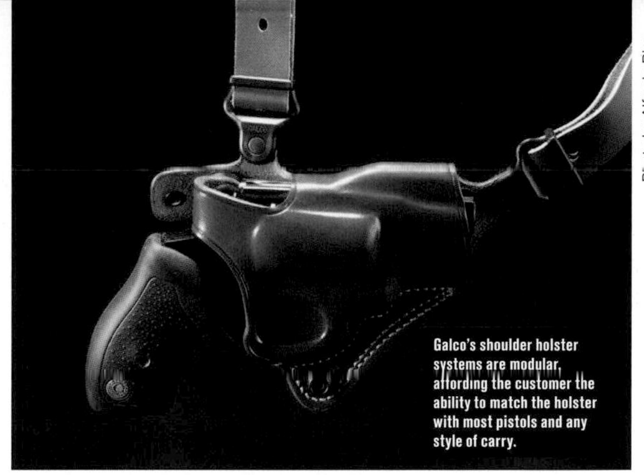
Photo by Alfredo Rico

Galco's shoulder holster systems are modular, affording the customer the ability to match the holster with most pistols and any style of carry.

RETENTION

When you're carrying a concealed handgun, your primary safety mechanism is the fact that the sidearm remains concealed. If no one can see your gun, no one's going to try to take your gun. However, if you're facing a would-be assailant who has caught a glimpse of your firearm—whether a wardrobe malfunction or someone with knowledge of your carry habits—that would-be thief arguably has better access to your gun than you do.

In an episode of "Personal Defense TV," Massad Ayoob demonstrated a gun retention technique he learned from police defensive tactics instructor Terry Campbell. The technique is designed to thwart disarm attempts from the front, since the shoulder holster itself provides a degree of security against a rear disarm attempt. The premise of the technique is to bring your nonshooting hand upward in a scissor-like motion to pin the assailant's hand to your gun. This traps the assailant's arm and prevents him from being able to draw your gun from its holster. The conclusion of this technique is dependent on whether the assailant grabbed your gun with his right hand, his left hand or both hands.

Against a right-handed gun grab (when your gun is worn under your left shoulder), after pinning the assailant's hand to your gun, step to your right with your left leg and pivot around 180 degrees while gripping your gun. This action should completely dislodge the bad guy's grip and potentially break his wrist in the process.

If the assailant grabs with either his left hand or both hands, you step forward at a 45-degree angle with your right leg and cup the assailant's left forearm with your hand, pulling it into your chest. Then, reorient your hand so your palm is under the assailant's elbow. Direct his elbow upward, then downward to achieve an arm lock and fully extract the bad guy's hand from your gun. Obviously, these techniques take practice to attain proficiency. A less complex gross-motor-based alternative would be to simply deliver palm strikes to the assailant's face after trapping his wrist with your arm.

CONCLUSION

The shoulder holster, like every concealed carry method, has its strengths and weaknesses. The draw from a shoulder holster tends to be slower than from a belt-mounted holster and can more easily be fouled in an arm's-length deadly force encounter. However, for some, including those who are seated for extended periods or suffer from lower back or shoulder injuries, a shoulder holster is a comfortable and practical alternative to waistline carry.

If you opt for a shoulder holster, you need to become familiar with the Galco product line. Make sure your decision to utilize a shoulder holster is based on your perceived needs and not a desire to emulate a Hollywood hero.

Photo by Alfredo Rico

OFF-BODY CARRY

Sometimes concealed carry requires you to think beyond the holster.

BY RICHARD NANCE // PHOTOS BY ALFREDO RICO

Carrying a concealed handgun can be a pain—figuratively and literally. For many people, the discomfort associated with wearing a holstered firearm soon outweighs their desire to carry. As a result, their handguns get left at home or in a vehicle, where they're probably not going to do much good.

As an alternative, some opt for off-body carry methods such as a purse, an over-the-shoulder pack or even a disguised day planner. It's easy to see how off-body carry could be more comfortable and convenient than wearing a holstered gun all day, but is it a viable option for personal protection?

While you're not going to win any quick-draw contests drawing a firearm from your day planner, it's certainly better than going unarmed. Having access to a concealed handgun and being aware of your environment could be a life-saving combination when your daily routine is interrupted by an assailant who threatens to do you harm.

There are bound to be times when even the most hardcore advocates of holstered concealed carry will find it uncomfortable or just plain inappropriate. For instance, a day at the beach will probably not lend itself well to wearing a belt-mounted holster because you would need to wear an overgarment to conceal your gun (and it's pretty hard to hide that ankle holster when you're wearing shorts).

If you're in workout attire, wearing a holster or even a belt would be laughable. Let's face it: For most people, strict adherence to holster carry is not feasible. When traditional carry methods are impractical, here are some off-body alternatives to consider.

PURSE

For women, carrying a concealed handgun in their purse is a natural choice. After all, women typically carry purses anyway, and it's a lot easier to add a gun to the mix than redesign a wardrobe to accommodate

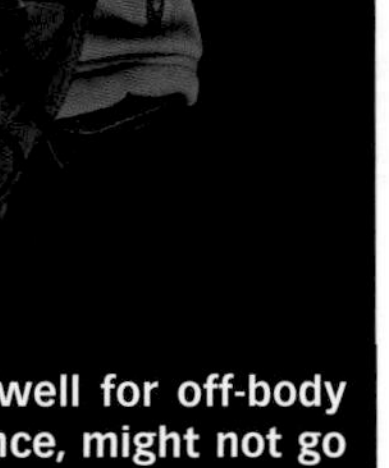

An over-the-shoulder pack such as Elite Survival's Avenger Gunpack works pretty well for off-body carry. Just be sure to pick a style that goes with your setting. A camo bag, for instance, might not go well with business attire.

Photos by Alfredo Rico

carrying a handgun in a belt-mounted holster.

Besides the fact that there's nothing unusual about a woman carrying a purse, it's also not odd for her to keep that purse close by at all times, and that's important. One of the dangers associated with off-body carry is the possibility of someone gaining access to your firearm. If you decide to carry your gun in a purse, you must maintain physical control of your purse at all times. Complacency in this regard could have tragic consequences.

Despite the benefits of carrying a gun in a purse, there's more to this carry method than simply dropping a gun into the purse's main compartment along with your keys, makeup, wallet, etc.—items that could interfere with your ability to quickly access your gun.

Your best bet is probably to purchase a purse specifically designed for concealed carry. These days there is quite an array of well-made, fashionable and practical holster purses on the market. (Editor's Note: Galco's DEL holster handbag is what our model is drawing from in the lead photograph—and, no, her finger is not on the trigger, although her indexing technique needs some work.) Make sure the purse actually looks like a purse. If you're wearing a nice dress and heels, an OD green purse with nylon straps and hook-and-loop closures might appear a little too obvious.

As with traditional purses, it would make sense to own a couple of different holster purses to match your attire. While concealed carry purses aren't cheap, you can't afford to skimp on quality.

In purse carry it's vital to have a separate compartment for the gun. Do not keep anything else in this compartment. An eyebrow brush or an ink pen that finds its way into the triggerguard is a recipe for disaster. When the gun is secured in a properly oriented integral holster, you are well on your way to a smooth and efficient draw stroke.

The purse's gun compartment should be secured by a zipper. Don't rely on snaps, hook-and-loop fasteners or magnets to contain your firearm. The last thing you want to have happen is for your gun to fall out onto the ground.

If possible, reserve a spot in the purse for a compact, but strong flashlight that you can locate quickly in an emergency. The purse should be able to conveniently store your concealed carry permit (if applicable) and a spare magazine or speedloader. Keep these items in the same location so you're not digging through your purse when you desperately need them.

Keep in mind that drawing a gun from a purse takes practice. You need to consider how your gun is best accessed and carry your purse to facilitate a smooth draw. For instance, a right-handed shooter using a purse with a side-zippered pocket would be best served carrying the purse over her left shoulder, with the zippered gun compartment within easy reach.

Off-body carry methods such as purse carry require perhaps even extra attention to your surroundings. If you're walking to your vehicle, for example, and notice someone rapidly approaching from behind, you could

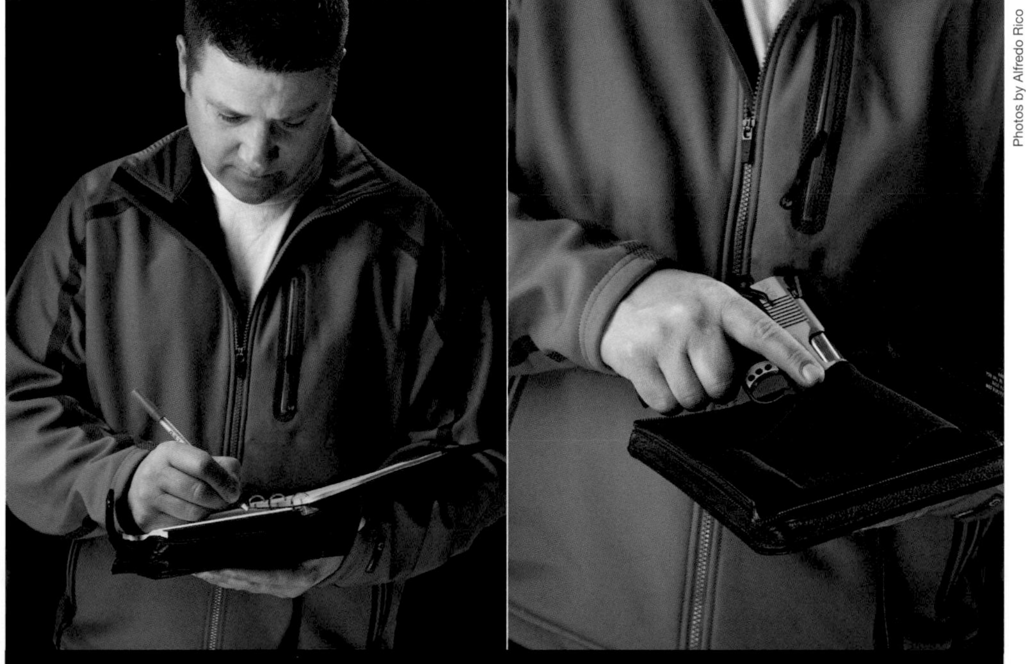

Photos by Alfredo Rico

Day planners such as Galco's Hidden Agenda are a commonplace accessory in which to stash a handgun. Unlike a purse or pack that you wear, there are times when you will set down a day planner. Just don't let it out of your sight.

afford yourself a much-needed head start by unzipping your holster compartment and acquiring a shooting grip on your firearm. In fact, the ability to covertly grip a handgun in anticipation of danger is perhaps the only tactical advantage to off-body carry.

PACKS

When I first became a police officer in 1997, I purchased a huge black fanny pack in which to tote my department-issued Glock 22. I carried that thing with me wherever I went. Over time, the proverbial "big black fanny pack" has become symbolic of either a concealed carry aficionado or an off-duty cop. Add to the mix short hair, sunglasses and (God forbid) a moustache with no other facial hair and you may as well be wearing a badge. I still have a buddy or two who carry their guns in fanny packs, but it is definitely a less popular option than it was a decade ago.

A step up in the concealment department is an over-the-shoulder pack, which can often be worn on the belt (for you die-hard fanny-packers). Sometimes referred to affectionately as a "man purse," these packs actually work pretty well for concealed carry. The fact that they are slung over the shoulder and head (as one would sling a long gun) offers a welcome degree of gun retention. These packs are also much more likely to remain on your body, so the chance of inadvertently leaving your gun behind is minimal.

Over-the-shoulder packs come in a variety of shapes, sizes and colors. You'll want to be sure that your pack goes with whatever it is you're wearing. A camouflage gun pack might not blend in really well at a business meeting or formal affair, but it might be perfectly suited for hiking or any number of other outdoor activities where more casual attire is the norm.

When selecting a gun pack, make sure it has a separate, zippered compartment for the gun. Be sure to keep your concealed carry permit handy, if applicable. Another benefit to carrying a gun pack is that there is probably ample room in which to store a small flashlight.

Adjust the straps so the pack is properly oriented for drawing the gun. Another key is to prestage the zipper so you won't have to fumble with it when you need it most.

I prefer to leave the zipper slightly open. This allows me to obtain a solid grasp of the exterior flap and rip it open for access to my gun. As you can imagine, having to unzip the holster compartment could significantly slow your draw. The draw stroke from a pack can be very smooth, but it requires extensive practice.

DAY PLANNER

A day planner offers a very covert carry method. You could probably walk around with one all day and not get a second glance. A quality day planner is made of full-grain leather and blends with either business or casual attire. Like the other off-body carry methods, a day planner/holster should have a separate zippered compartment for storing the firearm. Some even have a designated elastic strap to store an extra magazine, but you'll be hard-pressed to find room for a flashlight.

On the downside, since the day planner/holster is carried in-hand, there are bound to be times when you set it down. If you become complacent and let it out of your sight, you are tempting fate. Granted, it probably won't be apparent that the day planner contains a firearm, but they often contain credit cards and other valuables that would appeal to a thief.

Some day planners are equipped with a strap that can be secured to your wrist, but securing the day planner to your wrist could draw unwanted attention.

Drawing your gun from even the best-designed day planner is challenging. As with the purse or gun pack, it's best to prestage the zipper to save time when drawing.

In certain circumstances you might be able to acquire a shooting grip on the gun in preparation for drawing it from the day planner. When you can grip the gun in this manner, you can greatly expedite your draw stroke. In fact, this technique will probably allow you to present your gun to the target faster than if you had to contend with an outer garment concealing your holstered firearm.

Of course, none of these carry methods is worth much if you don't place the right handgun inside them. While selecting the right gun will largely be a matter of personal preference, you want to choose a gun that fits your hand and that you can shoot accurately.

Off-body carry doesn't relegate you to carrying a pocket gun, but a full-size handgun might be overkill. The extra bulk and weight inherent in a full-size pistol or revolver could nullify the advantage of off-body carry, making it heavy and cumbersome.

A compact handgun is probably a more sensible pairing. I find that my Springfield Armory EMP 9mm fits well in the off-body holsters I employ. And today's 9mm ammunition makes for a very capable personal protection round.

Make no mistake: off-body carry offers less security and typically a slower presentation of your handgun than traditional holstered carry. But if you choose the right gear and gun, are aware of your surroundings and practice diligently, off-body carry is a viable option. If the convenience of this mode of concealed carry results in you being armed more often, then it's well worth the investment of time and money.

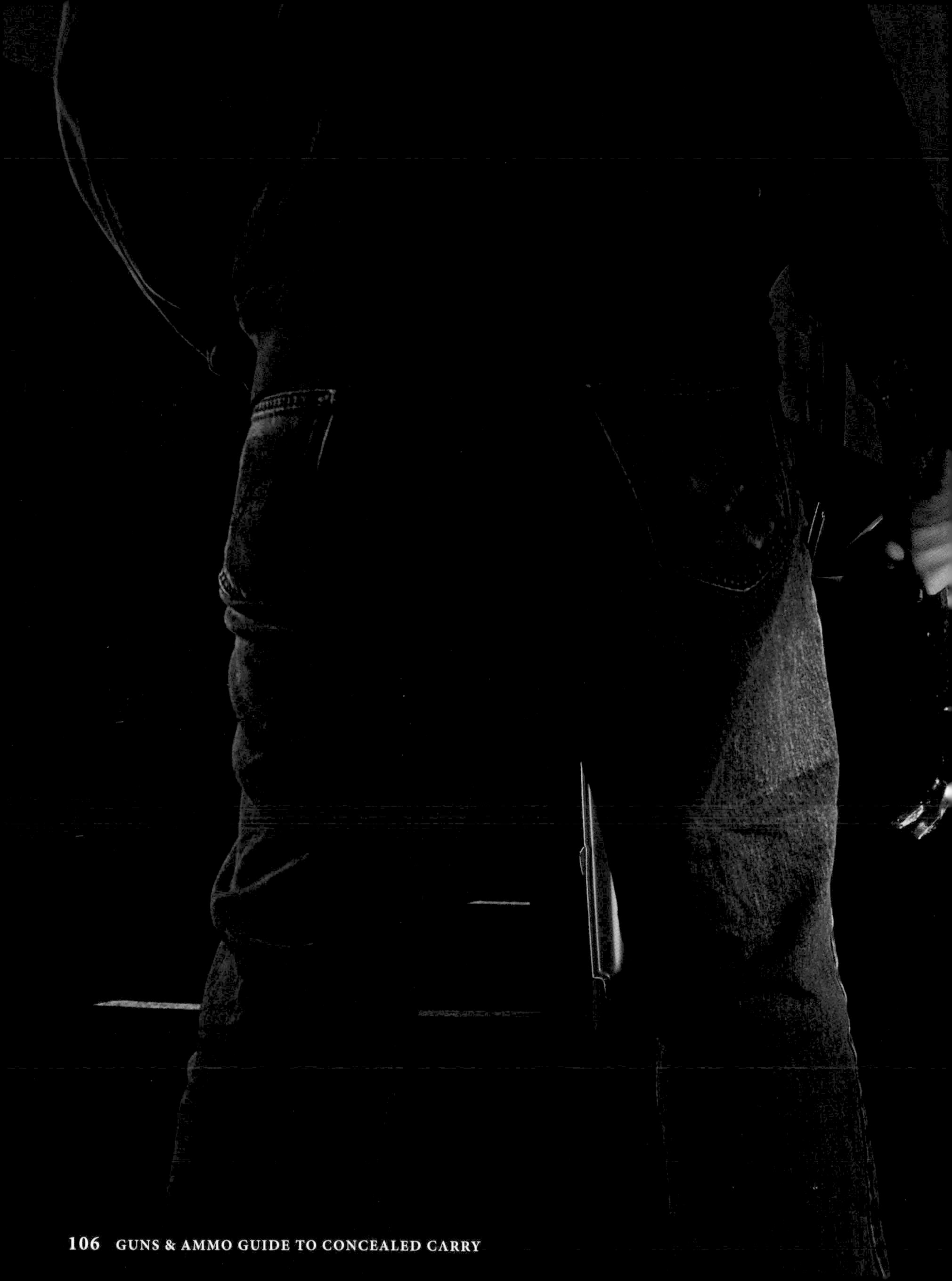

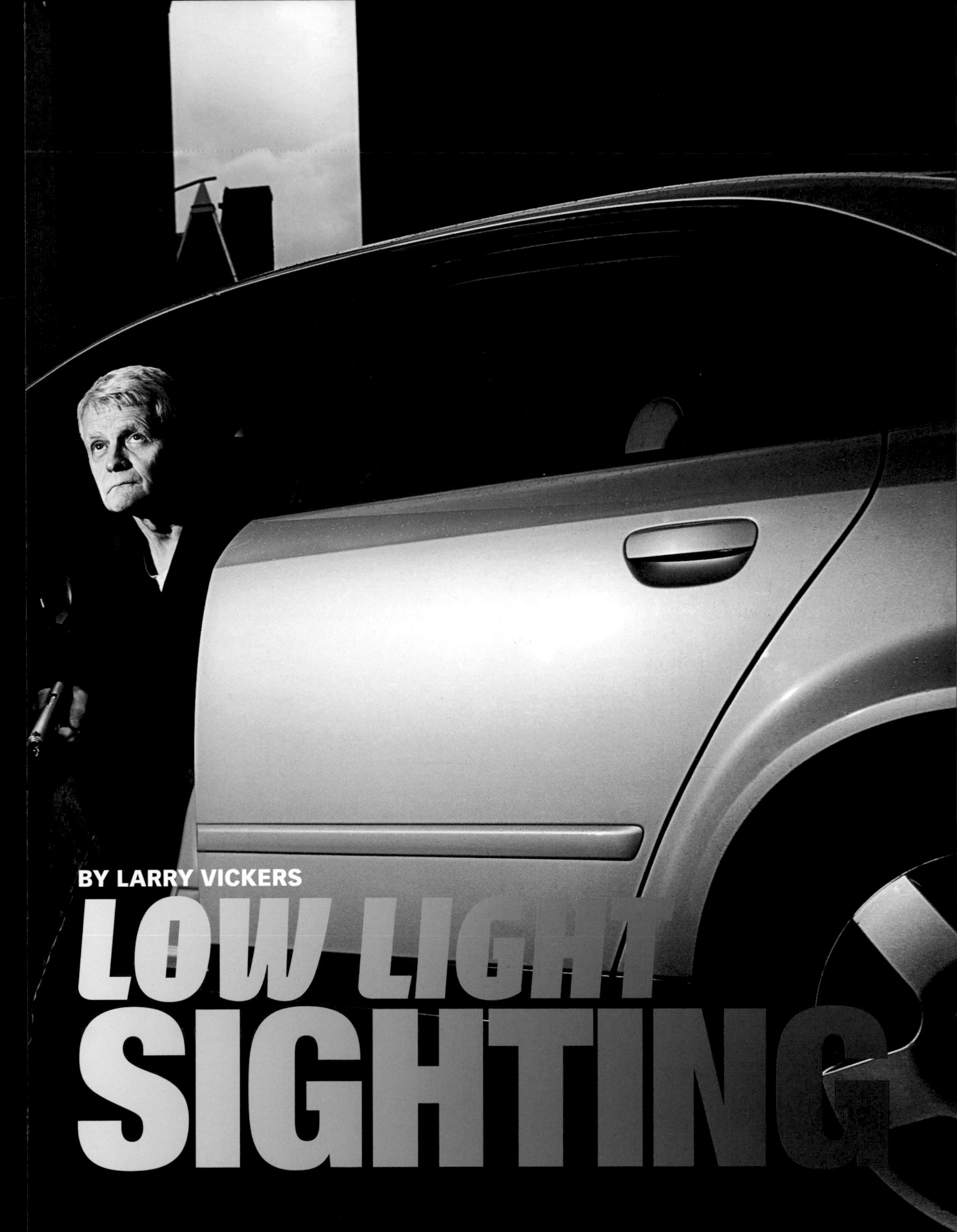

BY LARRY VICKERS

LOW LIGHT SIGHTING

Crimson Trace Corp. offers laser grips for virtually all popular defensive handguns in numerous configurations. Their product line has also grown to include vertical grips for long guns.

As anyone who has taken one of my classes can attest, I am very accuracy oriented. My classes always stress a high degree of accuracy. That's because in a gunfight accuracy will almost always suffer. There are many reasons for this, not the least of which is that you may very well be receiving fire from your assailant. Additionally, there is a high likelihood that you will be moving, your enemy may be moving, and it could be in an environment of limited visibility.

Night Sights

Night sights on handguns have become standard issue on many service pistols in use today. In fact, many people would not think of using a pistol without night sights. Contrast this to just 10 years ago and it would be safe to say that night sights have taken the market by storm.

There are many excellent night sights on the market but the overwhelming majority of my personal handguns have either Heinie or Novak sights installed. Most of my handgun sights carry tritium inserts. The Heinie Straight Eight, my personal favorite, only features one tritium dot on the rear sight, which allows you to focus more easily on the front sight (versus the types that have two dots, which tend to overpower the front tritium dot). Novak also offers a wide variety of sights with tritium inserts and between these two vendors you pretty much have your bases covered.

As far as a recommended supplier of tritium inserts, my personal experience has led me to favor Trijicon. Trijicon has a very good reputation of long lasting, durable tritium vials that are easily adapted to different types of sights but there are a couple of things to remember with night sights:

Night sights on handguns have become standard issue on many service pistols in use today. In fact, many people would not think of using a pistol without night sights.

1) You need to practice at night with night sights to determine how well you can shoot with them. Many shooters have the attitude that with tritium sights on their pistol, they are ready for night fighting. Not quite. I have seen many

Depending on the model, Crimson Trace Corp. lasergrips can be grip-activated by depressing a button on either flank of a grip panel, a button on the frontstrap or one at the backstrap.

shooters who struggle shooting at night, even with tritium sights. Two factors that are often overlooked are having to shift ocular focus from the target to the sights with the resulting loss of target definition and eyesight limitations at night. Both of these can lead to bad hits and complete misses during low light conditions.

2) During the day, completely ignore the night sights and use them as standard black pistol sights. The reason being that very rarely do the dots correspond with a traditional sight picture of standard pistol sights. What can happen under stress is a shooter lines up the dots instead of the iron sights creating shot groups that are low, high, left or right depending on how the tritium sights line up in relation to the standard sights. This is just another reason why I favor the Heinie Straight Eights since this is not as much of a factor.

Tritium night sights are like any other accessory attached or installed on your weapon having distinct pros and cons. I feel the pros greatly outweigh the cons but, as always, failure to understand the cons of night sights can come back to bite you when you least expect it.

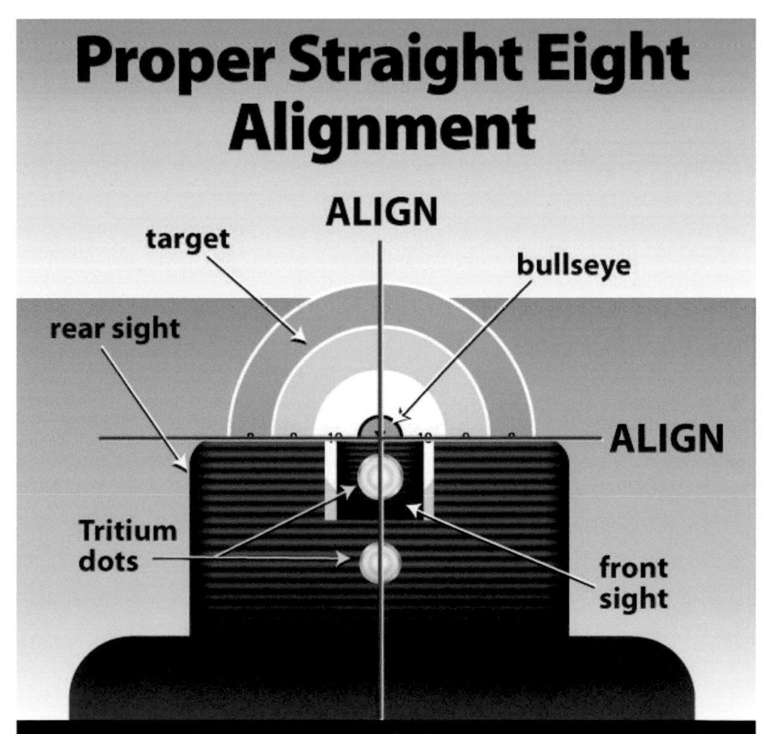

Heinie Straight Eight sights consist of a front tritium dot and a slightly smaller tritium dot at the rear. To align the sights, one dot is placed on top of the other making an elongated figure eight.

In addition to his famous LoMount carry sights, Wayne Novak is also well known among the 1911 community for his talent in creating custom pistols. Whatever the requirement (duty, self defense, or competition), Novak Custom Guns can create an application that accommodates a handgunner's needs. Only recently, Novak has announced that they are Colt suthorized distributors. Visit www.novaksights.com.

The Thin Red Line

Pistol lasers offer a distinct advantage at night, just as do night sights. As many of you know, I'm a consultant for Crimson Trace Corp. (CTC) Lasergrips, which means that some of you will quit reading immediately expecting this to be a "puff piece" in celebrating how great they are and not admitting to any downsides. Those of you in that category certainly don't know me very well. The following is the reality of visible lasers and CTC Lasergrips according to Larry Vickers. No punches are pulled.

I used to think, like many others, that lasers on sidearms were a joke. Fortunately for me, I have not had to eat as much crow over this topic as my good friend Ken Hackathorn but I have had my fair share. After giving them an honest assessment, here is what it really boils down to: a laser on a pistol offers much the same advantages as red dot reflex sights on a carbine or submachine gun. Under stressful shooting scenarios, they make firing a handgun a much easier task.

I highlight CTC lasers in my night fire portion of handgun instruction along with night sights, white light principles and techniques. At night and in conditions of limited visibility, they are nothing short of awesome. They make accurate handgun shooting easier than any other sighting system. Don't get me wrong, night sights and white light have their place but a visible laser at night rules. Period. Anyone who has had one of my classes or been taught by Ken Hackathorn can attest to that. They dramatically improve the shooter's ability to get accurate hits at night. Of course, like anything else, visible lasers do have pros and cons that we'll highlight in detail.

A rule of thumb is that any time you have any degree of difficulty seeing your pistol sights then a visible laser will be an advantage. For instance, coming into a building from outside (even during the day) the laser will be of value indoors. Out in bright daylight I prefer my iron sights and find the laser a bit of a distraction. Anytime you combine low or reduced visibility with shooting on the move or unconventional shooting positions, the laser is a distinct advantage. Police in particular have found that visible lasers offer an advantage while using cover, like a shield. This example would fall back to the category of unconventional shooting positions mentioned above.

Lasers are excellent training aids for watching a shooter's trigger control as any movement during the trigger squeeze will display on target. When first using the laser shooter's will try and eliminate all movement causing shooters to snatch or jerk the trigger early in training. Once the student learns to accept a wobble zone (which is now more visible due to the visible laser on target) then fast and accurate shooting comes more naturally. Once mastered, a handgunner can shoot faster and more accurately under low light conditions than ever possible with regular pistol sights, even night sights.

As with any battery-operated device, lasers will occasionally need new batteries. CTC advertises a 4-hour continuous run time with their laser grips, sufficient time for most use as I can attest (I have not had to change any batteries to date). Oil, solvents, water and dust can all play a part in making the visible laser less than 100 percent functional. Because of this, they do occasionally need maintenance and cleaning. I know that's a shocker to many but it's probably a good idea once in a while to make sure your pistol is properly cleaned, lubricated, and maintained. That would include your visible laser-aiming device.

CTC has sold thousands of Beretta grips to the US military for the standard issue M9s but a downside is that they don't make grips for every pistol out there. Since being used by troops, they have been received with overwhelming positive feedback. Remember that the M9 doesn't have night sights so the lasergrips add a low light capability that simply did not exist. This is a huge advantage and many of the troops appreciate it.

The visible laser is also a very useful crowd-control device as the red dot seems to cross all cultural and language barriers. As we know, combat is the ultimate test bed and CTC has taken the lessons learned from the sandbox and continues to move forward with a true Mil Spec M9 model, one that's water- and dustproof.

Parting Thought

I will close by saying that if you have not tried a visible laser or night sights, you should. Remember they are meant to augment the standard sights, not replace them. These aids are simply another tool in the toolbox.

PART IV
GUN GUIDE

Compact .380 pocket pistols, clockwise from top: Sig Sauer P238, Kahr P380, Micro Desert Eagle, Kel-Tec P-3AT and Ruger LCP.

BY CLAIR REES

DEEP CARRY .380s

Considered by most authorities as the bare minimum for self defense, this little cartridge is gaining new respect.

Long considered the "weak sister" of defensive handguns, the .380 ACP has suddenly become the pistol everyone's talking about. The cartridge owes its newfound popularity to three recent developments.

First, more and more security-conscious people (including women) are applying for concealed carry permits. Once they have a permit, they need a gun. If they try carrying a mid- or full-sized 9mm or .40 S&W pistol, they soon learn what a chore this undertaking can be. It doesn't take them long to start looking for a handgun that's light and unobtrusive enough for comfortable daily carry. That's one reason the .380 is suddenly in such demand.

While concealablity is important, savvy gunners also want something they can rely on to do the job. The .380 ACP has been regarded both as "sufficiently potent" or "not potent enough" for self defense. Generally relegated to the role of hideaway backup, the .380 has long shared Rodney Dangerfield's "I get no respect" lament.

Second, ammunition manufacturers have developed more effective loads through better bullets that narrow the performance gap between the .380 and the 9mm or .38 Special. The larger rounds are still preferred, but now by a smaller margin.

And most recently, firearm manufacturers have begun offering an expanding array of improved .380-chambered pistols. Most of these models are smaller, lighter and better made than the pocket pistols on the market just a few years ago. These .380s are proving to be popular and don't linger long on dealers' shelves.

Browning Heritage

When John Browning designed the .380 Automatic Colt Pistol cartridge a little over a century ago, it boasted

Specifications

Model: Kel-Tec P-3AT
Type: Autoloading pistol
Caliber: .380 ACP
Operation: Short recoil
Trigger: Double-action only
Safety: Transfer bar
Overall length: 5.2 inches
Barrel length: 2.5 inches
Height: 3.5 inches
Width: 0.77 inches
Weight: 8.3 ounces
Finish: Blued 4140 steel slide; frame is machined from 7075-T6 aluminum
Magazine capacity: 6 rounds
Price: $338.18
Manufacturer: Kel-Tec CNC, Inc., 1475 Cox Road, Cocoa, FL 32926; www.keltec.com.

At just 8.3 ounces, Kel-Tec's P-3AT was the lightest of the guns tested. This was the first of the superlight .380 pocket pistols.

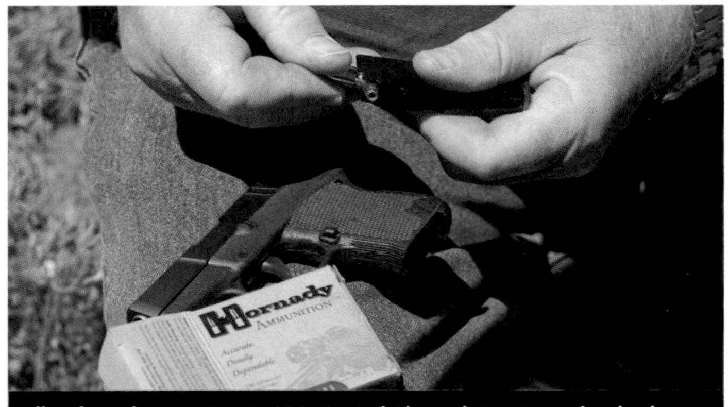

Like the other compact .380s tested, the Kel-Tec magazine had a 6-round capacity.

Compact .380s like the Ruger LCP are a good fit for women's hands.

Specifications

Model: Ruger LCP
Type: Autoloading pistol
Caliber: .380 ACP
Operation: Short recoil
Trigger: Double-action only
Safety: No manual safety
Overall length: 5.16 inches
Barrel length: 2.75 inches
Height: 3.6 inches
Width: 0.82 inches
Weight: 9.4 ounces
Finish: Blued steel slide; black glass-filled nylon grip and frame.
Magazine capacity: 6 rounds
Price: $259.00
Manufacturer: Ruger Firearms, 1 Lacey Place, Southport, CT 06890; Web www.ruger.com.

significantly more power than the first auto pistol cartridge he developed. Introduced in 1899 by Fabrique Nationale, Browning's first pocket pistol digested the then-new .32 ACP (7.65mm) ammo. The gun and cartridge were soon adopted by many European police agencies.

In 1908, the Colt Pocket Automatic was chambered for the more potent .380 round that Browning designed for that gun. Four years later, FN introduced the same cartridge called the 9mm Browning Short in Europe. It was quickly adopted as the official military cartridge of Italy, Sweden, and Czechoslovakia, and became a favorite of European police.

In the U.S., the .380 was overshadowed by the .38 Special, which had just been introduced in 1902. One of the most popular handgun rounds ever developed, it was universally favored for police, military and civilian use. For several decades, virtually all police officers in America wore .38 Special revolvers as their primary duty guns. If they carried a .380, it was tucked in a pocket or an ankle holster, reserved for last-ditch emergencies.

Now, innovative designs have put the .380 in the spotlight once again. While new 9mm, .40 S&W and .45 ACP pistols continue to appear, .380s are getting the lion's share of attention. Everyone seemingly wants to get their hands on one. While the guns are in short supply, I succeeded in obtaining five of the hottest .380s currently available and managed to round up a supply of .380 ammo.

Kel-Tec P-3AT

The Kel-Tec P-3AT was the pistol that restarted an interest in the .380. Basically, the company redesigned its P-32 .32 ACP pistol to digest .380 ACP ammo and did so without a substantial difference in size and weight. At just 8.3 ounces, this gun is a real featherweight.

Kel-Tec eliminated the slide stop and reduced magazine capacity to six rounds. The gun features Browning's short-recoil, locked-breech design. A transfer bar connects the trigger to the hammer, which is powered by a free-floating extension spring. After firing, a hammer block prevents further contact between hammer and firing pin. Both barrel and slide are made of SAE 4140 ordnance steel and the frame, which contains the firing mechanism, is machined from 7075-T6 aluminum. Dupont high-impact ST-8018 polymer forms the grip, magazine well and trigger guard.

Lilliputian size, combined with light handling and a .380 punch, make the P-3AT a winner. When I first began shooting the Kel-Tec, I experienced a couple of feeding failures. However, once I'd put 32 rounds of Black Hills 90-grain JHP ammo through the gun, the prob-

The Micro Desert Eagle is built to last and faintly resembles the lineage to the Desert Eagle and Baby Eagle pistols.

Rees with Magnum Research's Micro Desert Eagle—known as the "Kevin" in Czech military units.

Specifications

Model: Micro Desert Eagle
Type: Autoloading pistol
Caliber: .380 ACP
Operation: Gas-assisted blowback
Trigger: Double-action only
Safety: No manual safety; DAO trigger
Overall length: 4.5 inches
Barrel length: 2.2 inches
Height: 3.7 inches
Width: 0.90 inches
Weight: 14 ounces
Finish: Steel slide and aluminum frame, both with nickel-Teflon finish
Magazine capacity: 6 rounds
Price: $479.00
Manufacturer: Magnum Research, Inc., 12602 33rd Avenue SW, Pillager, MN 56473. Website: www.magnumresearch.com

lem disappeared. All five of the pistols I tested choked on certain ammo, but switching to a different load usually solved the problem. Each gun had its own individual preferences. No one should fully trust a new carry gun until it has fired at least 200 consecutive rounds without a hiccup.

In spite of its size and lack of heft, the Kel-Tec is a performer. Recoil is snappy, but not distracting. I had trouble seeing the vestigial sights but still managed to fire 3 1/2- to 4-inch groups with both Hornady and Cor-Bon 90-grain JHP loads.

Ruger LCP

Everything I've said about the P-3AT applies to Ruger's LCP (Lightweight Compact Pistol). At first glance the two guns look nearly identical. And while they share the same basic design, there are differences. Most immediately obvious are the extractors. The Kel-Tec extractor is an elongated arm that extends 1 3/8 inches back from the chamber, diminishing the ridged gripping area at the rear of the slide. The extractor is locked in place by a hex-head screw. The Ruger extractor is just 9/16 inch long. The LCP has a manual slide hold-open latch on the left side of the frame that allows the action to be locked open. The P-3AT lacks this refinement.

The Ruger's grip is a little thicker—0.754 vs. 0.714 inch—providing a larger gripping area and somewhat better control. Too, the LCP is just over an ounce heavier—9.4 vs. 8.3 ounces. The beefier grip and extra heft gives the Ruger a slightly more substantial feel.

Comparing trigger action was a toss-up. Both triggers had a long, double-action pull, with some stacking. Both broke at 7 to 7 1/2 pounds. Again, the triggers worked only when the actions were cocked. If the gun fails to fire when the trigger is pulled, you have to manually cycle the slide, ejecting the chambered round, before pulling the trigger again.

MORE EFFECTIVE AMMO

Good ammunition is the key to pistol performance. Because .380 ammo (like most ammunition these days) has been in short supply, I was unable to get samples of every .380 load currently manufactured.

Chronographed loads included Federal 90-grain Hydra-Shok ammo averaging 768 feet per second (fps), Winchester 95-grain Brass Enclosed Base loads (701 fps), Winchester 85-grain Silvertip hollowpoints (804 fps), Cor-Bon 90-grain jacketed hollowpoints (980 fps) and Cor-Bon 80-grain DPX ammo (1010 fps).

Others included Federal's Low-Recoil Personal Defense load with 90-grain Hydra-Shok jacketed hollowpoints, Hornady's 90-grain JHP/XTP, Black Hills's 90-grain jacketed hollowpoints, Remington's 102-grain brass-jacketed hollowpoints, Federal American Eagle 95-grain full-metal-jacket load, and 94-grain copper-jacketed hollowpoints from Wolf.

Not having enough for extensive testing with every load, each gun digested a mix of brands and bullet weights. Of particular note, Cor-Bon's "Deep-Penetrating" DPX loads featuring Barnes's 80-grain all-copper bullets and Hornady's 90-grain JHP/XTP ammo turned in stellar performances. Fired through 10-ounce denim into a block of 10 percent ballistics gelatin, these bullets expanded to nearly twice their original diameter with penetration between 9 and 11 inches. Properly placed, any of the loads used in the test would be lethal, but bullets that expanded caused the most damage.
—Clair Rees

Hornady's Critical Defense load integrates a flex-tip polymer fill within the cavity of the hollowpoint. As a bullet passes through clothing, uniform expansion occurs because material cannot disfigure the expanding bullet once it's entered the flesh.

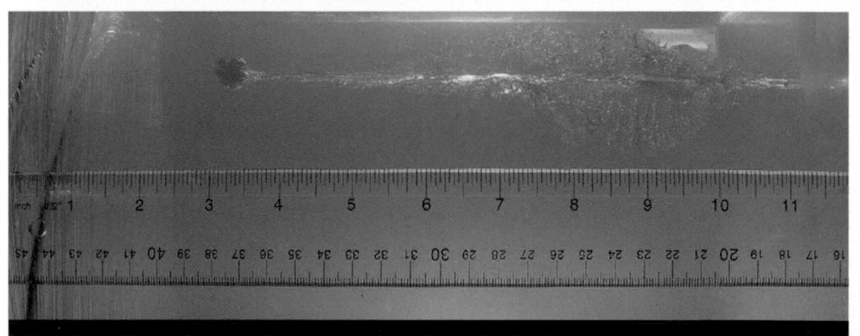

Cor-Bon 80-grain DPX (Deep-Penetrating X bullet) loads expanded well while passing 10-ounce denim and 9 inches of ballistic gelatin.

The LCP delivered very good accuracy. At 7 yards, Cor-Bon 80-grain DPX loads punched 2 3/4-inch offhand groups. The Ruger's rear sighting notch was slightly deeper and than front sight and slightly taller than the Kel-Tec's aiming equipment, giving the LCP a small edge with respect to sights.

Micro Desert Eagle

Only recently introduced by Magnum Research, the Micro Desert Eagle is a modified and refined version of the gun the Europeans call the ZVI Kevin. Manufactured in Prague in the Czech Republic, the Kevin has been issued to Czech pilots and other military units for use as a backup pistol. Featuring a stainless steel slide and an aluminum alloy frame, the Micro Desert Eagle is made in Minnesota by Magnum Research, Inc., under license from ZVI.

One unique feature of the Micro Desert Eagle is the gas-assisted blowback system. A pair of ports in the top of the barrel vent firing gases forward, adding push to the gun's blowback operation. The unusual design positions the trigger bar (connecting the hammer and trigger) on the frame's outside, not inside as you would expect.

With its hammer-forged 2.2-inch barrel, the gun measures 4.5 inches long and 3.7 inches tall. It's a scant 0.88-inch wide and weighs 14 ounces. Like the Kel-Tec P-3AT, the Micro Desert Eagle has no external safety or slide release. While its DAO trigger displayed stiff stacking and a 10-pound letoff, a little practice proved it to be surprisingly controllable. Firing offhand at 7 yards, I was able to print five-shot groups measuring just 2 3/4-inches, center-to-center with Cor-Bon's 90-grain JHP factory loads. One advantage of the Micro Eagle's trigger is that you can simply pull it again if the gun fails to fire (for another attempt at igniting the primer).

The Kahr P380 feels good in the hands and shoots very well. Added marks for good sights.

Specifications

Model: Kahr P380
Type: Autoloading pistol
Caliber: .380 ACP
Operation: Short recoil
Trigger: Double-action only
Safety: No manual safety
Overall length: 4.9 inches
Barrel length: 2.5 inches
Height: 3.9 inches
Width: 0.820 inches
Weight: 10 ounces
Finish: Stainless steel slide, matte black polymer frame.
Magazine capacity: 6 rounds
Price: $667.00
Manufacturer: Kahr Arms, 130 Goddard Memorial Drive, Worcester, MA 01603; Web: www.kahr.com.

Recoil was agreeably mild, making fast follow-up shots possible. The fixed rear sight nestled between the frame's sturdy "ears" was easy to see but the stainless 3/32-inch-high front sight was less visible under adverse lighting. Twin recoil springs create enough resistance to make cycling the slide by hand difficult for many women or men with a weak grip. The pressure required to retract the slide also makes taking the gun apart—and putting it back together—a challenge. The problem

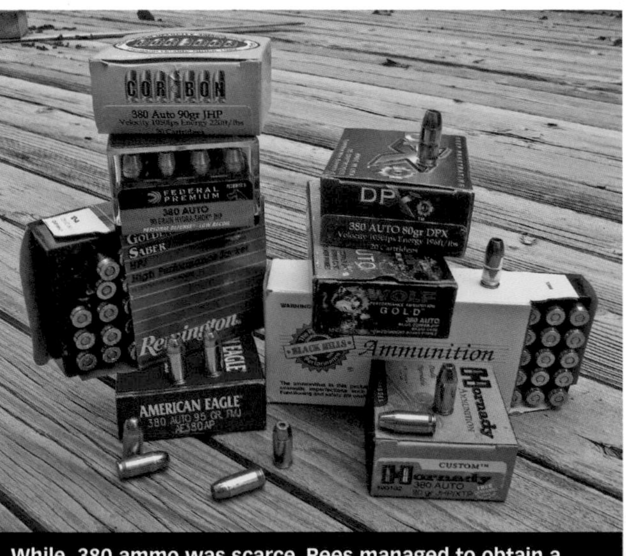

While .380 ammo was scarce, Rees managed to obtain a small supply of these factory loads.

comes in lining up two witness marks on the slide and frame, then holding the frame rigidly in that position with one hand, while using the fingers of your other hand to rotate the octagonal barrel clockwise 180 degrees. This unlocks the action, allowing the slide to move forward off the frame, so you can dismount the barrel. I managed to field strip the gun—but to put it back together, I had to wait until a second pair of hands were available.

The Micro Desert Eagle digested a total of 140 factory rounds without any real problem. Two feeding failures were attributed to me not having the magazine fully inserted in the gun. Cor-Bon's Pow'R Ball ammo was too long for the magazine but other Cor-Bon loads worked fine.

Kahr P380

The Kahr P380 is lighter and smaller then the other compact Kahrs we know. Measuring 4.9 inches long, 3.9 inches high and weighing barely 10 ounces, it slips easily into the front or back pocket.

Ergonomics are excellent. In spite of the gun's dimensions, its grip feels more substantial than all but one of the other .380s tested. This is a real aid to accuracy with pocket pistols. Trigger action is very manageable with a double action letoff of just 6 pounds.

Fired offhand from a range of 7 yards, this little pistol proved capable of 1 5/8-inch five-shot groups with both Federal's 90-grain Hydra-Shok jacketed hollowpoints and Black Hills 90-grain JHP factory loads. Accuracy is enhanced by the Kahr's excellent, easy-to-see sights. A short white post is visible under the rear sighting notch, while the front sight features a matching white dot. This makes aiming easy under most light conditions. Both front and rear sights are drift-adjustable for windage and night sights are an available option.

None of the guns tested have magazine safeties. If a round has been chambered, they will still fire even if the magazine is removed. With the P380, there is no manual safety. The only controls are the trigger, slide stop (the slide locks open when the last round is fired), and magazine release.

Sig Sauer P238

While the other guns tested are double-action designs, the Sig Sauer P238 fires in single-action only. It's similar to the discontinued Colt Mustang and is basically a miniature version of the 1911, complete with a beavertail frame. The primary operational difference is the lack of a grip safety. The familiar thumb-operated safety lever is there, making this the only .380 tested that has a manual safety and the only one I tested that features an exposed hammer.

The P238's sights are the best of the group—a squared-off, sharply defined rear notch with a white bar underneath. The prominent front blade carries a visible white dot. Both sights can be drifted in their dovetail slots for adjustments in windage and again, night sights are an option.

The trigger has no discernible stacking, breaking crisply at 7 pounds. With Remington's Golden Saber 102-grain JHP loads, the P238 punched 2-inch groups for me when fired offhand at 7 yards.

Pocket Defenders

Of the .380s tested, the Sig Sauer P238 had the best handling qualities. It points naturally and shoots well. On the other hand, the P238's hammer—particularly when cocked—could snag on clothing. For my tastes, I would prefer the long DAO trigger with little exposed for deep carry.

Specifications

Model: Sig-Sauer P238
Type: Autoloading pistol
Caliber: .380 ACP
Operation: Short recoil
Trigger: Single-action only
Safety: Manual, thumb operated + firing pin safety
Length: 5.5 inches
Height: 3.9 inches
Width: 1.1 inches
Barrel length: 2.7 inches
Weight: 14 ounces
Magazine capacity: 6 rounds
Grips: Fluted aluminum
Finish: Black anodized frame, stainless steel slide
MSRP: $558.00
Manufacturer: Sig Sauer, 18 Industrial Drive, Exter, NH 03833; Web: www.sigsauer.com.

Sig Sauer's P238 has the best sights of the pistols tested. This .380 functions like a 1911.

The 17.1-ounce LCR-357 is the optimal weight, light enough for concealed carry and just heavy enough to make shooting the .357 Magnum a practical reality.

CARRY MAGNUM

Putting fear to rest with the Ruger LCR in .357 Magnum.

BY ERIC R. POOLE
PHOTOGRAPHY BY MIKE ANSCHUETZ

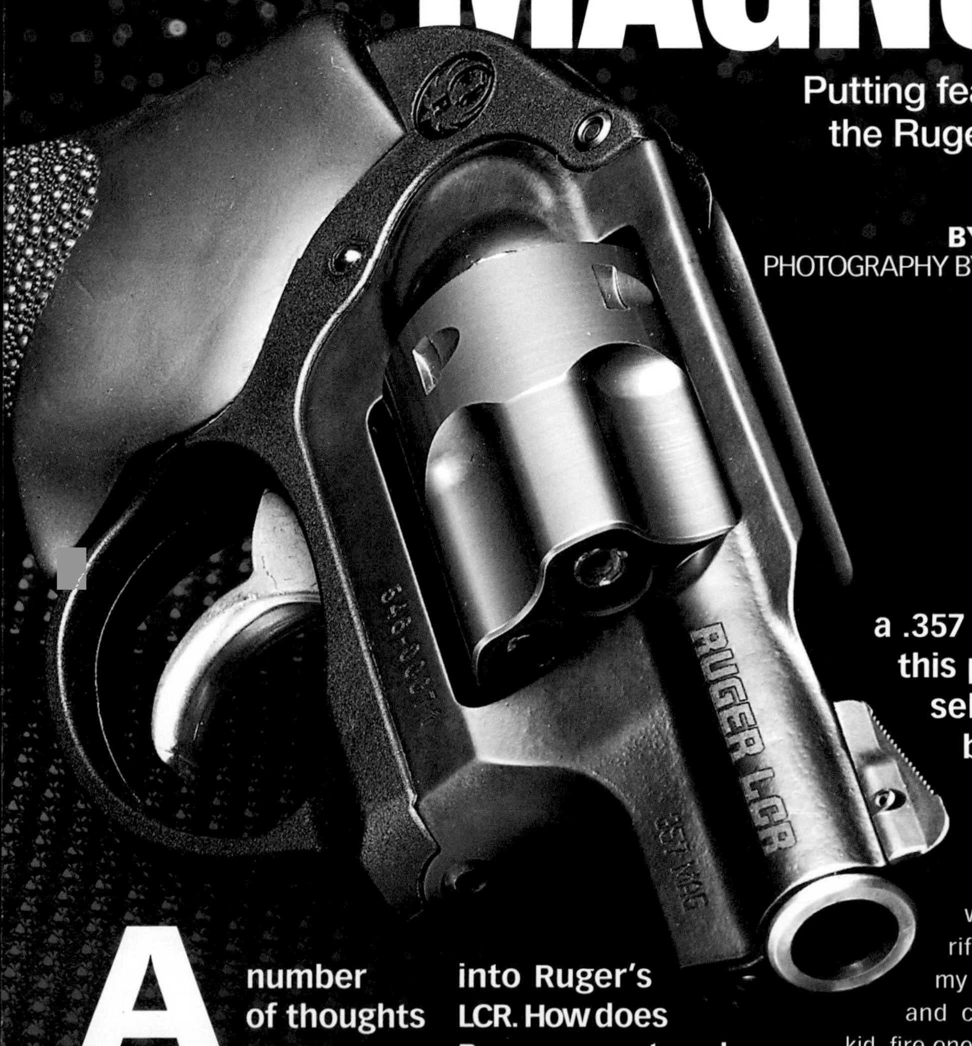

A number of thoughts came across my mind when I first loaded five rounds into Ruger's LCR. How does Ruger expect such a small revolver to harness the forces from a .357 Magnum? Will this pistol shoot itself into pieces before exploding in my hand?

Then my mind wandered to a terrifying memory when my dad had me, a brave and curious six-year-old kid, fire one of his make-my-day magnums to reemphasize the fact that I wasn't to touch any gun without his supervision. For

The stainless steel frame provides additional strength and weight to better manage .357 Magnum loads. The LCR's cylinder is a mere 1.283 inches in diameter, making it the narrowest revolver in its class, better enabling discreet carry.

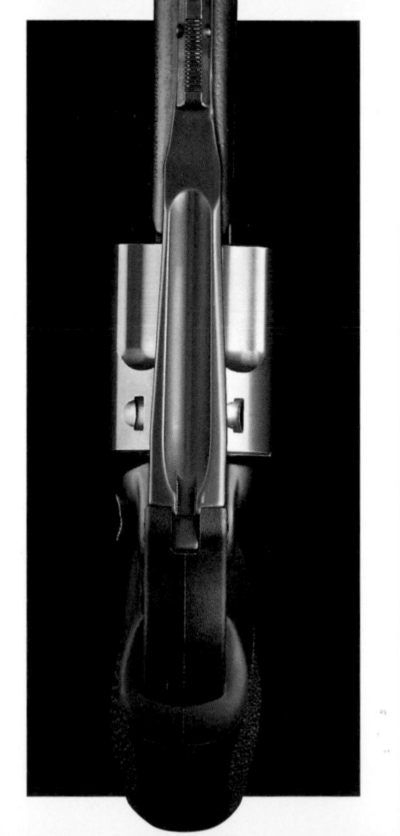

me, that negative reinforcement actually worked. Focusing back to the LCR, I put sights on target and mentally prepared myself for the inevitable: "Damn, this is going to hurt."

But it didn't. The shot went off, and it was over. I had one hole centered nicely on my eight-inch target 15 yards away. It hit point of aim, point of impact. Further, I assessed that the LCR was still intact and my hands weren't throbbing. I thought, *What the hell? Did I mistakenly throw in a .38?* I opened the cylinder to check. Nope. Four rounds of .357 remained. Then I concluded, "Why, this isn't so bad."

SPECIFICATIONS

RUGER LCR-357
TYPE: Revolver
CALIBER: .357 Magnum
CAPACITY: 5
WEIGHT: 17.1 oz.
BARREL: Stainless 1.875 in., six-groove, 1:16 RH twist
OVERALL LENGTH: 6.5 in.
HEIGHT: 4.5 in.
WIDTH: 1.28 in.
FRAME: Stainless steel, black oxide finish
CYLINDER: Fluted stainless, Target Gray finish
FIRE-CONTROL HOUSING: Polymer
FINISH: Black polymer
SIGHTS: Integral U-notch rear, replaceable pinned ramp front
TRIGGER: Double action
MSRP: $669.00
MANUFACTURER: Sturm, Ruger & Co., ruger.com

KEEPING A SECRET

You know something has to be good when you have to sign a nondisclosure agreement before a company like Ruger let's you see a new product. That's what happened before I was allowed to see the original Lightweight Compact Revolver chambered in .38 Special. It was officially unveiled shortly thereafter to the public at the 2009 SHOT Show in Orlando, FL.

After a thorough briefing, I joined a few other industry writers on Ruger's indoor test range to validate the revolutionary concept I'd been presented. None of the samples exhibited any problems while digesting hundreds of +P loads from Cor-Bon and Remington. I could keep five-shot groups hovering an inch while shooting offhand from seven yards. Switching to a different model featuring Crimson Trace Lasergrips, my best group witnessed by my peers measured .98 inch. The Hogue-equipped LCR was much more pleasant to fire than the Crimson Trace version. However, more accurate results were undeniably obtained while using the laser and Remington ammo.

Versatility in the LCR-357 means that it can be loaded with easy-shooting .38 Specials, the defense-ready .38 +P or full-house .357 Magnums.

THE NEXT STEP

Ruger revealed the LCR-357 at the 2010 NRA Annual Meetings and Exhibits in Charlotte, NC.

"After we completed the .38-caliber LCR, we thought about the next step," says Ken Jorgenson of Ruger. "We performed extensive testing on the LCR using 158-grain .38 Special +P ammunition, and it performed very well. In order to build an LCR to resist the stress from the .357 Magnum, we decided that the frame should be made out of steel instead of aluminum like the original. Then we completely tested the LCR on a computer program before we even built one. To change the stresses, we just had to change some numbers."

The Ruger LCR and the LCR's innovative assembly stations (called cells) are the ideas of Ruger's highly respected Joe Zajk, chief engineer, revolvers. Most LCR components are built in the Newport, NH, facility, and the parts that are

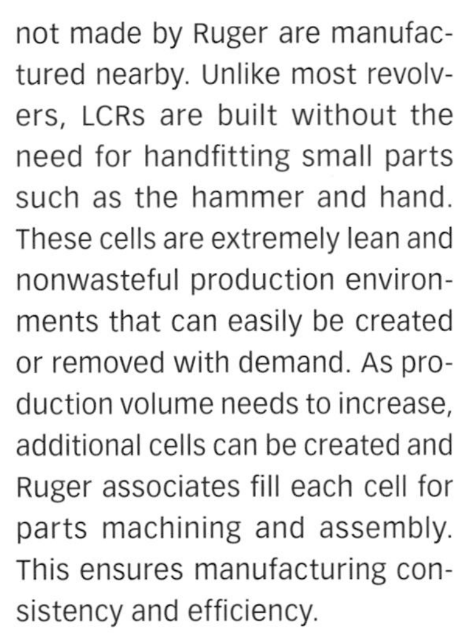

not made by Ruger are manufactured nearby. Unlike most revolvers, LCRs are built without the need for handfitting small parts such as the hammer and hand. These cells are extremely lean and nonwasteful production environments that can easily be created or removed with demand. As production volume needs to increase, additional cells can be created and Ruger associates fill each cell for parts machining and assembly. This ensures manufacturing consistency and efficiency.

The .38 and .357 LCR models share a lot in common. The largest commonality is the fire-control housing. However, due to the different metal making up the cylinder frame, the .357 is a little more than 3½ ounces heavier than the 13½-ounce original. You can call those four ounces recoil management. Both are made of three main subassemblies (if you discount the removable grip): the frame, the fire-control housing and the cylinder.

FRAME

The monolithic frame on the original LCR is created from an aerospace-grade, 7000-series aluminum forging that is treated with a black synergistic hardcoat. Ruger successfully tested 30 different aggressive chemicals and found that this hardcoat exceeded the Mil-Spec salt-spray tests to survive longer than hardcoat anodizing. The .357 Magnum utilizes a frame investment cast from 410 stainless steel and finished in black oxide.

Specific cylinder flutes and barrel shroud bevels help direct BC gap flame and debris away from the shooter.

FIRE-CONTROL HOUSING

Both versions of the Ruger LCR feature the same recoil-reducing polymer fire-control housing. The lightweight material is a weight saver over traditional carry revolvers and also resistant to corrosion or deterioration from things such as harsh solvents. Having fire-control components located within a single housing, dimensional relationships can be held tighter than those divided by traditional double-action revolver components. And to reiterate the previously stated point, there is absolutely no handfitting involved with the LCR.

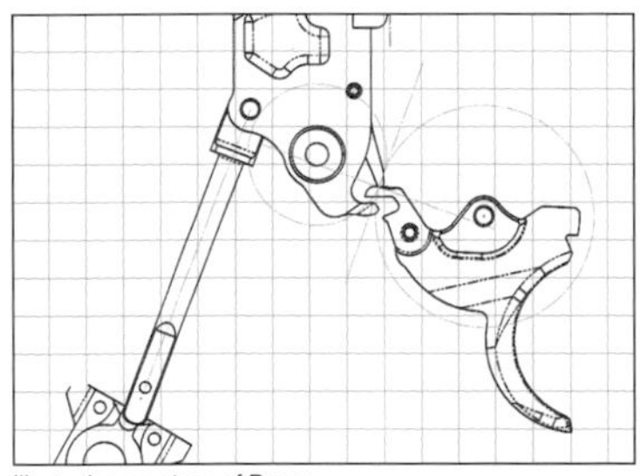

Illustration courtesy of Ruger

TRIGGER

The double-action trigger pull is quite different on the LCR from any other revolver, and that's because a cam has been introduced to reduce friction on the engagement surfaces. Using Ruger's friction-reducing cam, the trigger can be smoothly drawn without stacking to a resistance of about 10 pounds. The force required to draw the trigger builds gradually and peaks later in the stroke at the point when the finger benefits from mechanical advantage. The result is a trigger pull that feels lighter than it actually is.

"The double-action trigger has to do two jobs," says Ruger Product Manager Mark Gurney. "The first job is to rotate the hammer, and the second is to release the sear. The second job isn't that hard. It's the first job in small double-action revolvers that's the hardest. This type of gun typically struggles with the early part of the work. The lever at the back of the trigger is lifting on the hammer sub-assembly. In classic revolvers, friction stacks up without much rotation. In the LCR, we have a cam on the trigger lever and a corresponding follower shape on the hammer dog that allow one to roll over the other."

Once the hidden hammer is drawn back in the LCR, the trigger finger is close to the frame and benefits from mechanical advantage to finish the trigger pull process.

ACCURACY RESULTS

.357 Magnum	Bullet Weight (gr.)	Avg. Velocity (fps)	Standard Deviation	Avg. Group (in.)
Remington Golden Saber	125	1,133	37	2.53
Remington Express	158	1,137	34	2.07
.38 Special	**Bullet Weight (gr.)**	**Avg. Velocity (fps)**	**Standard Deviation**	**Avg. Group (in.)**
Remington Golden Saber (+P)	125	794	24	1.74

Notes: Accuracy tested from a Shooter's Ridge pistol rest on a bench from 15 yards. Results are the average of five 5-shot groups. Velocities are 5-shot averages recorded at 12 feet with a Master Gamma Shooting Chrony chronograph.

That's why people perceive a lighter and more consistent trigger pull in the LCR. For newcomers who are used to anticipating the release point just before a hammer falls forward, don't be surprised if the LCR takes some getting used to.

GRIP

The LCR in .357 Magnum comes standard with the Hogue Tamer grip that features a cushioned insert to help reduce perceived recoil. The fire-control housing's grip peg allows for a variety of grips to be installed, but unless you're a glutton for punishment, I wouldn't recommend shooting the .357 Magnum variant with anything besides the Hogue grip. In a joint effort, the LCR's standard grip was designed using U.S. military anthropomorphic data on hand shape so the LCR could be comfortably held by a broad spectrum of hand sizes. In May 2010, Ruger announced the development of the Hogue LCR Boot Grip that saves a half ounce in weight.

"The LCR has been a phenomenal success for us," says Chris Killoy, Ruger's vice president of sales and marketing. "The new Boot Grip for the LCR gives our customers a slightly more concealable option for discreet carry, yet gives up very little in terms of controllability and recoil management."

CYLINDER AND BARREL

Using the same material as that found in the powerful Ruger .454 Casull revolvers, the LCR's cylinder and barrel are created from Carpenter 465 stainless steel. This particular stainless steel was chosen for its strength and dimensional stability during machining and heat treatment. The barrel measures 1$\frac{7}{8}$ inches long and carries a 1:16-inch twist rate. The cylinder is then finished with Ruger's Target Gray.

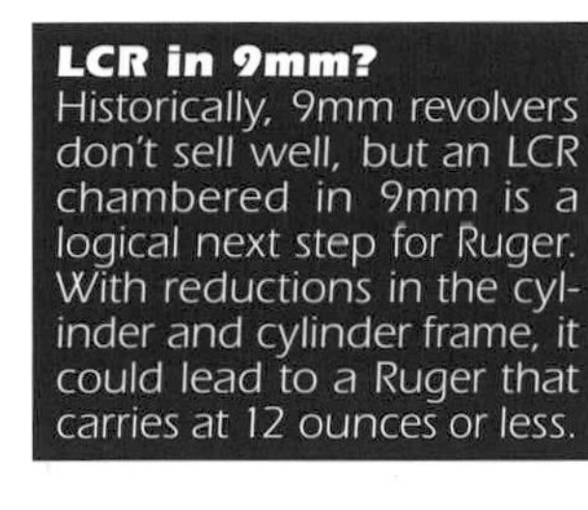
LCR in 9mm?
Historically, 9mm revolvers don't sell well, but an LCR chambered in 9mm is a logical next step for Ruger. With reductions in the cylinder and cylinder frame, it could lead to a Ruger that carries at 12 ounces or less.

A patented cylinder front latching system uses titanium components, optimized spring tension and enhanced lockup geometry to keep the cylinder locked in place during firing.

OTHER DETAILS

There are three details on the frame and cylinder of the LCR-357 that work together, but can easily be overlooked. Just behind the barrel shroud, there are two bevels and a small relief radius cut under the topstrap. And if you compare cylinders, the fluting is different. These details help to reduce spitting of debris and flame back toward the shooter. Ruger developed these subtle features while studying high-speed video.

Beneath the grip is an internal lock. It doesn't interfere with the fire-control mechanism when inactive, but it is there. It's one of those things that you might not notice if you never removed the grip.

The front sight is a replaceable serrated ramp, and the rear is a fixed notch. Ruger offers XS Sight Systems' 24/7 tritium standard dot front sights as an option for those who desire the fast, low-light target acquisition XS sights are known for.

The LCR-357 accepts all accessories available for the original LCR, including holsters, speedloaders and Crimson Trace Lasergrips.

SHOOTABILITY

The LCR-357 is something of a dichotomy, a contradiction of sorts. Common sense tells me that 128-grain bullets traveling at 1,100 fps from a 17-ounce revolver with a sub-two-inch barrel is going to be about as much fun as it was when I caught my hand on fire after spewing Bacardi 151 over a lighter and choking on the leftover (dumb). Comparing photos, the awesome fireball does bear a slight resemblance, but in actuality, firing the Ruger LCR is much safer and the flash of fire is over in the blink of an eye.

In the accompanying photos, you can see the difference between shooting a .38 Special (+P) and a .357 Magnum from the same gun using Remington Golden Sabers loads, but don't misinterpret the images. The flash and bang are directed away from the shooter, and you can get a sense of the

.38 Special

.357 Magnum

(Top) **The Remington Golden Saber 125-grain .38 +P load produces minimal flash and blast, and reduced recoil when fired in the steel-frame LCR-357. It chronographed at 794 fps from the 1⅞-inch barrel. Yes, we did capture the bullet in flight on camera.** ***(Bottom)*** **The Remington Golden Saber 125-grain.357 Magnum produces far more blast and flash, but clocked at 1,133 fps. Recoil is heavier than the .38 +P, but still manageable.**

Photos by Eric R. Poole

awesome power a .357 possesses. Even if you're going to be shooting more .38s than .357s, why not own something capable of safely shooting both? I fired a little more than 400 rounds from three different loads to check my point of aim without experiencing one hint of malfunction. With that round count, it shouldn't be a surprise if your hand is sore for three days.

Shooting +P .38s in this steel-frame LCR is much gentler than it is in the original aluminum-frame model. I know it's only a four-ounce difference, but the handling is noticeable, an added bonus for the LCR in .357. It's like roughhousing with a neutered Doberman—still impressive, just a little more friendly.

Ruger's .357 LCR is optimized for a 158-grain cartridge. On the range, I found that the sights were on target out to 15 yards with both Remington's Golden Saber 125-grain .357 HPJ and Remington Express 158-grain .357 loads. When switching to Remington's Golden Saber 125-grain .38 Special, the rounds fell about four inches when I stood anywhere behind the seven-yard line. Accuracy was incredibly consistent across the board, but the difference in point of impact is just another reason to get to know the gun and the specific load you intend to task with guarding the life of you or yours.

I approached this evaluation with a bit of reluctance, but the LCR-357 is a shootable revolver. It does wear on you, but as I experienced using the Crimson Trace Lasergrip, it would be worse without the Hogue grip. I don't recommend strings more than 30 to 35 rounds at any given range session. As intimidating as it might seem, the experience really wasn't like wrestling a controlled explosion. Magnums are actually quite manageable as long as you're not shy of a little extra felt recoil. You do need more time to recover between shots, but the terminal ballistics from virtually any type of hit by a .357 Magnum modern defense load show it's potentially lethal. Even if the choice is to load five rounds of .38 Special, you still have a great carry piece. It's nice to have options.

CONSTANT

My choice of a carry gun

COMPANION

gets some refinements.

For nearly 13 years I have carried the same Glock 26. I know its serial number by heart, and the round count is up to around 6,000. Most of those rounds were +P+ jacketed hollowpoints.

Sure, I would prefer to carry a bigger pistol day to day, but my frame and ridiculously hot Southern climate do not allow for full-size guns. Hell, I'm lucky to get two months of jacket weather. The old Glock has worn through a premium leather holster, and a true gentleman would have had the slide refinished—but I like those silver streaks

By J. GUTHRIE

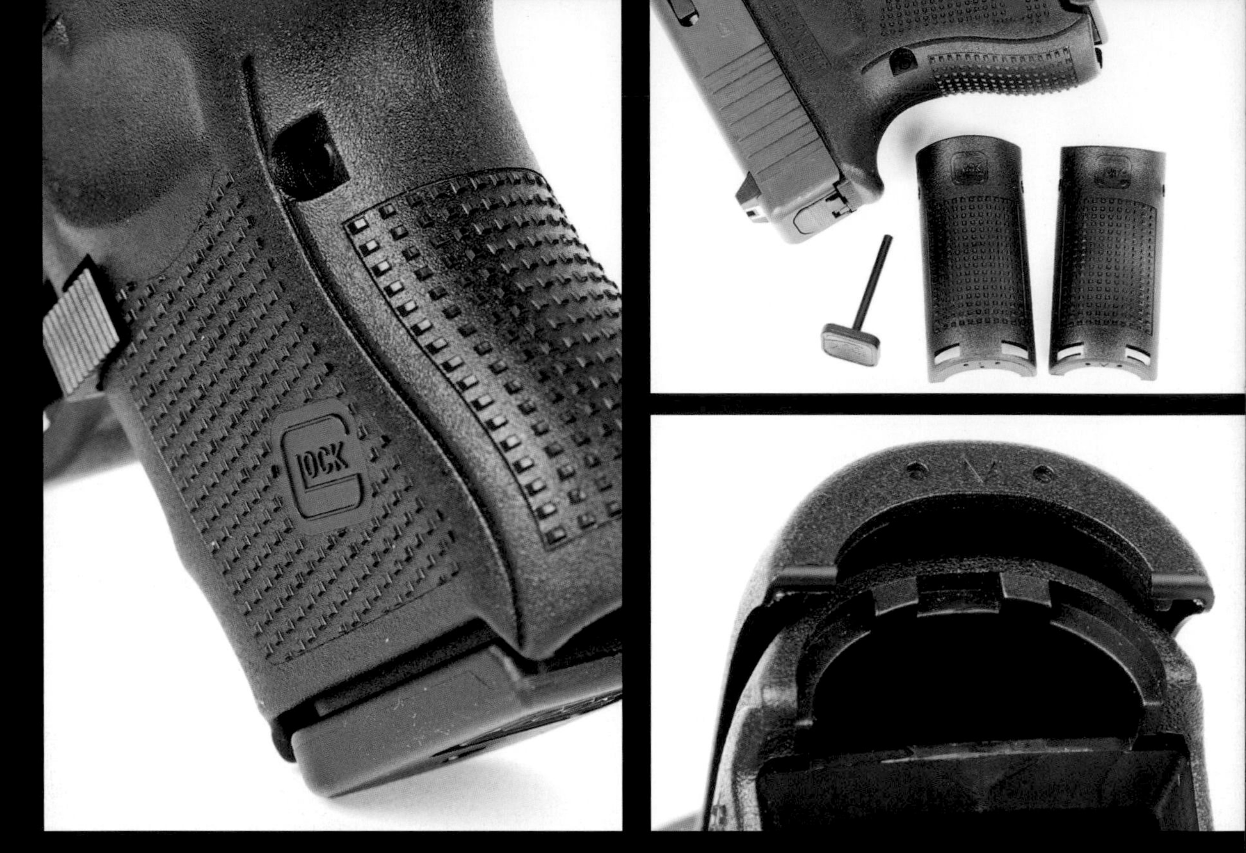

The Gen4 frame is shorter than previous models but accepts two different backstraps. The backstraps snap over the bottom of the frame and are secured along their length by a long groove in the frame. The trigger housing pin secures the backstraps up top, and a punch and longer pin for the large backstrap are provided.

down the slide and shiny corners. In fact, I like everything about this old girl. We both have taken a tumble or two across the pavement, and one spill on the range added a scar to my knee and one to her frame.

In 13 years, the only malfunctions came while I was learning to shoot with my weak hand, and nothing has been broken or replaced. My Glock 26 got a new recoil spring and a few new magazines every two years, but with careful and regular maintenance she has never wavered. Even after I started writing about guns, this old Glock was still snapped ahead of my back pocket before my boots were laced every morning. There was just no reason to mess with something that worked.

My Glock 26 and I have been in a few tight spots, and one of the few times I thought it was about to come down to them or me it was this pistol that my fingers wrapped around. It gave me the confidence to take all comers, and I went home that night no worse for wear. On a lighter note, the pistol has accounted for a couple of hundred armadillos, several dozen copperbacked timber moccasins and a half dozen hogs.

Internally, very little changed in the Gen4 pistols except the addition of a small bump on the trigger bar tab that disengages the firing-pin safety. The bump centers the tab on the safety and adds weight to the trigger pull. Full-size and compact Gen4s now use a dual-captive recoil spring, a feature that was always found on baby Glocks.

If you pulled up in the front yard with a pickup truck full of money and custom 1911s and wanted to trade, I would just have to laugh and go back to work. If you asked twice I might sic my old dog, Doc, on you. Nothing could make me part with this baby Glock, but I would be the first to put it down if I thought there was something better to keep me or my family alive in a fight.

After spending a couple of months with a Glock 26 Gen4, I have some very serious decisions to make.

A MODERN PISTOL

At first I wrote off the new generation of pistols as a "me too" product meant to give an old, but proven pistol a little flash in a market that is getting pretty crowded. I gave them a quick once-over at the SHOT Show and moved on to bigger news. Just about every pistol now has replaceable backstraps and "revolutionary" surface treatments that are supposed to improve grip. Five hundred rounds on the nose later, I decided that my initial conclusion was wrong.

Internally, at least on the 26 and 27 Gen4s, not much changed since Glock engineers reached self-proclaimed perfection out of the gate. The minor mechanical changes, save one, were meant to accommodate new features on the outside of the pistol. Like

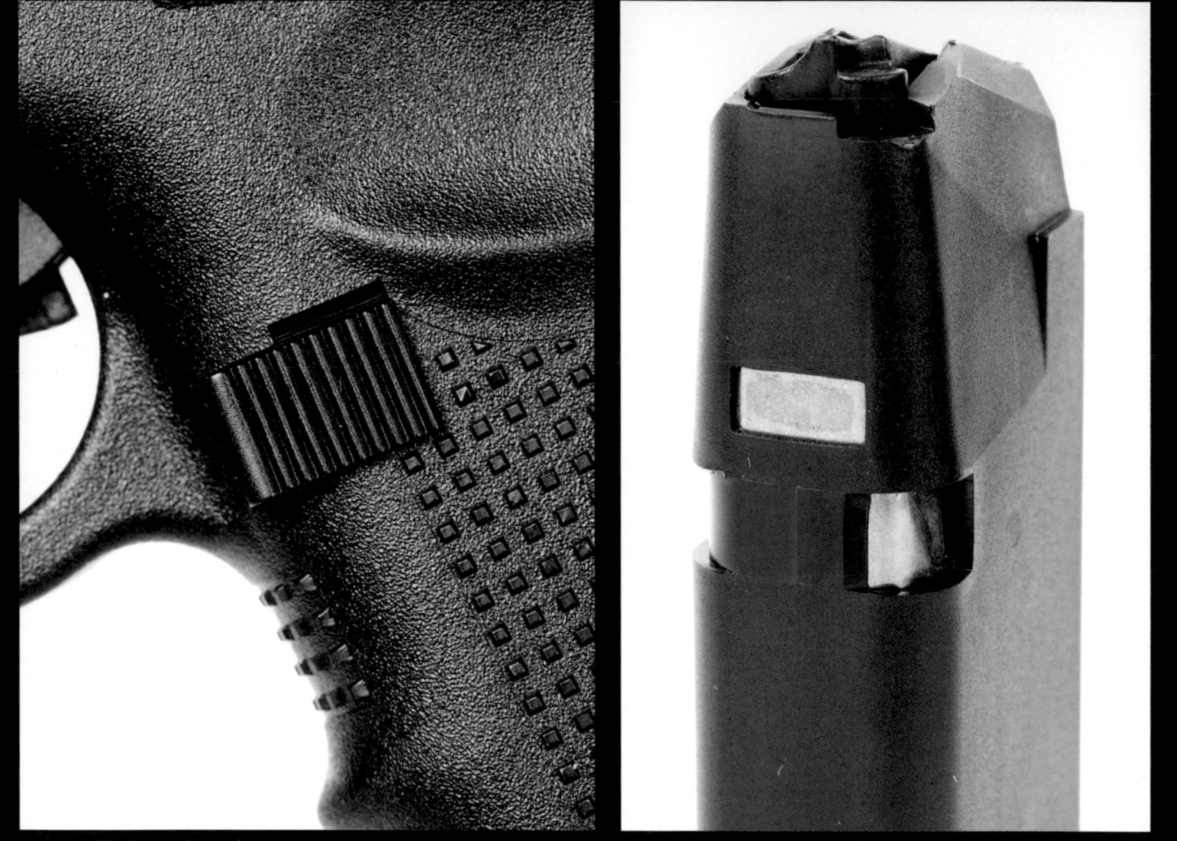
Another big Gen4 change is the reshaped magazine catch. It is larger but has a lower profile and can be easily swapped for lefties. New magazines have a corresponding slot, but older magazine will still work.

a little stamped metal shark, the trigger bar has a small tab that extends up above the frame to push up and disengage the firing-pin safety as the trigger is pulled rearward. The Gen4s have a tiny bump that makes contact with the slide and keeps the tab in position to cut across the firing-pin safety's center.

To be honest, I never really noticed where my old tabs were hitting the firing-pin safety, but after pulling apart a half dozen dirty guns, the tabs all seem to run along the outside edge. After smoking up the inside of the Gen4, I could clearly see where the tab scrapes the carbon fouling right down the middle of the safety. For the record, I have never had or heard of any issues with a trigger bar tab that missed the firing-pin safety.

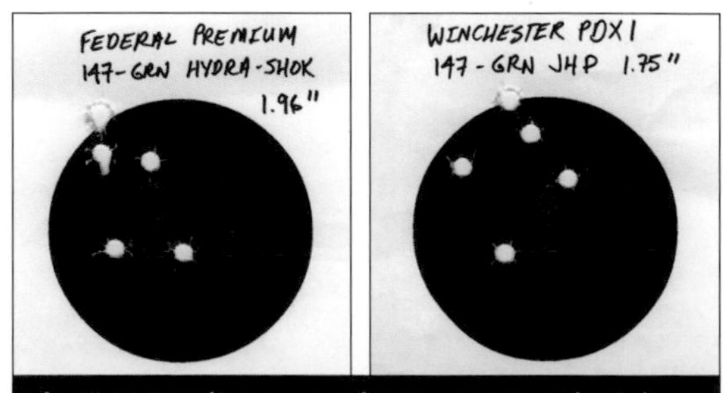

The Gen4 sample gun proved very accurate and consistent with a variety of self-defense loads from Federal, Black Hills and Winchester.

In addition to centering the tab, the new tumor also seems to increase the trigger pull by dragging along the slide. You can see the drag

Accuracy Results

Load	Group
Black Hills 115-grain JHP +P	2.32 inches
Black Hills 124-grain JHP +P	2.54 inches
Federal Premium 147-grain Hydra-Shok	2.13 inches
Remington 115-grain Golden Sabre JHP +P	3.40 inches
Winchester PDX1 147-grain JHP	2.22 inches

Averages are derived from 4 5-shot groups shot from a sandbag rest at 25 yards.

The Gen4 baby Glocks offer real improvements over older generations. The frame is easier to control and can be customized to suit, and the magazine catch has been greatly improved.

Glock 26 Gen4

Caliber: 9mm
Action: Striker fired
Capacity: 10 (factory), 12, 15, 17, 33
Weight: 19.75 oz.
Barrel: 3.46 in.
Overall Length: 6.3 in.
Height: 4.17 in.
Grip: Rough Textured Frame (RTF)
Finish: Matte Tenifer
Sights: Fixed, white dot (front), U-notch (rear)
MSRP: $549.00
Manufacturer: Glock, glock.com, 770-432-1202

marks on the slide's fouling, too. Using a Lyman electronic trigger-pull gauge, I measured the trigger weight of five different Glocks with standard everything and came up with five pounds, seven ounces. Then I stuck the gauge on my two Gen4 samples, which supposedly have the same pull weights, and came up with a 5-pound, 13-ounce average. After a couple of hundred rounds, Glocks usually lose 2 or 3 ounces, but the 26 Gen4 was stubborn and held firm.

If the extra weight is just too much, you could always install one of the many aftermarket trigger disconnectors, but you'll probably end up voiding your warranty in the process. Since they are "perfect," who needs a warranty anyway?

The biggest change in the Gen4 Glocks is readily apparent when you pick up the pistol. It has a short frame—Glock calls it the Multi Backstrap Frame (MBS)—that's smaller in diameter than the older models, not dramatically so, but instantly noticeable. Glock reshaped the grip's backside and used the trigger housing pin to hold backstraps of two different sizes if so desired. Changing the grip takes just 30 seconds with a little punch that's included. The backstrap's bottom hooks onto the frame, and it snaps into place, the edges matching frame grooves for a seamless transition. The larger of two backstraps requires using a longer trigger housing pin, which is also supplied.

I really like the short frame, and in side-by-side comparisons, I feel that I can manage the short-frame pistol better, especially when it's paired with the Rough Textured Frame (RTF), but more on that later.

Replacing the backstrap does not alter the grip's width. Rather, it lengthens the grip (and we aren't talking a huge difference either). The frame measures 2.80 inches from the trigger bow's front to the rear of the frame just above the trigger housing pin. Adding the medium backstrap increases that measurement to 2.88 inches, 2.96 inches if you install the large backstrap. The medium backstrap matches the old Gen3 frame if you are longing for that old familiar feeling.

While the math tells the mind that the difference between large and small is a paltry .16 inch, your strong hand is on another planet. You can completely change the pistol's feel, though the backstraps do nothing to change the grip angle. Something tells me an enterprising soul who knows plastic will soon do something about that for those who hate the Glock's much-maligned grip angle. I am all for a beavertail grip, so my pistol looks as cool and still runs better than all those 1911s on the line.

If you have gorilla hands, the backstraps allow you to actually hold the pistol and not swallow it. Another huge advantage would be to mimic your primary gun's grip on your backup pistol. Commonality of everything has always been a huge checkmark in the Glock's plus column, but carrying a Glock 30 with a doublestacked magazine of .45 on your ankle just because it feels like your fullsize Glock 21 is a bit much. You could turn a 26 or 27 into a backup pistol that feels exactly like your primary, but you would lose the ability to use big mags in your little gun.

Much has been made of the Rough Textured Frame (RTF). Glock calls it rough for a reason—it is rough as hell everywhere. I'm sure some engineer spent years and millions of Gaston Glock's money coming up with the perfect shape that takes a PhD in geometry to describe. At the end of the day, the RTF amounts to a an organized formation of tactile squares that grab your hand. More important, Glock was pretty liberal with the treatment and added it to the spaces between the finger grooves, side panels and backstrap.

I love the RTF because it helps me control the pistol when I am shooting fast, under stress or weak-handed. More and more I am realizing that maintaining a consistent and strong grip is paramount for accurate and fast shooting. You cannot control the pistol with your arms or body until you control it with your hands. Wearing the pistol concealed under a shirt without something between it and your skin is going to result in a rash, depending on just how flabby your love handles are.

Glock redesigned the magazine catch so it offers more real estate with a low profile. It sounds counterintuitive, but the magazine catch is much larger and extends farther back into the grip panel. The longer operating pad gave me a little more surface area to hit under stress. The end result is a magazine catch that's easier to operate, but will not inadvertently dump your mag like the extended catches can do.

The magazine catch can easily be swapped for left-handed shooters, and it just requires flipping the part over and reinstalling it. Gen4 magazines have a new, reciprocal notch opposite the old one. Gen3 and Gen4 magazines are interchangeable except in the case where a Gen4 magazine catch has been swapped to the opposite side. Gen3 mags do not have the corresponding notch to catch the magazine's latch.

Much has been made of the initial problems with the dual recoil-spring system impeding function in the full-size pistols. The 26 and 27 have always used dual recoil springs, and there appears to be little or no change from the old system to the new. I fired 500 rounds of all types of ammo, from heavy 147-grain stuff down to snappy 115-grain +P+ JHPs. There were no forcasts of any trouble.

Functionally, very little has changed on the 26 and 26 Gen4, and what did change was for the better. The Gen4 still waves high the banner of utter reliability because nothing changed that could make it unreliable. Gen4 owners have the option of experimenting with new frame sizes or sticking with what worked by punching one pin and swapping backstraps.

MY AFFAIR

The old Glock 26 I keep doesn't have feelings, but if she did, I'm sure that they'd be a little hurt. The tried-and-true battery of Gen3 carry guns will be phased out for Gen4 models as soon as the account matches the purchase price of new pistols—but I'm not trading her in on a whim. This is no midlife crisis. The Gen4 pistols offer some real advantages, and they could make all the difference when you draw and mean it.

CARRY

In a dark corner of a pub at an undisclosed location, two serious-looking gentlemen sit at a table solving all the world's problems. Lynyrd Skynyrd's "Mississippi Kid" is blaring on the jukebox as the blond waitress, clad in hot pants and a tight T-shirt, drops off another round. Conversation slows, and the short, chubby guy with the white hair and beard takes a sip of his martini, looks across the table and says, "What ya carrying?"

Placing his bottle of beer on the table, the clean-cut man with the cowboy hat says, "Colt 1911. You?"

The older man swirls his martini glass and contemplates picking out the olive with his fingers. "Same, 'cepting it's a Para, Long-Slide Limited. Forty-five, of course." He takes a sip and watches as their waitress bends down to pick up a tip. "I've got 14 230-grain Remington Golden Saber in the mag and another in the spout. What's your carr load?"

Skynyrd is replaced with "One Last Breath" fron Creed—it's a diverse crowd—and the man with th hat notices his drinking companion ogling the wait

Choose what you carry wisely.

BY RICHARD MANN

AMMO

The demand for increased terminal performance is producing a wide array of intensely engineered bullets from major manufacturers and small custom houses. You can find a load to do just about anything you want nowadays.

It's possible that some loads will not offer reliable expansion from some short-barreled handguns. These 88-grain Remington JHP bullets failed to expand when fired from an S&W BodyGuard.

Hornady's Critical Defense line of ammunition combines reliable but moderate expansion from short-barreled handguns with moderate penetration and the ability to defeat intermediate barriers commonly encountered in a defensive setting.

ress. "You're too old and ugly for her, and you both know it." He takes a swig from his beer and gently places the bottle on the table. "I figured you for a heavy-for-caliber—big gun—kinda guy. Goes well with your portly appearance. I prefer wide wound cavities to deep penetration. Mine is loaded with DoubleTap 185-grain Noslers."

And the argument begins.

When it comes to selecting a carry load for a defensive handgun, pistoleros have to choose the type of terminal performance they want. Thing is, there's no best answer for all situations.

By using bullets built from compressed metal particles, DRT is able to create a bullet that will work well on many barriers and still expand or uncompress inside soft tissue. With more engineering and testing, powdered-metal bullets may soon eclipse the performance of standard jacketed, lead-alloy-core bullets.

There's no magic bullet, and no load guarantees immediate assailant incapacitation. What we have to choose from is deep-penetrating loads, moderate-penetrating loads and those that offer shallow penetration.

The general rule of thumb is that the deeper a bullet penetrates, the less tissue it destroys. This may seem contradictory—shouldn't a deeper hole be bigger? No, and here's why. For starters, when bullets expand, their frontal diameter increases. The larger a bullet's frontal diameter, the wider the hole, the more resistance it has and the less it will penetrate.

Second, if you only consider the tissues that are damaged by the crushing effect of the bullet, you can calculate the size of the hole as you would the volume of a cylinder. The formula for this is (πr2d), with (r) being the radius of the bullet's frontal diameter and (d) being the depth of penetration. If we look at the loads favored by our arguing gun guys, the Golden Saber load drives to 16 inches in 10 percent ordnance gelatin and creates a crush cavity with a volume of 5.30 cubic inches. The shallower-penetrating DoubleTap load, which expands wider and hits harder, drives to about 10 inches and creates a crush cavity measuring 5.53 cubic inches.

How could this be? It's simple, really. The cavity size increases linearly with penetration but goes up exponentially with the frontal bullet diameter. It's just basic geometry. But there is more to it than just the crush cavity. As bullets impact liquefied materials, like the tissues humans are made of, they create a splash just like when you throw a rock into a pond. The size of this splash is a direct result of expansion—expanded frontal diameter—and velocity.

The effects of this splash are what some call hydrostatic shock, but it's probably better defined as hydraulic damage. Shoot a bullet into water and you'll get a splash, but the water recovers in seconds. With tissues that are saturated with liquid, like the tissues in the body, this splash and stretching tears and permanently damages the tissues. In some instances this damage is significant, and in others not so much. The wider the expansion and the higher the velocity, the more damage—bigger splash—the bullet causes.

There are other considerations, too. Some bullets fragment and send particles of the lead-alloy core and shrapnel from the bullet jacket out from the bullet's path. These secondary projectiles create additional, though small, cavities. To further complicate the way you might value wounding, some of our most modern bullets are manufactured with compressed cores of minute metal particles

The PDX1 loads from Winchester might just deliver the best performance of anything available when subjected to the FBI's testing protocol. However, unless you're a law enforcement officer, it's unlikely you will need all that barrier-defeating ability.

Law enforcement agencies are concerned with a bullet's ability to shoot through auto glass and other barriers. This might be ideal for their line of work, but bullets that perform well in these tests often are better at shooting through barriers than stopping bad guys.

If you think you may have to shoot through a car door to save your life, maybe you should select one of the bullet styles championed by the FBI. Otherwise, more conventional and less expansive ammo should serve you just fine.

that literally uncompress inside a liquid-based target. These particles drive through tissues and seem to almost purée living organs.

So where does that leave citizens who are trying to select what ammunition they should load in the handgun they have decided to bet their life on? Obviously, with a decision that is as complex as it is important.

Many believe that the best approach is to follow the FBI's lead and choose a bullet that performs to standards in its testing protocol. But here's the problem with the FBI's approach: the FBI subjects a load to eight tests, most of which are through intermediate barriers. Then all results are weighed equally. This means the "best" loads, according to the FBI, are those that are best at shooting through stuff but not necessarily at damaging tissue.

Others put a great deal of emphasis on velocity. Their contention is that tissue damage increases with velocity. All things being equal, this is indeed fact and good common sense. For example, if you fire the same bullet from a .38 Special and a .357 Magnum, which one do you think will damage the most tissue? But here's the problem with this approach: all things are never equal.

Bullets need a certain impact velocity to initiate expansion. If they impact below that velocity, they will not expand at all. If the velocity is too high, they can expand to the point that their final frontal diameter is actually smaller than it would have been had they impacted at a slightly slower speed. So, manufacturers design bullets to operate within a certain velocity window, and they will generally perform best when they impact somewhere in the middle of that window.

Testing in ordnance gelatin is a bit expensive and may be more work than one man should attempt. However, if you go together with some shooting buddies, you can share the effort and cost. You'll likely learn a great deal in the process.

Ideally, bullets are also designed for specific cartridges, at specific impact velocities. This is why we see some loads recommended for short-barrel revolvers or compact autos. Short-barreled handguns generate less velocity, so the load—and bullet—is engineered to work at those speeds. The thing is, the work one bullet does may be completely different from the work another bullet does, and what one shooter wants, another may not.

For example, the FBI believes in deep penetration and the ability of bullets to defeat intermediate barriers. This design requirement necessitates a bullet that will hold together and retain most all its weight. Building a bullet to do this

continued on 148

Winchester's PDX1 load for the Taurus Judge uses the multi-projectile concept to increase wounding. Recoil is stiff, especially out of lightweight revolvers.

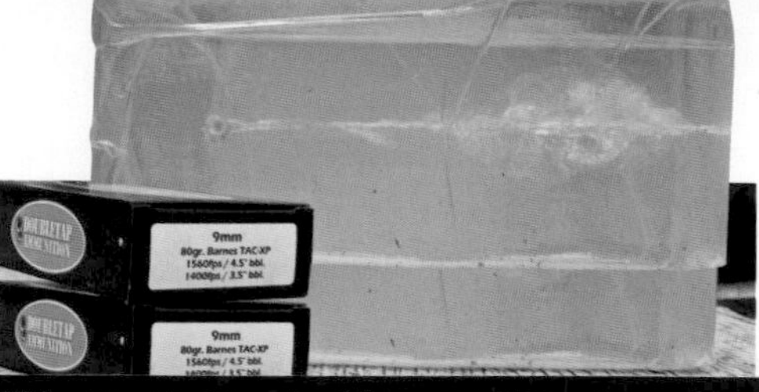

This 80-grain 9mm load from DoubleTap has a blistering speed of 1,500 fps. That, combined with moderate expansion, helps this bullet create a good-size wound cavity and still drive deep. Recoil is very mild, making it a great choice from supercompact 9mms.

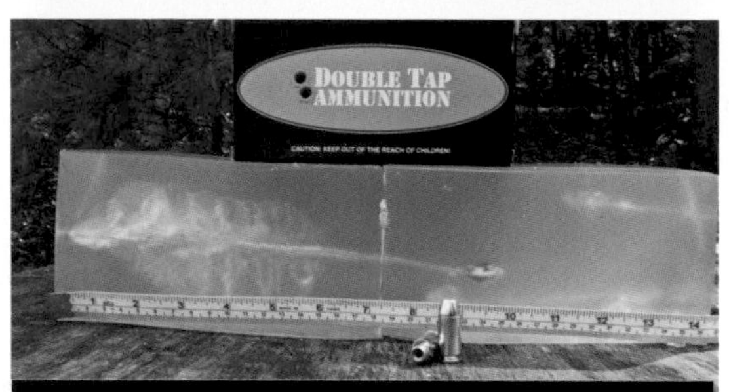

By driving the 185-grain Nosler bullet to more than 1,100 fps, DoubleTap has created what might be the most devastating .45 ACP load available, at least in terms of wound cavity size. This load offers wide expansion and moderate penetration, a perfect combination for the destruction of a lot of tissue.

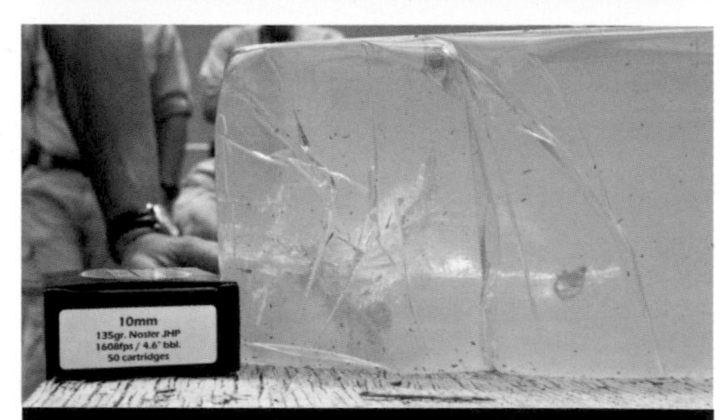

DoubleTap's hypervelocity 10mm load utilizing a 135-grain Nosler bullet is an example of a load you might select if overpenetration and maximum tissue damage are at the top of your list.

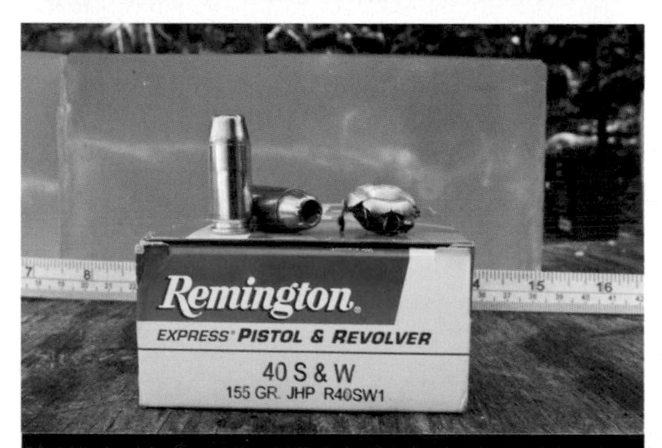

A standard hollowpoint bullet at standard velocities is not a bad thing. This Remington 155-grain .40 S&W load offers moderate to deep penetration and average-size wound cavities.

Cor-Bon's 165-grain .45 Auto +P load is a handful to shoot and creates a wicked, but shallow wound cavity in gelatin. If overpenetration is one of your concerns, this load is a good option.

Remington's 185-grain JHP load for the .45 Auto is a perfect example of moderation. It penetrates to about 12 inches and creates medium-size wound cavities without excessive recoil.

Federal's EFMJ bullet is a unique approach to terminal performance. Because of their profile, these bullets feed reliably, and because of their light weight, recoil is moderate. They are also one of the most reliably expanding bullets available.

Many claim that .32-caliber handguns are not suitable for self-defense. This 60-grain load from DoubleTap uses a special Barnes TAC-XP bullet designed just for DoubleTap. It will outperform most any .380 ACP load with regard to wound cavity size and penetration.

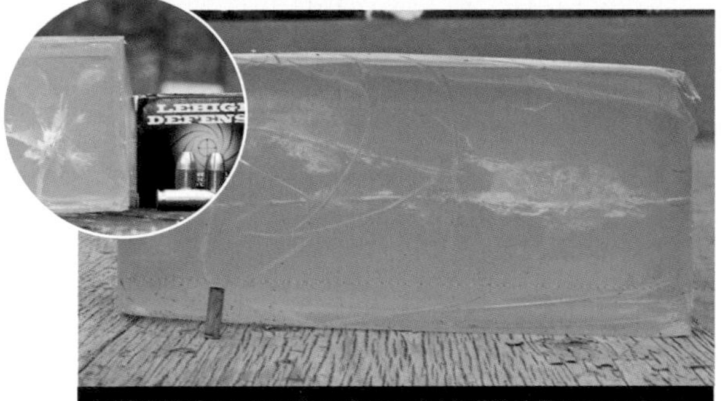

Lehigh Defense's unique four-petal bullet delivers moderate recoil and penetration. Because the bullet expands to such a wide diameter, wound cavities are of medium to large size.

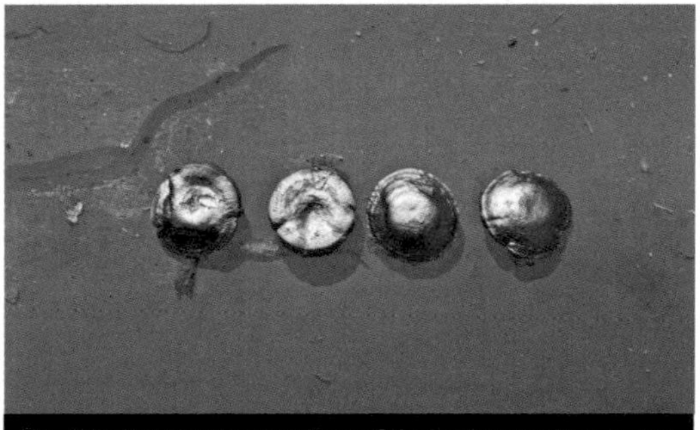

One thing you want, regardless of the load you select, is consistency, the same level of expansion and penetration from every shot.

Standard shotshells are not a bad option as a defensive load in a Taurus Judge or S&W Governor revolver, especially if you want to limit penetration. However, these can be a handful to shoot.

By combining bullets that expand widely with high velocity, large wound cavities like these are easy to create in gelatin. This 135-grain Nosler bullet fired from a .40 S&W handgun will penetrate to about 11 inches.

Most Judge and Governor revolver loads are built around the .410 shotshell case. Cross Outdoors, in conjunction with LeHigh Defense, offers a multi-projectile load for the .410 revolver but uses a .45 Colt case. Recoil is very manageable.

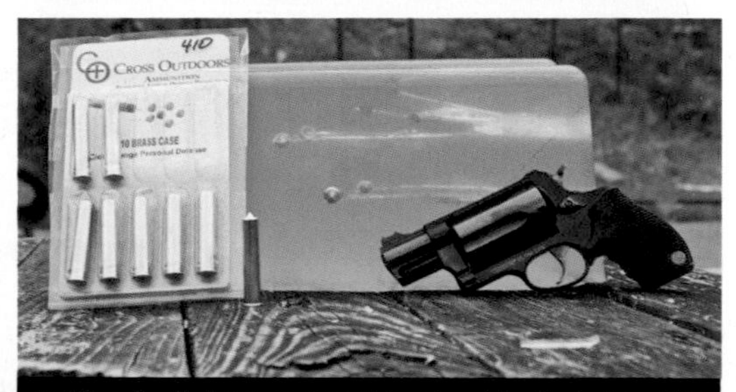

Multi-projectile loads such as this one originally designed by Cross Outdoors and now offered by Lehigh Defense are a unique way to damage a lot of tissue with one shot. This .410 shotshell load from a Judge has six projectiles.

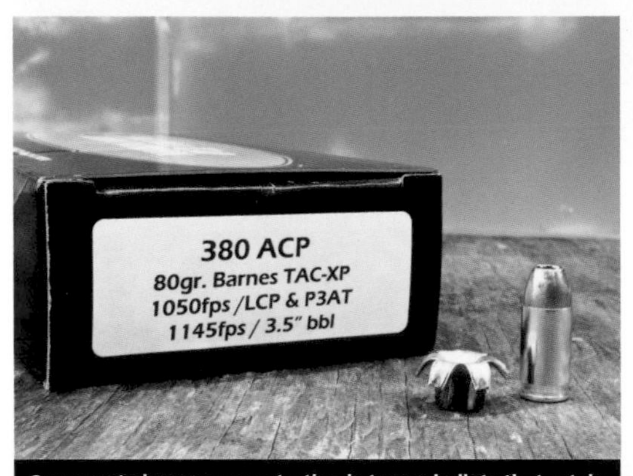

One way to increase penetration is to use bullets that retain all their weight. This can make wound cavities a bit smaller than what is seen with conventional hollowpoints. However, total weight retention allows the use of a lighter bullet that can be driven faster, which increases wound cavity size.

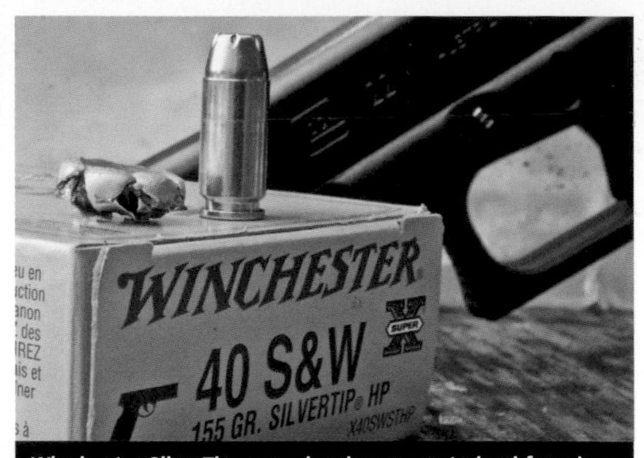

Winchester SilverTip ammo has been a go-to load for a long time in several defensive handgun cartridges. Even though it received a bad rap at the FBI's Miami shootout in 1986, it is still a good choice if you like moderate penetration. This 155-grain SilverTip load in .40 S&W will drive to about 11 inches in 10 percent ordnance gelatin.

Because .38 Special handguns operate at low velocities, modern bullets such as the Gold Dot along with +P loads have really increased the terminal performance of this cartridge.

It's possible that some loads will not offer reliable expansion from some short-barreled handguns. These 88-grain Remington JHP bullets failed to expand when fired from a Smith and Wesson Bodyguard.

continued from 145

is not hard, and several manufacturers do it very well. The Speer Gold Dot, Federal Hydra-Shok and EFMJ, Hornady XTP, Winchester PDX1 and Remington Golden Saber are all perfect examples of bullets that offer this type of performance, regardless of the cartridge they are loaded in.

A good number of citizens who carry for personal protection are not so concerned about shooting through a car windshield or door. Instead, they want to create a massive wound cavity that damages the maximum amount of tissue. It's hard to argue with this concept. The more tissue that is damaged, the sooner blood will be lost. The sooner the brain runs out of the blood that carries oxygen to it, the sooner collapse is imminent.

If this is the wounding path you want to follow, standard JHP bullets, especially those pushed to high or even +P velocities, are where you want to look. Old standby loads such as the Winchester SilverTip, Remington hollowpoints and most of the DoubleTap loads using Nosler JHP bullets will provide very large wound cavities with moderate penetration.

If wicked but shallow wound cavities are what you want, look to bullets such as the Glaser Safety Slug, Extreme Shock AFR round and high-velocity, light-for-caliber bullets such as the DoubleTap 135-grain Nosler 10mm load and the Cor-Bon 165-grain +P .45 ACP load. These bullets speed along at blistering velocities and generate a great deal of energy. Wound depth for all these loads is about six to seven inches, practically eliminating all overpenetration concerns.

Even though it has changed in design over the years, Federal's 230-grain .45 Auto Hydra-Shok is one of the most respected defensive handgun loads of all time for personal defense. They are often the most reliable option, but they create small wound cavities and penetrate very deep.

With this flatnose, hardcast bullet, Buffalo Bore takes a different approach to terminal performance in a .380 ACP. These bullets will drive beyond 31 inches in 10 percent gelatin and still make a modestly impressive wound cavity. They do not expand.

When selecting a defensive handgun cartridge, you'll want a consistent load, one that works the same way every time. This comes from repeatable velocities and well-engineered bullets.

There is nothing wrong with standard hollowpoints at standard velocities as long as you don't try to shoot them through robust barriers. These loads generally offer controllable recoil and minimal wear on a gun.

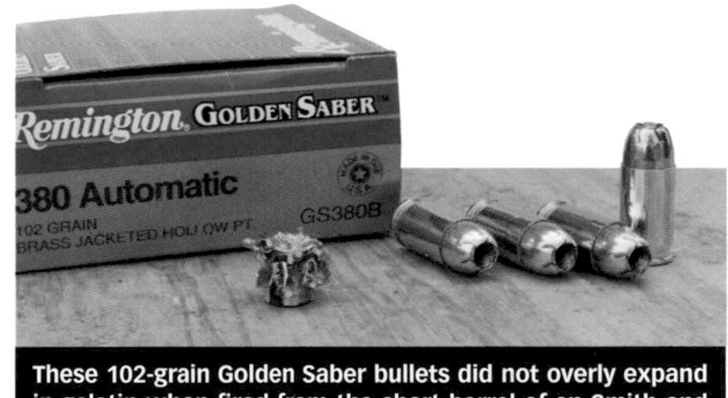

These 102-grain Golden Saber bullets did not overly expand in gelatin when fired from the short barrel of an Smith and Wesson Bodyguard handgun, but they did open up to a .59 caliber; not bad for a .380 Auto load.

Other examples of shallow-to-moderate-penetrating loads are some of the offerings from Lehigh Defense. These expensive specialty loads utilize an all-copper bullet that develops four wide petals during expansion. Tissue damage is massive, but penetration is limited. For example, the .380 Auto 68-grain bullet only drives to a depth of about seven to eight inches, but expands to almost .70 caliber.

The sensible solution seems to be a compromise, especially for the armed citizen who will not necessarily need to shoot through the passenger door of a '72 Pontiac. These are the loads I turn to for my carry guns. I'm generally happy with between 8 and 12 inches of penetration in 10 percent ordnance gelatin, if bullet expansion is substantial. But in this performance category you will still need to make choices.

For example, the Winchester 185-grain Silvertip load is what I carry in my Lightweight Commander, because at about 950 fps it is very controllable to shoot. The 185-grain DoubleTap load I carry in my full-size 1911s uses a Nosler bullet and is 200 fps faster. (This is not a +P load, but it does reach +P velocities. DoubleTap achieves this with a special powder.) Both bullets penetrate to about the same depth; however, because of the higher velocity and wider expansion, the DoubleTap load creates a wound cavity almost twice as large.

Similarities exist for every cartridge when you are comparing loads that penetrate to the same depth. In most cases the load with the higher velocity will damage the most tissue. These higher velocities are often the product of +P ammunition. This is not a bad thing, but it almost always brings with it increased recoil and wear

Wilson Combat is now offering a line of ammunition. Most cartridges are available loaded with Hornady's XTP bullet, which has a reputation for deep penetration and an ability to defeat intermediate barriers. These bullets perform this way because of their moderate expansion and how well they hold together.

Remington's Golden Saber is an example of a bullet designed to go deep and penetrate intermediate barriers. These bullets show moderate to wide expansion, but just as important, they are consistent in their performance.

Buffalo Bore Ammunition is one of the few companies that offers +P .380 Auto loads. These bullets will expand well even when fired from handguns with very short barrels.

By loading a bullet like the Barnes TAC-XP, Black Hills ammunition can create moderate recoiling loads that drive deep. Several ammunition companies are turning to Barnes's all-copper bullets for defensive handgun loads.

COMPARISON OF VARIOUS CARRY LOADS

LOAD	VELOCITY (fps)	PEN (in.)	RD (in.)	RW (gr.)	CAVITY (cu. in.)
Various .32-Caliber Loads					
.32 NAA / .32 H&R / .327 Federal Magnum					
.32 NAA 60-gr. Cor-Bon JHP	1,193	7.10	.44	32	1.08
.32 H&R DoubleTap 60-gr. Barnes	1,400	15.00	.52	60	3.18
.327 Mag. Federal Hydra-Shock 85-gr.	1,396	12.90	.52	84	2.74
.327 Mag. Federal 110-gr. JSP	1,572	15.00	.71	97	5.94
.327 Mag. Speer Gold Dot 115-gr.	1,483	17.50	.65	113	5.80
.32 H&R Federal Hydra-Shok 85-gr.	1,046	18.00	.38	81	2.04
.380 ACP					
DoubleTap 80-gr. Barnes XPB	1,144	8.25	.62	80	2.49
Lehigh Defense 68-gr.	1,150	6.00	.68	68	2.25
Winchester PDX1 85-gr.	860	9.75	.59	95	2.66
Buffalo Bore 90-gr. JHP +P	1,129	11.00	.61	90	3.21
Federal 90-gr. Hydra-Shok	891	11.50	.59	89	3.14
Winchester SilverTip 85-gr.	831	11.50	.56	85	2.83
9mm Luger					
DoubleTap 80-gr. Barnes XPB	1,545	13.00	.60	80	3.67
Federal EFMJ 105-gr.	1,254	9.50	.61	105	2.77
Hornady Critical Defense 115-gr.	1,119	10.00	.57	115	2.51
Speer Gold Dot 124-gr.	1,182	13.25	.71	124	5.71
Federal 115-gr. JHP	1,177	14.50	.57	114	3.70
Cor-Bon DPX 115-gr.	1,262	16.00	.50	115	3.14
.38 Special and .357 Magnum					
Winchester SilverTip 110-gr.	1,043	8.50	.40	60	1.07
.357 Mag. Federal Hydra-Shok 130-gr.	1,482	9.25	.68	68	1.47
Hornady Critical Defense 110-gr. +P	955	10.00	.52	109	2.12
.357 Mag. Remington SJHP 110-gr.	895	10.25	.61	110	2.99
Hornady Critical Defense 110-gr.	870	10.50	.48	109	1.90
Remington Golden Saber 125-gr.	883	13.00	.60	125	3.67
Speer Gold Dot 135-gr.	865	14.50	.58	134	3.83
.357 Mag. Winchester 158-gr. SWC	1,255	26.00	.36	158	2.65
.40 S&W					
Winchester SilverTip 155-gr.	1,209	10.25	.76	155	4.65
DoubleTap 135-gr. Nosler	1,315	10.75	.54	80	2.46
Remington 115-gr. JHP	1,125	13.00	.71	155	5.14
Wilson Combat 140-gr. DPX	1,195	14.25	.73	140	5.96
Remington 180-gr. JHP	957	16.75	.61	180	4.89
.45 ACP					
Winchester 185-gr. SilverTip	942	9.00	.76	178	4.08
Lehigh Defense 175-gr.	1,100	10.00	.88	152	6.08
DoubleTap 185-gr. Nosler	1,144	10.00	.84	183	5.54
Federal 230-gr. Hydra-Shok	897	15.00	.73	230	6.27
Remington Golden Saber 230-gr.	927	16.00	.65	230	5.31
Federal 230-gr. FMJ	839	31.00+	.45	230	2.37

Terminal performance data were obtained by firing each load into a block of 10 percent ordnance gelatin positioned 5 to 10 feet from the muzzle. Velocity was established by firing over an RCBS AmmoMaster chronograph positioned 10 feet from the muzzle. Crush cavity volume in cubic inches, based on the recovered diameter (RD) of the bullet and total penetration (PEN) depth. "RW" represents the recovered weight of the bullet.

Sources

Black Hills Ammunition
605-348-5150
black-hills.com

Cor-Bon
800-626-7266
corbon.com

DoubleTap
866-357-1066
doubletapammo.com

DRT
660-564-2331
drtammo.com

Federal
800-831-0850
federalpremium.com

Lehigh Defense
267-217-3539
lehighdefense.com

Remington
800-243-9700
remington.com

Speer
800-627-3640
speer-ammo.com

Winchester
618-258-2000
winchester.com

and tear on your handgun. Both are things that need to be considered.

Then there are the specialty loads such as the aforementioned Glaser Safety Slug. And, since the introduction of the Judge revolver by Taurus, we have seen an entirely new breed of specialty ammunition loaded with multiple projectiles. Lehigh Defense is perfecting these multi-bullet loads for common cartridges such as .45 Auto and .45 Colt. Are these loads viable self-defense options? Sure. But, like with any of the other conventional handgun cartridges, the same considerations exist. How deep do you want to drive the bullet, and how much tissue do you want to destroy?

Regular shotshells are nasty from a Governor or Judge, and they're not very much fun to shoot either. The Winchester PDX1 load shows a lot of promise, but it, too, is a handful. Lehigh Defense took a different, multibullet approach for these .410/.45 revolvers and other cartridges by using light projectiles, and it has created deadly, light-recoiling options.

In the end, it comes down to you selecting a load that will do the damage you want. It's no different from selecting a new car. We all have our likes and dislikes, and we are all a product of our experience and perceptions. There is, however, another very important consideration when selecting defensive handgun ammunition: reliability. Even if there were a magic bullet or load, it would be worthless if it was not reliable in your handgun.

How many rounds of a particular ammunition do you need to fire in your handgun to determine reliability? That's a good question. Obviously, the more the better, but let's say you test 1,000 rounds for this purpose. Do you clean your gun after every one or two magazines of ammunition fired? You probably should. After all, you'll likely be carrying a clean gun.

The reality is that few of us can afford to fire 1,000 rounds of expensive carry ammunition. A more realistic and appropriate number is something between 50 and 100 rounds. If your gun is broken in and will reliably cycle 50 to 100 rounds of a certain load without any hint of a hiccup, you should feel relatively confident in the combination's reliability. Also, you should swap out your carry ammo about once per year, and this will give you another opportunity to run a reliability test.

Regardless of the gun, caliber or load you choose, the most important aspect of employing a defensive handgun will always be getting a hit, in the right spot, first. And this requires something you cannot buy at the local gun shop: practice.

That said, I would offer some common-sense advice to anyone who is serious about selecting a load for his defensive handgun. Start by choosing several loads that offer controllable recoil in your handgun. Next, verify that any load you are considering passes your reliability test. Then test these loads in some sort of media to make sure they will expand from your handgun. You can shoot them into a 55-gallon drum of water to test expansion or in ordnance gelatin to discover penetration depth. It's a great learning experience, and if you share the cost with some shooting buddies, it's not that expensive.

Unlike many other arguments that can be solved with math or science, the best defensive handgun load is a subjective thing. We cannot go out and test these loads on the targets we ultimately intend to shoot, so we have to substitute various mediums and make decisions based on what we learn from these experiments. We're working with hypotheticals. Still, the solution can be simplified with three rules:

Rule 1: Carry the largest-caliber, highest-capacity handgun you can comfortably conceal on a daily basis.

Rule 2: Load it with flawlessly functioning ammunition, utilizing an expanding bullet, delivering high energy levels for your cartridge of choice.

Rule 3: Practice, practice, practice, with the ultimate goal being consistently putting five shots in a five-inch circle at five yards in less than five seconds.

The truth of the matter is that we are all living—at least financially—somewhere between one box of ammo and a bodyguard. Follow these three rules and your gun and the ammo you have shoved in it will not be nearly as important as your mindset. Regardless of your gun or ammo, shoot center mass, first and until the threat no longer exists.

Back at the bar, the argument went on for hours. Problem was, neither man could demonstrate proof that the other was wrong. In the end, the waitress went home with the cowboy. The short, fat guy managed to convince several patrons that he was a famous gunwriter, and they bought him martinis until he began a political rant that continued until the bar closed. Nothing new here; the cowboy always gets the girl, and everyone knows that gunwriters don't pay for ammunition or their drinks. And they think they know everything.

THE NEXT BRAVE ONE

High quality, low cost.

BY DOUG LARSON

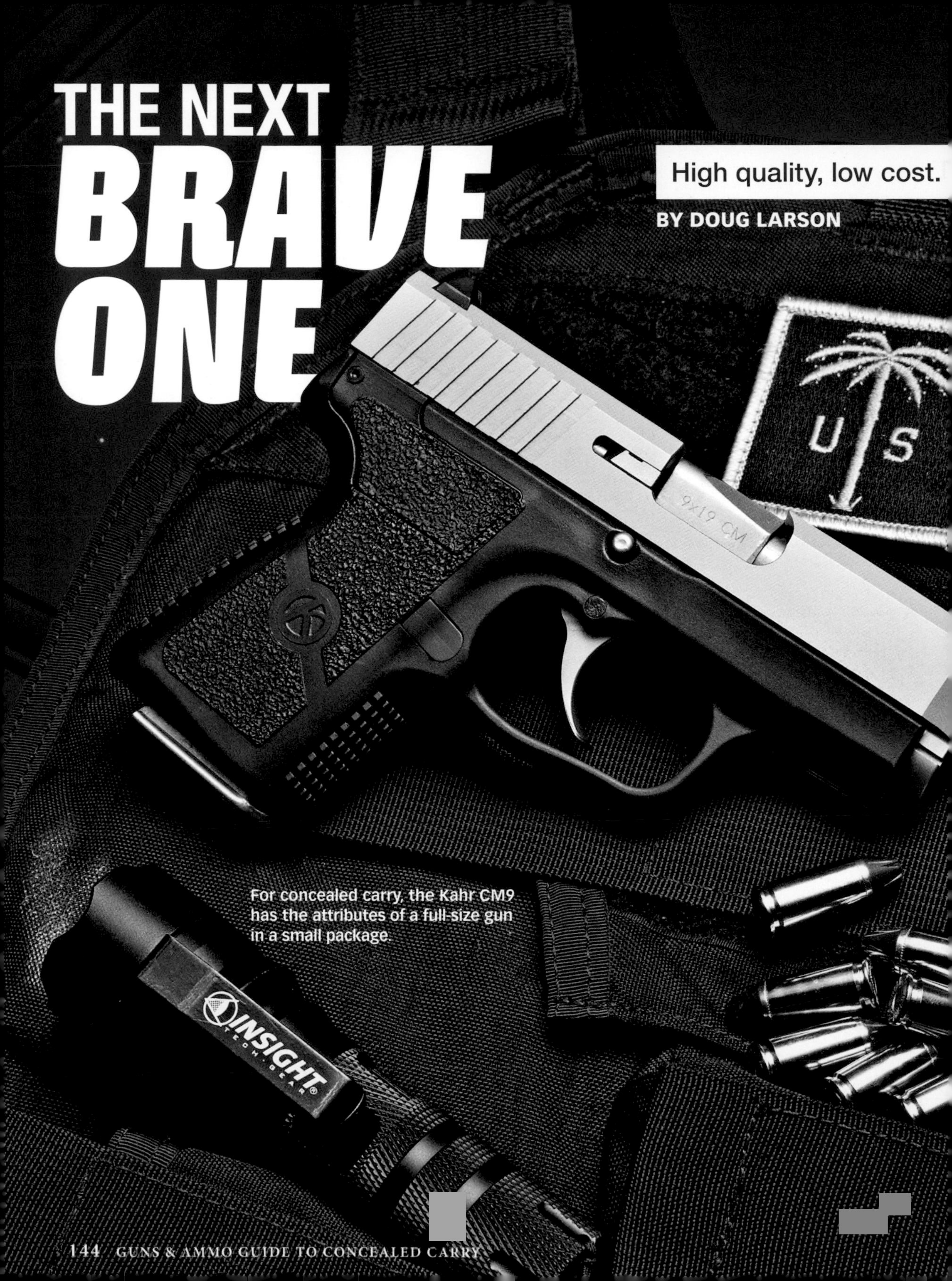

For concealed carry, the Kahr CM9 has the attributes of a full-size gun in a small package.

This is a realistic pocket gun.

It was not long ago that most people who carried guns for a living shunned the 9mm. However, modern ammunition and bullet design have changed the minds of many, and now the 9mm has resurged as a popular self-defense round. Just as well, demand is increasing for small, easily carried and concealed handguns.

Kahr Arms of Worcester, Massachusetts, was a bit ahead of the curve when it introduced its K9 in 1995. It's a pocket-size 9mm pistol with many features once found only in full-size pistols. The gun was a hit with law enforcement and others who carry concealed because it put useful firepower in a small package. The design evolved, others followed, and Kahr continued to develop similar guns based on that success. Eventually, in 2001 the company came out with the PM9, which was smaller than the K9 and built on a polymer frame.

The PM9 had a lot of appeal because it was much lighter than an all-steel gun and it was thin and short—about the size of a classic .32 or .380 ACP-chambered Walther PP series. Many used to consider the PPK the ultimate pocket pistol. In contrast with Walther's blowback operation, Kahr pistols are locked-breech, modified Browning actions, so they can better handle the more powerful 9mm in such a small package. However, due to the fact that other pocket pistols of the time were considered cheap throw-aways, many consumers didn't realize that the most expensive PM9 wasn't a cheap piece made from pot metal and plastic. Nevertheless, sales and demand steadily remained, but Kahr realized that another segment of the market could be reached if it could find a way to reduce the price.

There wasn't much savings to be realized by modifying the PM9's frame. It's polymer, after all. However, Kahr determined that the steel slide and barrel, which required expensive machining, could be made more efficient and still offer the same attributes

KAHR ARMS CM9

Type: Locked-breech, modified Browning operation, semiauto
Caliber: 9mm
Capacity: Six-round magazine, seven-round (available)
Barrel: 3 in., stainless steel
Overall length: 5.42 in.
Weight: 15.9 oz.
Finish: Black polymer frame, matte stainless steel slide
Sights: Drift-adjustable rear notch with bar, pinned front blade with white dot
Trigger: Double-action only
MSRP: $460.00
Manufacturer: Kahr Arms
508-795-3919
kahr.com

Photo by Mike Anschuetz

A variety of holsters are available from Galco, including, clockwise from bottom left, the Pocket Protector, the Speed Paddle and the Stinger. The gun is large enough that it is easy to grasp and draw without fumbling for a grip.

that attract those who continued to buy the PM9. So the engineers and designers went to work and developed the CM9.

GUN DETAILS

The CM9's slide and barrel are made from stainless steel and have a subdued matte finish, but the slide is about ⅛ inch longer than the PM9. That is the only difference in overall dimensions I could find when comparing the two models, but there are other subtle differences.

Instead of the rounded corners found on the PM9, the CM9 slide has beveled edges along the top and front, and the front sight blade is pinned to the slide instead of drifted in a dovetail. Both carry a white dot, and both rear sights are dovetailed wearing a white post to sit the front dot on when sighting. This bar-dot sight configuration has proven to be very effective and is much better than the nearly nonexistent tiny sights found on some other guns of this size. The only other money-saving external machining that I could find was the lack of a dimple that's cut into the front lower corner of the CM9 slide.

Kahr did find another subtle way to save the end user some money in doing away with the PM9's rollmark in favor of simple engraving of the CM9 slide. It is likely that most buyers won't care about these differences as long as the CM9 remains dependable.

Internally, the slide and barrel assemblies are nearly identical to the one found on the PM9 except for the recoil-spring guide assembly, which consists of a recoil-spring guide that's about ⅛ inch longer than the PM9s. The spring guide telescopes and has an internal spring, all of which are surrounded by the main recoil spring. Only the outer spring can be removed for cleaning, but this has never been a problem with the several Kahr pistols I've tested. Instead of the PM9's machined slide catch, which rotates freely on the shaft, the CM9's unit is a one-piece metal injection-molded (MIM) part. This part costs less to make than the

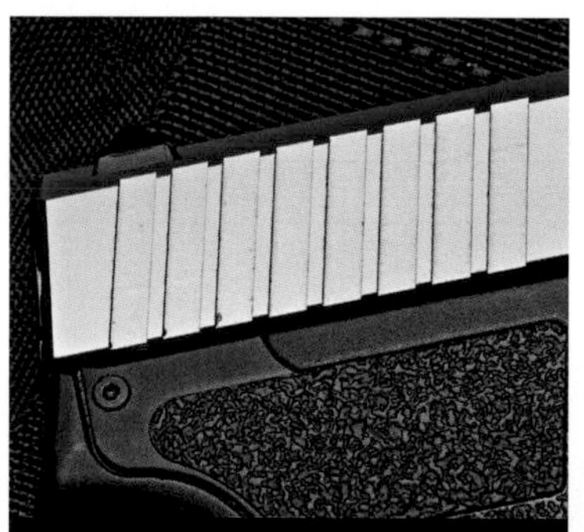

The slide is easily grasped by forward raking and tactile serrations.

For its intended duty as a carry piece, the magazine release is low profile enough that it doesn't drag when the pistol is drawn. It's still easy to reach and press when needing to change magazines.

The CM9 comes with real sights: a dovetailed rear that is drift adjustable and a pinned front. The bar and dot configuration is easily picked up by the eye.

Accuracy Results

Load	Weight (gr.)	Avg. Velocity (fps)	SD	Avg. Group. (in.)
Speer Gold Dot HP	124	1,113	07	1.85
Hornady Critical Defense FTX	115	1,008	10	3.72
Black Hills JHP +P	124	1,226	03	3.75
Double Tap Brass Jacketed HP +P	124	1,216	12	4.60

Velocity recorded 15 feet from the muzzle with a PACT Professional chronograph. Accuracy tested off a pistol rest. Results are the average of 3 5-shot groups at 25 yards.

PM9's and is another cost-saving measure that allows Kahr to offer the gun for less money.

The barrel, besides being slightly longer than the one found on a PM9, has conventional land-and-groove rifling instead of polygonal rifling. While polygonal rifling is easier to clean and is said to deliver higher velocity at the same pressure, it is more expensive to manufacture. For practical purposes, I've never noticed a difference between the two types of rifling, so if it means less cost for the buyer, it's a good thing.

The barrel lug and its highly polished feed ramp are offset to the left of the boreline. This offset allows the trigger bar to run along the side of the lug instead of beneath it, which does two things. First, it allows the boreline to be set lower to the frame, which in turn results in the recoil line of thrust being lower in the hand, which reduces muzzle rise. That's a particularly useful attribute in a small defensive sidearm because it means that the sights can be brought back on target much quicker for a follow-up shot. The other advantage that the offset lug brings is the fact that the trigger bar can be set farther inboard, making the gun slimmer. Translation: better concealability.

The CM9 is equipped with an external extractor that also serves as a loaded-chamber indicator by protruding from the side of the slide when a round is chambered. It's a nice feature, but an experienced shooter will not rely on that to make sure his gun is loaded—or unloaded. That man will instead physically check the chamber. Safety is paramount.

The steel trigger on the test gun is typical of a Kahr pistol. It has a long, smooth pull and a little stacking just before breaking cleanly at about 6½ pounds. Stroking the trigger draws the striker that is already partially cocked by the action of the slide the rest of the way to the rear, where it is released to strike the primer. It's a good draw, made so in part by the patented cocking cam. The gun is equipped with a passive striker block designed to allow the striker to move forward and hit the primer only if the trigger is pulled. Some people refer to this as a drop safety, and it's added peace of mind since there is no external safety.

The ejector is a metal device that is fixed to the polymer frame and positively kicks expended brass well clear of the gun. The extractor and ejector work well together and functioned properly every time during testing.

To strengthen the black polymer frame and prolong the service life of the gun, the slide reciprocates on steel rails that are molded inside the dustcover and on small steel inserts at the rear of the frame rails. The grip is nicely textured on the sides and features the Kahr logo, while the front- and backstraps are aggressively checkered through the mold to provide a very slip-resistant surface. This is important on a small gun with an abbreviated grip

After the last round is fired, the slide catch locks the slide to the rear. The recoil-spring guide is a compound device that telescopes and includes an internal spring to complement the outer recoil spring.

The extractor has a large claw to positively grasp the empty cartridge case and pull it free of the chamber. The metal wedge on the opposite side of the gun is the ejector.

The slide and barrel assembly are ready to be mated to the frame. Note the kidney-shaped slot in the barrel lug, through which the slide catch shaft is inserted. The two recoil springs are clearly visible.

At the rear and residing inside the slide is the spring-loaded striker. Next to it, the metal protrusion is the passive striker block that is designed to prevent the striker from contacting a primer until the trigger is pulled.

where the pinkie of the firing hand is left to dangle. The triggerguard is roomy, so there is plenty of room for beefy fingers.

The serrated magazine-release button is where Americans expect it to be—on the left side at the junction of the triggerguard and the grip. It protrudes enough that it is easy to activate and allows magazines to drop freely when pushed. Initially, empty magazines did not drop freely from the test gun, but after the first seven rounds are fired, the problem went away. This illustrates why the Kahr owner's manual recommends a 200-round break-in period.

The CM9 is supplied with one six-round stainless steel magazine with a flush baseplate and witness holes so the round count can be quickly determined. Kahr has seven-round versions with extended baseplates available that provide more gripping surface but are a little harder to conceal. The follower is polymer with a metal insert that engages the slide catch after the last round is fired, locking the slide to the rear. When a fresh magazine is inserted, the slide catch can be pushed down with the thumb, but if an empty magazine is in the gun, it is difficult to do so. This is by design, probably to signal that the gun is empty. If racking the slide is your preferred way to recharge the gun after inserting a loaded magazine—and this is the way most savvy profes-

For disassembly or reassembly, the slide must be retracted to this position where the slide lock can be removed or inserted past a notch cut into the bottom of the slide.

Even though the gun is small enough to easily conceal, it shoots like a full-size gun and is not difficult to control even with full-power +P 9mm loads.

The CM9 is an inexpensive version of the PM9, but handles the same way and can actually be shot for fun despite its diminutive size.

Sources

Crimson Trace
800-442-2406
crimsontrace.com

Galco International
800-874-2526
usgalco.com

Kahr Arms
508-795-3919
kahr.com

sionals do it—the slide has plenty of gripping surface and serrations at the rear to make it work.

TAKEDOWN

Fieldstripping the CM9 is similar to other Browning modified-action guns and starts with making sure the gun is unloaded. Check it at least twice. Then, holding the slide partially to the rear so the witness marks on the left side of the frame and slide align, push the slide catch from right to left and remove it. You may need to tap the slide catch shaft with a plastic screwdriver handle to knock it free because mine was a tight fit. Next, with the gun pointed in a safe direction, pull the trigger. The slide can then be removed from the front of the frame, after which the recoil-spring assembly and barrel can be separated from the slide. The outer recoil spring is then pulled off the recoil-spring guide.

Reassembly is in reverse order, but when mating the recoil-spring assembly with the barrel and slide, be sure it is centered laterally in the slide. Because the recoil lug is offset to the side, it can look centered when it isn't. Also, the slide catch should be installed so that the spring in the frame pushes the catch down, not up. Otherwise the slide catch can lock the slide to the rear at a bad time.

Since my aging eyes aren't what they used to be, to test the practical accuracy of this pistol I attached a Crimson Trace Laserguard. I've found that the laser aids in shooting accurately because it eliminates the need to stop and focus on the front sight while aligning it with the target and the rear sight. It also makes it easier to shoot from unusual positions, which can happen if the user is knocked off his feet in a fight and cannot quickly acquire or line up the sights with his eye. Lasers are not the solution to every aiming problem, though, and even Crimson Trace will tell you that they are not a substitute for iron sights. Any mechanical device can fail.

As expected, the gun worked reliably well. Regardless of the load or brand, all ammunition—even +P—ran, there were no malfunctions, and recoil was never a problem. Although the CM9 is a small gun, it has enough gripping surface that it's not uncomfortable to shoot. Testing with a variety of Galco holsters, I also found that the gun is large enough that no fumbling or searching for the grip were necessary when presenting from a belt holster or the pocket.

Kahr Arms recognizes that this gun will be used for self-defense and wisely cautions that it or any gun to be used in that way be tested with the ammunition that the user intends to carry. Kahr suggests that at least 100 rounds be tested for reliability before that brand and load are adopted for self-defense. It can be expensive to test this much ammunition, but your life is worth it. Keep in mind that the government fires thousands of rounds when evaluating new guns for police or military use.

The manufacturer's suggested retail price is more than $200 less than that of the PM9, but it performs, functions and feels the same. I've put thousands of rounds through a couple of PM9s and many more through this gun, and I can see no practical difference between the two. This gun represents a great value.

POC

BY RICHARD NANCE I PHOTOS BY ALFREDO RICO

With the Kimber Solo Carry, you're never alone.

Every firearms manufacturer vying for a piece of the ever-expanding concealed carry market is trying to produce a pistol that's reliable, lightweight and of a substantial caliber while maintaining an adequate ammunition capacity for personal defense.

With so many sizes, calibers and options available, selecting a pistol for concealed carry can be a daunting task. Choose a gun that's too big and it'll probably be somewhere other than with you in your time of need. And although a smaller pistol is easier to carry, it's also going to be more difficult to shoot, thanks to its short sight radius, oftentimes nearly nonexistent sights and minimal grip surface.

In recent years, there has been a resurgence of the "pocket pistol." Initially, these pistols were chambered in .380 ACP, but several companies soon developed 9mm offerings. Kimber, a company synonymous with high-quality pistols, entered the fray with their Solo line.

The highest evolution of the Solo is the Carry DC (LG) model, which features Crimson Trace Lasergrips. The Solo Carry is a lightweight pistol that's heavy on performance. It's equally well suited for pocket or belt carry and sports a slew of user-friendly features designed to give the shooter a welcomed edge during a deadly force encounter.

As with all Solo models, the Carry DC (LG)'s 7075-T7 aluminum frame is topped with a stainless steel slide coated with a self-lubricating DLC (Diamond-like Coating) finish for optimal durability and corrosion resistance. The Solo Carry is extremely lightweight for a 9mm pistol, tipping the scales at a mere 17 ounces, and its stainless steel barrel is just 2.7 inches long.

Serrations on the front- and backstrap aid the shooter in recoil control, which is a concern with a 9mm pistol as light as the Solo Carry. Just as important, these serrations are beneficial in establishing and maintaining a proper shooting grip, which is of the utmost importance given the minimal gripping surface on the Solo Carry.

The Solo feels and points like a 1911, and its controls are intuitive for anyone familiar with John Browning's combat-proven design. This little pistol has all the right curves, and a Carry Melt treatment helps ensure a snag-free draw from concealment.

Surprisingly, the Solo series of pistols are actually a hair smaller in height and length than the Kimber Micro pistol series. Of course, the Solos are slightly wider and heavier because they're chambered in 9mm rather than .380 ACP.

Photos by Alfredo Rico

Keep in mind that reloading a micro-compact pistol is more challenging than a full-size pistol because there's less gun and magazine to hold on to.

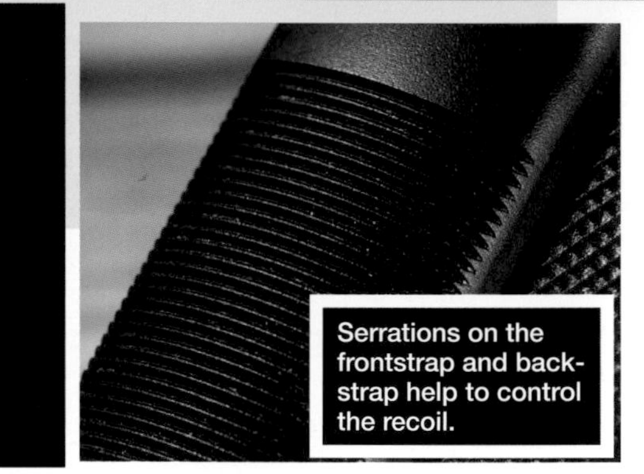

Serrations on the frontstrap and backstrap help to control the recoil.

TRIGGER TIME

Unless you have tiny hands, your pinky will dangle below the grip when firing.

Photos by Alfredo Rico

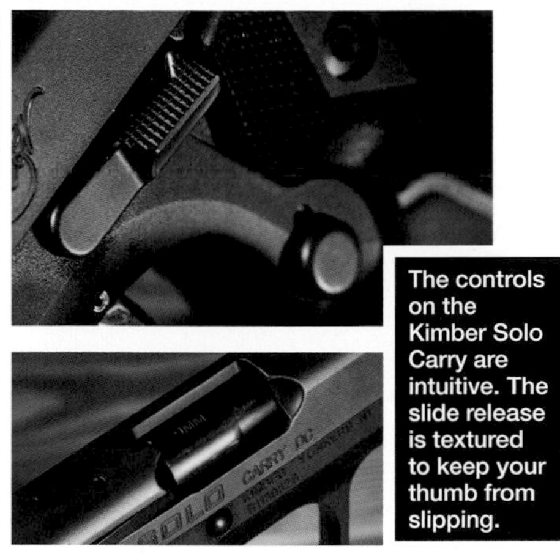
The controls on the Kimber Solo Carry are intuitive. The slide release is textured to keep your thumb from slipping.

As the name implies, Kimber designed the Solo from the ground up for concealed carry. Despite its lightweight and compact stature, it is not the least bit chintzy. And its subdued finish serves as a reminder that this little gun is all business.

The Solo Carry points naturally, not unlike the 1911s that helped establish Kimber's reputation for quality. While there's no grip safety, the ambidextrous thumb safety is very much like a 1911. Although the thumb safety seemed a little small, it was easily manipulated, and its functionality was identical to those you'd find on any of Kimber's acclaimed 1911s.

The slide-release lever was within easy reach and operated smoothly. Its size, slope and checkering provided excellent purchase for the shooter's thumb when sending the slide home to chamber a round. Although I prefer to use the thumb of my support hand to manipulate the slide-release lever, the Solo Carry is small enough that the lever can be activated with the shooting-hand thumb if you so desire.

Having a magazine release on either side of a pistol designed for concealed carry is not a bad idea when you consider that sustaining an injury could relegate you to fighting with one hand behind your back, so to speak. And if ol' Mr. Murphy has anything to say about it, it will be your dominant hand that's taken out of the fight.

The Solo Carry boasts an oversize ambidextrous slide release that's easily accessible with your thumb. However, the magazine release on the gun I tested was a little stiff. This, coupled with the fact that the six-round magazine fits flush in the pistol, made extracting the magazine from the pistol a little cumbersome.

The last thing you want in a gunfight is to be struggling to get rid of an empty magazine to make room for a fully loaded one. I would imagine that the Solo's magazine release would loosen up a bit over time. That being said, this potential problem could be avoided altogether by purchasing the eight-round magazine and carrying it in the pistol. This larger magazine extends below the bottom of the grip, which would make it easy to strip from the pistol. Then the six-round magazine could be carried as a spare, affording you a total of 15 rounds.

Like all Solo models, the Carry DC (LG) is a single-action, striker-fired pistol. According to the Kimber catalog, the trigger breaks out

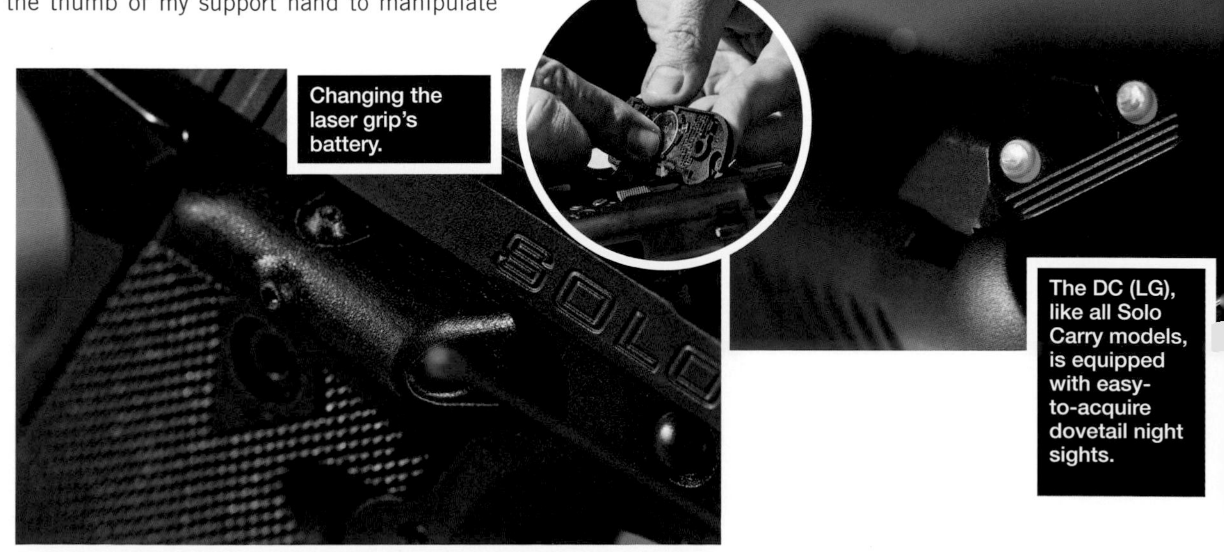

Changing the laser grip's battery.

The DC (LG), like all Solo Carry models, is equipped with easy-to-acquire dovetail night sights.

Crimson Trace Lasergrips offer several advantages over iron sights, but in bright sunlight the laser can be difficult to see. The laser is activated by the middle finger when you acquire a proper shooting grip.

between 6½ and 7½ pounds, but it felt lighter than that. While the Kimber Solo may feel and point like a 1911, its trigger bears little resemblance.

The Solo's trigger moves rearward along an arc as opposed to straight back, as is the case with a 1911. While this was certainly no 1911 trigger, it was nothing to be ashamed of either. There was no significant takeup or overtravel, and you could feel and hear the trigger reset from shot to shot.

Given the Solo's intended purpose as a concealed carry gun, I decided to shoot it off-hand from the 10-yard line rather than from a benchrest at 25 yards, as has become the standard measure of accuracy for a full-size pistol. I decided to fire 5 5-shot groups using Federal 124-grain Hydra-Shok jacketed hollowpoint ammunition with the three-dot sights, then again using the laser.

As expected, recoil management was a factor in shooting this 17-ounce 9mm pistol. It's often said that you don't get something for nothing, and although Kimber's engineers are to be commended for developing such a lightweight 9mm offering, it was inevitable that the Solo Carry would have a little kick to it. Don't get me wrong, the recoil was by no means unbearable or painful, but it was enough to notice a delay in recovery from shot to shot.

Recoil control is another area in which the optional eight-round magazine may come in handy. Since this magazine protrudes slightly from the bottom of the pistol, it provides just enough room to incorporate your pinky, which improves your grip and enables you to better control the pistol during recoil.

In my opinion, having night sights on your concealed carry pistol is not a luxury, but rather a necessity. Unlike with most pocket pistols, the three-dot Meprolight night sights were big enough to actually see, yet since they are dovetail mounted, they have a low-profile, snag-resistant design.

Using the three-dot sights, my average five-shot group was 1.82 inches, with my best group measuring 1.42 inches. While these groups are not going to win any bull's-eye competitions, they were pretty impressive from such a compact, lightweight 9mm pistol designed to prevail in lethal combat as opposed to winning matches.

I'm a big fan of lasers on pistols. It baffles me when I hear old codgers — who, by the way, would probably benefit the most from a laser because of their diminished eyesight — dismiss the laser as a gimmick. Sure, for some a laser can be used as a crutch that prevents their marksmanship skills from ever moving forward. But for the shooter who is capable of shooting with iron sights, adding a laser can give you a significant advantage.

It's well documented that during a gunfight the tendency is to focus on the threat rather than your pistol's sights. Can this tendency be overcome through training? I believe it can be mitigated through training, but I also doubt that the average gun owner is going to devote the training time necessary to clearly see the pistol's sights when presented with a close-range deadly threat. With the laser, you can effectively aim your pistol even while focused on the threat.

The Solo Carry's Crimson Trace Lasergrips feature "Instinctive Activation." In other words, the laser is activated by your middle finger when you achieve a shooting grip on the pistol. If, for some reason, you

The Solo Carry proved plenty accurate for 10-yard protection.

Photos by Alfredo Rico

Performance

Type	Velocity (fps)	Standard Deviation	Extreme Spread	Avg. Group (in.)	Best Group (in.)
Federal 124-grain Hydra-Shok JHP	982	n/a	n/a	1.82 (1.60 w/ Lasergrips)	1.42 (.88 w/ Lasergrips)

don't want to use the laser, the unit can be easily deactivated by the on/off switch located on the bottom rear portion of the left grip.

With the Crimson Trace Lasergrips, the laser emits from the right side of the grip, just under the slide. Unfortunately, when I index my finger along the frame, the laser is completely obliterated. Therefore, I have to consciously lower the position of my index finger along the frame for the laser to be of any benefit.

As I fired the Solo in direct sunlight, it was difficult to see the red laser, which makes the case for being proficient at shooting with iron sights.

Another issue I had with the Lasergrips was that, due to the Solo's sharp recoil, I had to reacquire my grip frequently in order to maintain sufficient rearward pressure to activate the laser. Of course, laser-mounting options are limited because of the pistol's size.

Kimber Solo Carry DC (LG)	
Type	Single action, striker fired, semiautomatic
Caliber	9mm
Capacity	6+1 (8-round magazine sold as an accessory)
Barrel	2.7 in., stainless steel w/DLC (Diamond-like Coating) finish
Overall Length	5.5 in.
Weight	17 oz. (w/empty magazine)
Grip	Crimson Trace Lasergrips
Finish	Aluminum frame with DLC finish/stainless steel slide with matte-black finish
Trigger	Single action, striker fired (6.5–7.5 lb. pull)
Magazine	6 round (flush-fit type)
Sights	Meprolight 3-dot, tritium filled
Safety	Ambidextrous thumb safety
MSRP	$1,204.00
Manufacturer	Kimber 888-243-4522 kimberamerica.com

Using the laser, my average group size shrank to 1.60 inches. My best group measured a respectable .88 inch. All in all, the Crimson Trace Lasergrips significantly benefit the shooter in aiming the Solo Carry. Just remember, if you have a high trigger-finger index, using this laser will take some getting used to, and due to the recoil impulse, even this well-designed laser grip might not stay activated from shot to shot.

A pistol designed for personal defense simply has to go bang when you pull the trigger. If it's not reliable, nothing else matters. The Solo Carry functioned flawlessly throughout my evaluation. Of course, using premium ammunition helps. But why would you carry anything but high-quality hollowpoint ammunition from a trusted manufacturer in your concealed carry pistol anyway?

CONCLUSION

The Kimber Solo Carry DC (LG) is about as much gun as you could reasonably carry in a pocket. In fact, depending on the type of pants you're wearing and the cut of the pocket, it may be too big. But the Solo Carry with its optional eight-round magazine would make an exceptionally discreet belt-mounted gun if pocket carry isn't your thing.

With ergonomics similar to the venerable model 1911 and ambidextrous controls, the Solo makes for easy gunhandling. The three-dot night sights and Lasergrips help ensure your aim is true, and the smooth, single-action trigger makes it easy to hit what you're aiming at. If you're in the market for a top-quality 9mm pocket pistol, consider going Solo.

A quality carry pistol deserves quality ammunition. Enter Federal.

The Solo Carry comes with a six-round flush-fit magazine. Note the on/off switch for the laser on the lower rear portion of the grip panel.

Photos by Alfredo Rico

THE ONE THAT DOES IT ALL

BY TOM BECKSTRAND
PHOTOS BY MARK FINGAR

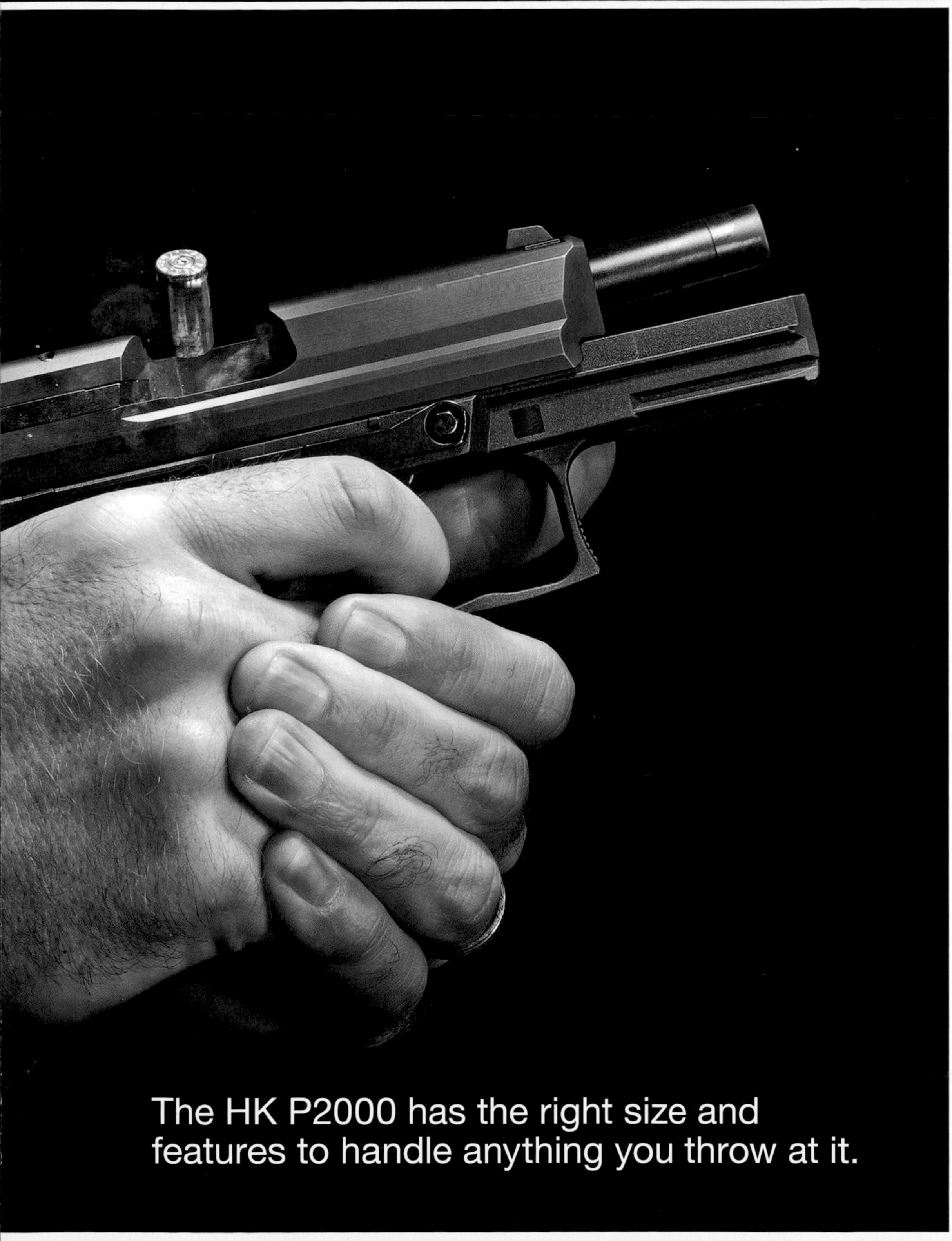

The HK P2000 has the right size and features to handle anything you throw at it.

Few choices can seem more daunting than buying a new handgun, especially for a first-time or fairly new shooter. Everyone has an opinion as to what makes the perfect handgun, and some of the metrics include price, quality, feel, reliability and caliber. I've overheard more than one firearms debate where both parties involved worked themselves into states of near hysteria trying to convince the other that he was right and his antagonist was wrong. Most of the emotional debates seem centered on the subjective terms listed above, so we'll try to avoid speaking in those terms.

What makes choosing a handgun so difficult is that a large part of our decision can be based on emotions or impressions that one pistol provides that another may not. While emotions are great in relationships and romance, I can't think of a single example where my emotions led me to make a good career or financial decision. So it is with buying guns.

When I look at pistols and evaluate them for their features and physical properties, one stands out from the pack. The HK P2000 has become a personal favorite of mine because of its size, ambidextrous controls, action and caliber. While I hesitate to bring a subjective characteristic such as reliability to the argument, I believe there is enough empirical evidence to make a compelling argument on the P2000's behalf, so we'll briefly discuss that as well.

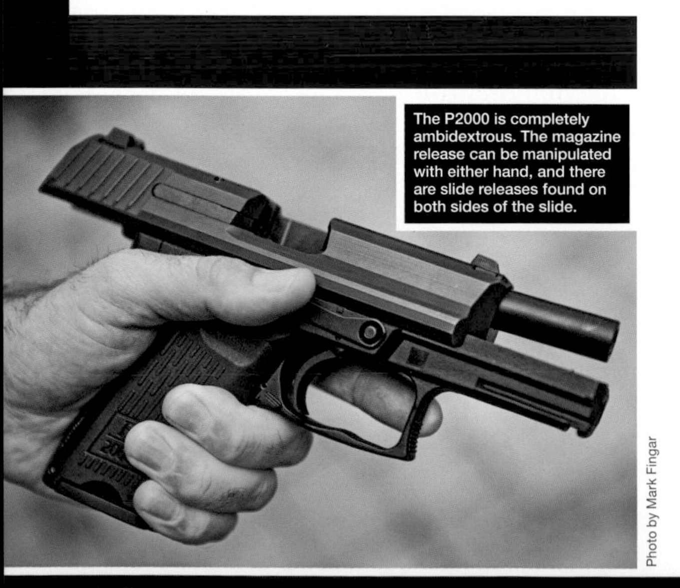

The P2000 is completely ambidextrous. The magazine release can be manipulated with either hand, and there are slide releases found on both sides of the slide.

Photo by Mark Fingar

SIZE MATTERS

If we all got what we wanted with a pistol, it would be small enough to conceal in our bathing suit, large enough to comfortably fit our hand, weigh two ounces, be heavy enough to make the recoil controllable and allow for mounting a light so we could use it effectively in dark areas. Obviously, no pistol will ever fit this description. Our goal then becomes to find a pistol that can do all things well, knowing that it will never be the best at any one specified task.

A pistol destined for a little bit of everything should allow us to get our entire hand on the grip without our pinky falling off the bottom. Our pinky provides an enormous amount of leverage and grip strength, both important for controlling recoil. While few new shooters really care about shooting fast at the start of their shooting career, as we get better, we desire to shoot faster. Being able to quickly deliver accurate second, third and fourth shots can also be the determining factor should we ever need to defend our lives.

Getting all of our fingers on a pistol also makes the shooting experience much more comfortable. With our pinky firmly planted on the pistol's grip, it's not getting beat to death by the magazine's floorplate every time we fire.

The P2000 has just enough grip to allow all our fingers to fit without having any excess material hanging below our hand. This means we can shoot the pistol fast and well but there isn't any extra length that makes the pistol hard to conceal.

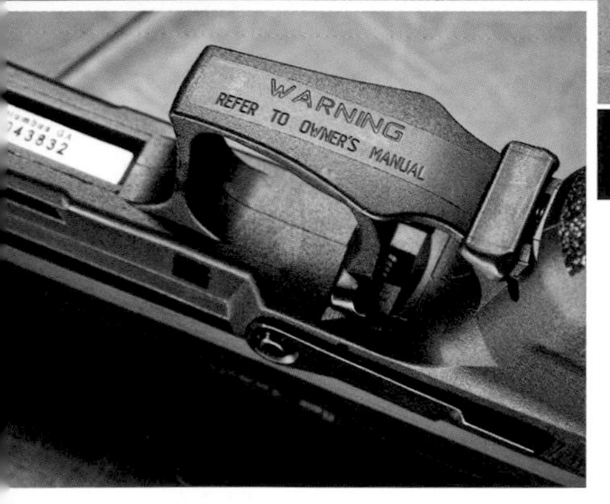

Photos by Mark Fingar

The P2000 field-strips by removing the slide release. The recoil spring is captured and has a polymer buffer to prevent slide/frame wear. The metal magazine is much faster out of the magazine well than a polymer one would be.

When we stick a pistol in our waistband for concealed carry, the part that is going to protrude the most (or "print") is the grip. Slight increases in grip length make a pistol exponentially more difficult to conceal. This is why we want just enough grip for our whole hand without any extra in a general-use pistol. No pistol I've found fits my very average-size hands better in this regard than the P2000.

The P2000 also has removable backstraps that let us tailor the grip thickness to fit our hand. The backstraps are easily removed by driving out one small roll pin, sliding off a strap, exchanging it with another and replacing the roll pin. It is a quick and easy way to ensure that we get the most comfortable fit for our hand.

USE BOTH HANDS

Ambidextrous controls are a significant advantage for any shooter. Once we master the basics with one hand, it's important to learn to shoot with the other. The biggest reason we really need to know how to shoot with both hands is that it gives us a way to use any cover we might have available if we ever need to defend ourselves. Shooting effectively with both hands mandates that we also be able to manipulate all necessary controls with either hand to keep the gun running.

As an experiment, do the following. If you're a right-handed shooter, imagine having to use a right-turn corner in your

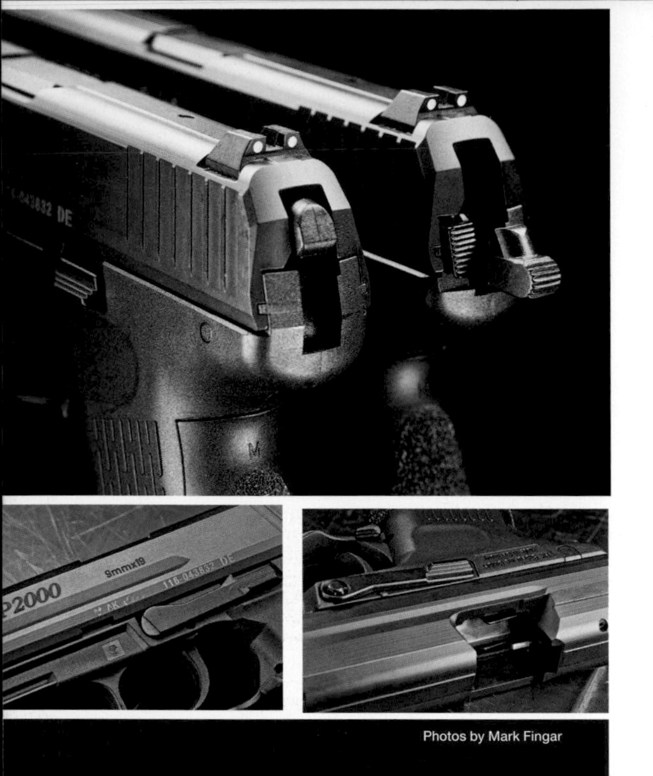

Photos by Mark Fingar

There are two versions of the P2000 available in the U.S. Version 2 on the left is the LEM model and is the author's favorite. Version 3 is a traditional DA/SA and is easily recognizable thanks to its exposed hammer and rear-mounted decocker.

house for cover in a shooting engagement. Because of our right hand and right eye dominance, we have to expose much more of our body to position our right eye and right hand where we can see around the corner to engage the threat, especially if we hug the corner. Left-handers can do the same exercise with a left-turn corner. We never know what might transpire when called upon to defend ourselves, so it's best to know how to use both hands and have a pistol that can accommodate the practice.

Many pistols on the market today have magazine releases that can be put on either side of the pistol for left- and right-hand shooters. The problem is that shooters need to know how to change it around if the pistol they purchase isn't set up properly for them. Some are easy and some are complicated, but the bot-

The P2000 comes with a truly ambidextrous magazine release that works for lefties and righties out of the box. It is a small paddle that rides underneath the triggerguard and is easy to work with either hand. For those desiring a larger paddle, an extended release can be found online and swaps out by removing a roll pin.

What the P2000 offers that painfully few other pistols do is an ambidextrous slide release. Most pistols are set up for right-handed shooters and either have no way for a lefty to use the slide release or make it very difficult to switch the pistol over for left-hand use. The P2000 comes with a slide release on both sides of the pistol to accommodate left- and right-handed shooters equally well.

LEM ISN'T JUST FOR COPS

Customers can find two variants of the P2000 sold in the U.S., the V2 and V3. The V3 is a traditional DA/SA semiauto pistol and is the easier to find of the two. Odds are, if you swing by your local HK dealer he'll have the V3. It is easily recognizable by the decocking lever located next to the hammer.

The version that I prefer and would pick if I could only have one pistol to do everything is the V2, or the LEM model. Yeah, LEM means "Law Enforcement Modification," but it's a great action type for all shooters. The design works by means of two firing mechanisms. The pistol's internal firing mechanism cocks automatically each time the slide operates. A small external hammer is the second firing mechanism, located at the pistol's rear. Each time we pull the trigger, the hammer moves through its full range of motion and fires the pistol when it drops onto the firing pin.

Photos by Mark Fingar

Purchasers of the P2000 can choose between 9mm and .40 S&W. The 9mm is cheaper, generates less recoil and can fit an additional round in the magazine. With modern bullets like the Barnes, it is every bit as lethal as the .40.

HK P2000	
Type	Recoil operated, semiautomatic
Caliber	9mm, .40 S&W
Capacity	12 (.40), 13 (9mm)
Barrel	3.66 in.
Overall Length	6.81 in.
Weight	1 lb., 8 oz.
Trigger Pull	V2: 6 lbs., V3: 4.5/11.5 lbs.
Grip	Textured polymer, interchangeable backstraps
Finish	HK Hostile Environment
Trigger	V2: LEM, V3: DA/SA
Sights	Fixed, three-dot
MSRP	$999.00
Manufacturer	HK USA 706-568-1906 hk-usa.com

The allure of the LEM trigger is that it is light and consistent. The V2 has a trigger pull of approximately six pounds, and the weight never changes. It's also a long, deliberate pull that can be cut short when we're in a hurry by only allowing the trigger to return far enough to reset between shots. With some practice we can become very fast with this trigger type.

Many shooters are unfamiliar with the V2 trigger, so few will ever recommend it over the traditional V3 model. For a pistol meant to do everything, the V2 is the way to go because its simple operation requires no safety or decocker manipulation while handling and shooting the pistol. There are few steps to screw up with a V2 trigger.

Also, unlike any of the popular striker-fired pistols, the P2000 has an external hammer that we can cover with our thumb when holstering the pistol. That option offers an additional way of controlling the pistol that the striker guns don't allow. When carrying a loaded pistol concealed (usually in our pants), anything we can do to prevent a negligent discharge is an advantage upon which we should capitalize.

Performance

Type	Velocity (fps)	Standard Deviation	Extreme Spread	Avg. Group (in.)	Best Group (in.)
PNW Arms 115 gr.	1,092	20	56	1.65	1.4
Barnes 115 gr.	1,059	13	35	1.6	1.51
Hornady 124 gr.	1,080	4	12	1.61	1.3

RANGE TIME

I've owned one P2000 since 2007 and have always enjoyed shooting the others. They are small and easy to carry, and the controls are intuitive and truly ambidextrous. HK pistols also have a hard-earned reputation as one of the most reliable pistols on the market.

Everyone likes to think they make a reliable pistol, but few ever get shot enough to really know for sure. A well-known pistol trainer, Todd Green, has done a couple year-long evals on HK pistols, putting more than 50,000 rounds through one and an incredible 91,000-plus through another. In both cases the pistols experienced an average round count between failures of more than 25,000 rounds. If ever there were an argument that a pistol was reliable, Todd's work is it.

I put three different loads through the P2000. The PNW Arms 115-grain TMJ load exited the muzzle at 1,092 feet per second, had a best group of 1.4 inches and had an average group of 1.65 inches. All groups consisted of 5 shots fired at 15 yards. The Barnes 115-grain ammo had a muzzle velocity of 1,059 fps, a best group of 1.51 inches and an average group of 1.6 inches. Hornady's 124-grain XTP had a muzzle velocity of 1,080 fps, a best group of 1.3 inches and an average of 1.61 inches.

ODDS AND ENDS

The P2000 is an exceptional pistol for general use. Its size and action type make a lot of sense for beginning shooters on up to accomplished professionals. While the model is available in 9mm and .40 S&W, I prefer the 9mm. It holds more rounds than the .40 S&W, the ammo is cheaper, and it recoils less. While some will argue that the .40's heavier bullet gives it more lethality, I'd argue that shot placement and adequate penetration are what really carry the day with pistols; caliber be damned.

Every time I shoot the P2000 I'm also reminded of why I prefer metal magazines over polymer ones, especially when the pistol frame is polymer. Polymer mags in polymer frames make for superslow reloads. Watch a group of polymer pistol shooters trying to reload quickly, and I can almost guarantee that one of the shooters will be flicking his magazine out of the pistol to try and speed things along. Polymer is just slow out of the magazine well. It's light, and it likes to stick to itself. The P2000's metal mags, on the other hand, leap out of the mag well even with the slide locked back and the barrel pointed skyward.

The P2000 is my "one and only" if I could only have one pistol for the rest of my life. It isn't the cheapest handgun on the market, nor is it the easiest to find. However, it is the only pistol I've found that does a wide variety of pistol chores well.